PRESCOTT 27,24
8/97

EFFECTIVE PSYCHOTHERAPY WITH BORDERLINE PATIENTS
Case Studies

ROBERT J. WALDINGER, M.D.
Assistant Director
Residency Training Program
McLean Hospital
Belmont, Massachusetts

Clinical Instructor in Psychiatry
Harvard Medical School
Boston, Massachusetts

JOHN G. GUNDERSON, M.D.
Director
Psychotherapy Program
Psychosocial Research Program
McLean Hospital
Belmont, Massachusetts

Associate Professor of Psychiatry
Harvard Medical School
Boston, Massachusetts

MACMILLAN PUBLISHING COMPANY
New York

Collier Macmillan Canada, Inc.
Toronto

Collier Macmillan Publishers
London

Macmillan Publishing Company
866 Third Avenue, New York, New York 10022

Collier Macmillan Canada, Inc.
Collier Macmillan Publishers • London

Library of Congress Cataloging-in-Publication Data

Waldinger, Robert J., 1951–
    Effective psychotherapy with borderline patients.

    Bibliography: p.
    Includes index.
    1. Borderline personality disorder—Case studies.
2. Psychotherapy—Case studies. I. Gunderson, John G.,
1942–   . II. Title. [DNLM: 1. Personality Disorders
—therapy—case studies.   2. Psychotherapy—methods—
case studies.   WM 420 W163e]
RC569.5.B67W35   1987   616.89   86-33258
ISBN 0-02-423900-3

Printing: 2 3 4 5 6 7 8   Year: 7 8 9 0 1 2 3 4 5

This book is an investigation of psychodynamic therapy of Borderline Personality Disorder. In it, we present and analyze reports of five intensive treatments of borderline patients conducted by five different therapists. Our aim is to address the question of whether and to what extent Borderline Personality Disorder can be "cured" by psychotherapeutic means. In an effort to understand the ways in which psychotherapy might effect favorable change in borderline psychopathology, we selected cases in which patients and therapists deemed significant progress to have been made over the course of treatment.

This book is designed to give psychodynamic psychotherapists a view of what their colleagues actually do in the treatment of severely disturbed borderline patients, and how entire treatments proceed over the course of several years. We have analyzed the material in these cases to arrive at some hypotheses about the markers of successful psychotherapy, such as when patients' self-destructive behavior should be expected to cease, when severely dysfunctional patients should begin to be gainfully employed, and how the tone of the therapeutic relationship is likely to shift over the course of therapy. In this respect, we hope to provide clinicians with some rudimentary yardsticks for the assessment of progress in these long and complicated treatments.

The book is also written to stimulate further psychotherapy research. Investigation of the process and effects of psychodynamic therapy is a complex enterprise. To date, virtually all of the evidence supporting the efficacy of psychotherapy with borderline patients has come from testaments by expert clinicians based on their own experiences. On occasion these have been supplemented by case reports. The methods of inquiry used by these individual practitioners have been criticized as too subjective to allow us to draw general conclusions about the psychodynamic therapy of borderline patients as it is now practiced in the United States and abroad.

At the other end of the spectrum is a more quantitative empirical approach to the study of psychotherapy that employs large numbers of variables, subjects, and practitioners with an attempt made for statistical control and evaluation. While this approach holds out the promise of greater freedom from individual bias, it relies on operationalizing the therapeutic process in ways that rarely can do justice to its complexity. As a result dynamically oriented clinicians often find psychotherapy research has little relevance to what they actually do in their offices.

Our study of case reports remains close to the first type of inquiry, but with the difference that our qualitative analyses are systematized and applied to work done by several independent practitioners. In this way, we are attempting to bridge the gap between qualitative and quantitative modes of studying the psychotherapy of Borderline Personality Disorder, remaining close to the experiences of therapists and patients, but examining them in ways that may increase the generalizability of our conclusions. We attempt to look for characteristics of patients, therapists, and treatment processes that are common among therapies of borderline individuals which have good outcomes. We hope to contribute hypotheses in this area that can be investigated more rigorously in the future. We also hope to make a data base of detailed case reports on psychodynamic therapy available to other researchers.

The book is laid out in three sections. The first section consists of introductory chapters that outline the major theories of borderline psychopathology and treatment, and discuss current controversies in the literature regarding the technique of intensive psychodynamic therapy with borderline patients. The second section consists of case material. Each case report is followed by a case discussion in which issues particular to that individual therapy are briefly reviewed. These issues include patient and therapist characteristics, transference, countertransference, therapeutic techniques, and outcome. Finally, the third section consists of an analysis of the cases with respect to diagnosis, patterns of intervention in treatment, patterns of change, and the relationship of therapeutic processes to the type of outcome achieved.

This work comes out of the Psychosocial Research Program at McLean Hospital. We gratefully acknowledge the support of the hospital staff and, most notably, its past and present leaders: Drs. Shervert Frazier, Alan Schatzberg, and Francis de Marneffe. We are indebted to the three colleagues on the McLean Hospital staff who, along with each of the authors, contributed case reports to the book and participated in the study of these treatments. Leonard Glass, M.D., Phillip Isenberg, M.D., and Harry Penn, M.D. gave extensively of their time, ideas, and clinical expertise to make this volume possible. We are also grateful to the five people who are the subjects of these reports, who gave us invaluable assistance in the complicated task of rendering histories that remain accurate in spirit and at the same time protect the privacy of those involved. Finally, we wish to thank Sue Busa, whose administrative skills were essential in the preparation of this manuscript.

R.J.W.
J.G.G.

CASE CONTRIBUTORS
(in addition to the authors)

Leonard Glass, M.D.
Director, Attending Psychiatrists' Program
McLean Hospital
Belmont, Massachustts

Assistant Clinical Professor of Psychiatry
Harvard Medical School
Boston, Massachusetts

Phillip Isenberg, M.D.
Director, Residency Training Program
McLean Hospital
Belmont, Massachusetts

Assistant Professor of Psychiatry
Harvard Medical School
Boston, Massachusetts

Harry Penn, M.D.
Associate Attending Psychiatrist
McLean Hospital
Belmont, Massachusetts

Clinical Instructor in Psychiatry
Harvard Medical School
Boston, Massachusetts

CONTENTS

1

Introduction to the Case Study Approach

The Purpose of This Book

Intensive psychodynamic psychotherapy is widely employed in the treatment of borderline personality disturbances. A large body of literature has emerged in the last two decades that characterizes long-term insight-oriented dynamic therapy conducted two or more times per week as the treatment of choice for this patient population (see Chapter 2). Yet there is considerable debate about whether this modality can, in fact, bring about the fundamental personality changes that many authors claim.

Given the fact that borderline patients are notoriously difficult to treat, and that they are prone to develop severe and sometimes life-threatening transference reactions in exploratory treatment, the question of the efficacy of this modality is by no means idle. Moreover, while the borderline syndrome is a chronic illness that has enormous personal and social costs, long-term psychotherapy is also costly, and its benefits must be weighed against these costs in making any decision about the best allocation of a patient's (and society's) resources.

Reports of the efficacy of intensive treatment of Borderline Personality Disorder have come primarily from individual practitioners who use their clinical practices as the data bases for their writing. Most of the case material presented in the literature consists of individual clinicians' vignettes, which they employ to make specific points about psychodynamic principles or therapeutic technique. These vignettes are not generally expanded to give overviews of completed psychotherapies. More detailed reports of entire treatments are rare in the literature [reports by Chessick (1982) and Masterson (1976) are among the notable exceptions]. In only one instance has a series of lengthy case reports by different practitioners been described in detail and discussed under one cover (Abend, Porder, and Willick, 1983), and this series consists primarily of patients who are not diagnosable as borderline by modern criteria (see Robbins, 1985; Gunderson, 1985).

Discussions of the outcome of treatment are equally scarce in the literature on borderline personality, despite practitioners' convictions that good outcomes that encompass fundamental change are possible with borderline patients.

The aim of this book is to look at the process and outcome of intensive treatment of borderline patients by different therapists, using detailed case reports of completed (or nearly completed) treatments in which therapists and patients deemed significant change to have occurred and a favorable outcome to have been achieved.

The book represents a first attempt to study the psychodynamic therapy of severely disturbed borderline patients treated by several independent therapists. In this respect, it broadens the scope of previous studies beyond that of the individual practitioner. Moreover, by relying on detailed reports of entire treatments, we aim for more in-depth analysis of process and outcome than is possible in studies that employ isolated and selected clinical vignettes. Our case study approach is designed to give us access to the ways in which variability in patient characteristics, therapists' personalities, and therapeutic technique influences the outcome of therapy. Perhaps the greatest advantage of this method over the single-practitioner approach is that it enables us to look at patterns of patient response and therapeutic change that are common to different treatments conducted by different therapists.

This book has yet another purpose: There is a need for the publication of detailed reports of psychoanalytically oriented treatments so that more clinical material can be available to those who would study the nature and outcome of psychodynamic therapy. Our book aims to increase this data base by adding five cases to what remains a small number of published in-depth clinical reports on the psychotherapy of severely disturbed patients. Our hope is that these cases will serve as subjects for the analyses of other researchers besides ourselves.

Our study proposes to examine two basic questions about intensive psychotherapy with borderline patients:

1. *What constitutes a favorable outcome of treatment?* What sorts of changes occur in borderline patients as treatment proceeds, and what is the timing and sequence of these changes? Is it possible for fundamental aspects of borderline psychopathology to change sufficiently so that successful therapy results in the patient no longer being borderline?

2. *What factors contribute to a favorable outcome?* What are the elements brought to treatment by the patient and the therapist that promote a good therapeutic result? What types of interventions by the therapist during treatment contribute to favorable change?

Our hope is that by examining five cases conducted by five different therapists who used significantly different techniques, we can begin to generate hypotheses about common denominators in the successful psychotherapy of borderline disorders.

Selection of Cases

We began this project by searching for cases of Borderline Personality Disorder that were judged by the therapists to have been successfully treated with intensive psychodynamic therapy. McLean Hospital is a psychiatric facility whose staff includes nearly 200 psychotherapists in varying capacities. We approached approximately 25 staff members who were known to be interested in the practice of intensive psychotherapy with patients suffering from severe personality disorders.

The great majority of this group had several borderline patients in intensive treatment at the time we approached them. However, most could not report any successfully terminated cases, usually because they did not deem their terminated treatments to have been successful, or because their more successful patients had not terminated and showed no sign of doing so in the near future.

Our sample of therapists thus consists of a small subset of volunteers from among a group of practitioners in the local psychiatric community and includes the two authors of this book. All five of the therapists in our group are male; while we asked several women to participate, all declined for one or more of the reasons noted above. Similarly, while therapists from other mental health disciplines were asked to participate, it happened that all of those who had successful cases were physicians. All five of the therapists in our group are psychoanalytically trained, and all were in the early or middle phases of their careers at the time that these treatments were conducted. All worked at least half time at McLean Hospital in a variety of capacities during the years chronicled in these case reports.

The patients in our group consist of four women and one man. This female/male ratio is higher than that estimated among borderline individuals in the general population (see Vaillant and Perry, 1985). All of the patients were in their early twenties when the treatments began, all were unemployed, and all were severely dysfunctional in work and in interpersonal relationships (see Chapter 8). Three were hospitalized at McLean at the start of psychotherapy, while two were never hospitalized. All of our patients had financial support for long-term psychotherapy from family and/or third-party payers. Four patients had terminated treatment when this project began, but one of them (Susan) subsequently returned to treatment after a year-long hiatus. The fifth patient (Martha) had not terminated but had tapered her sessions to once a week and was moving toward termination when our cases were selected.

The Development of the Book

We began by asking each of the five therapists to write a report of the psychotherapy, using whatever notes they had compiled about the case to render a history of the treatment in as much detail as possible. Each therapist was provided with an outline of subjects to be discussed and the format for the report. They were asked to write introductory material about the patient's presenting problems and developmental history, followed by a year-by-year chronicle of the treatment. Each case was written in the first person from the therapist's perspective. The group of five therapists then met regularly over a 12-month period to discuss each case and elucidate issues of process and outcome to be further explored.

In the second year of the project, we presented the five cases at a series of conferences for the clinical staff at McLean Hospital. At each case conference, one therapist presented his report and a consultant (usually a senior psychotherapist from the Boston area) gave a prepared commentary on the case. This was followed by group discussion.

Subsequent editing was done to disguise the cases heavily in an effort to protect confidentiality. At this point, the patients were asked to review the case reports. All five had been informed of the project by their therapists, and all agreed to read the reports and to consider giving their consent for publication. Each patient made a significant contribution to the writing of the case reports with respect to both the ways in which the reports were disguised and the descriptions of the treatment process. All five gave their informed consent for the use of the case reports in this book.

The Methods Used in Studying the Cases

The cases were studied individually and collectively. Individual reviews by the therapists, patients, authors, and consultants helped generate the material included in the case discussions that follow each case report. Some data about patients and therapists that emerged during group discussions were included in the case discussions but not in the case reports.

The case reports were then used to rate patients retrospectively in the following areas:

1. *Phenomenologic diagnosis.* Patients were assessed diagnostically by the authors using the criteria for Borderline Personality Disorder enumerated in DSM III, as well as the retrospective version of the Diagnostic Interview for Borderlines (DIB) (Gunderson et al., 1981).

2. *Psychological characteristics.* Patients were also evaluated by the authors with respect to intrapsychic characteristics at the start of treatment, using Otto Kernberg's criteria for Borderline Personality Organization (Kernberg, 1967) and a modified version of Michael Stone's

scale for Amenability to Analytically Oriented Psychotherapy (Stone, 1985).

3. *Treatment process.* The therapists and the authors independently assessed the nature and frequency of the therapists' interventions in each case. This was done systematically using a scale developed expressly for this purpose to catalog the major types of interventions generally encountered in psychodynamic psychotherapy with severely disturbed patients.

4. *Change during the course of treatment.* The authors and the therapists used two separate instruments to rate each patient independently on a variety of behavioral parameters in order to assess change during the period of the therapy. One scale, which rates specific patient behaviors and affects, was developed expressly for the purpose of assessing these five cases (see Table 9–1). We used a second instrument employed in our previously published survey of good-outcome cases of psychotherapy with borderline patients (Waldinger and Gunderson, 1984) to rate patients on four global scales with regard to change in: behavior (behavior is one of the 4 scales), ego functioning, object relationships, and sense of self over the course of treatment.

The methodologic limitations of our work are considerable and must be stated at the outset. Our sample is obviously small ($n = 5$) and the reconstruction of psychotherapies conducted over several years using therapists' notes and memories leaves open the question of the accuracy of their recollections. This may be balanced, to some extent, by the patients' contributions to these reports. We are mindful that these cases are thought by therapists and patients to have been both successful and in some way special, and that these assumptions about the outcome cannot help but influence the recollection and reporting of the work they did.

With regard to our analyses of patient characteristics, processes of change, and therapeutic outcome, the authors made their ratings independently of one another, and in this way attempted to diminish the subjectivity of our retrospectve assessments. However, only the diagnostic criteria in DSM III and the DIB have been tested for validity and reliability. The other instruments used in our study have not been so tested. This leaves open the question of how accurately they measure what they purport to measure. Finally, this study has no control group.

All of these limitations give us cause to be circumspect about any conclusions drawn from the study of our five cases. Nevertheless, this is a step toward systematic empirical analysis of how psychotherapy works in the treatment of borderline patients. We hope that this endeavor will generate hypotheses and that it will inspire further empirical work on the process and outcome of psychotherapy of Borderline Personality Disorder.

2

Intensive Psychodynamic Therapy with Borderline Patients: An Overview*

The treatment of borderline patients has long been characterized as an arduous task. Indeed, the clinical description of the borderline syndrome developed by Knight (1953) and others arose out of treatment difficulties. Patients who were thought to be neurotic and eminently treatable in psychoanalysis decompensated on the couch and came to be labeled "pseudoneurotic" by their bewildered analysts. In hospital settings, patients who seemed superficially healthy but underwent severe psychotic regressions were described as "latent schizophrenics" or "pseudoneurotic schizophrenics" (Hoch and Polatin, 1949). Frosch's concept (1970) of the psychotic character highlighted these patients' propensity for primary process thinking.

For all of these clinicians, the borderline patient was one with whom treatment was to be undertaken with caution, because the results of mismanagement could be disastrous. As a group, borderline patients are characterized by the intense clinging, dependent, and/or hostile transferences they develop toward the therapist early in treatment and by their propensity to undergo severe regressive reactions in the course of therapy. They routinely act out transference feelings in the form of dangerous self-destructive and sometimes violent behaviors. They evoke intense countertransference reactions in the therapist, often using suicide threats, unreasonable demands, and a wide variety of other coercive behaviors to draw the therapist out of a position of psychotherapeutic neutrality and into the roles of caretaker, parent, persecutor, and adversary. Therapists frequently become exhausted by such pa-

---

*This is a modified version of Waldinger, R.J., "Intensive Psychodynamic Therapy with Borderline Patients: An Overview," *Am. J. Psychiatry*, **144**, March, 1987. Published by permission of the American Journal of Psychiatry.

tients. Suicide is an ever-present risk, and the abrupt interruption of treatment is common.

It is little wonder, then, that when patients were found to lapse into psychotic thinking and to develop unmanageable transference reactions in the unstructured setting of psychoanalysis, clinicians began to write about strictly limiting the treatment of borderline patients to supportive psychotherapeutic interventions (Grinker et al., 1968; Friedman, 1975). Zetzel (1971) was a particularly prominent advocate of a highly structured, supportive approach in which the patient is seen infrequently (generally no more than once a week). She emphasized stability, consistency, and the setting of realistic limits as being of primary importance, and cautioned therapists against acceding to patients' unrealistic demands or presenting themselves as omnipotent figures with inexhaustible resources. She argued that in this way, the therapy could proceed without the development of regressive transference reactions that could not be worked through. Even so, Zetzel was pessimistic about the borderline patient's capacity to internalize a sufficiently stable ego identification to become genuinely autonomous. Thus she concluded that the treatment of borderline patients would rarely be definitive. Rather, she believed that such patients might need access throughout their lives to a therapist or some other person who could perform those ego functions for the patient that the patient would never be capable of performing autonomously.

Those who have subsequently written about the psychodynamic treatment of borderlines have shared Knight and Zetzel's sense of the difficulty of this work. However, in the last two decades there has been a burgeoning of literature on the usefulness of intensive exploratory psychotherapy with borderline patients—treatment aimed not simply at crisis management or improved social role performance, but also at the resolution of the pathologic constellation of conflicts, deficits, and defenses that are thought to lie at the heart of this disorder.

Many have written about the intensive psychodynamic treatment of borderline personality. This chapter focuses on those who have made the most lucid presentations of distinct viewpoints regarding treatment strategies. In this sense, no attempt is made to give "equal time" to all active contributors to the field. Rather, the goal is to delineate the most important positions on controversial issues.

Definitions of intensive treatment vary. Some authors, such as Masterson (1972), Buie and Adler (1982), and Kernberg (1975) write about dynamically oriented vis-à-vis psychotherapy conducted two or three times per week. Others, including Boyer (1977), Giovacchini (1979), Volkan (in press), and Chessick (1977), conceive of intensive treatment as psychoanalysis conducted on the couch five times per week. Moreover, the labels used for intensive treatment differ. Intensive psychodynamic therapy is labeled "expressive" by Kernberg (1982), "reconstructive" by Masterson (1976), and "psychoanalytically informed" by Chessick (1982). However, virtually all of these clinicians agree on certain basic tenets concerning what is safe and effective intensive treatment of the borderline patient:

1. *Stability of the framework of treatment.* This includes scheduling regular appointment times, beginning and ending sessions on time, and making clear from the outset what the therapist's expectations are concerning the keeping of appointments, payment of fees, and other framework issues. Any deviations from the framework by the patient or by the therapist (e.g., missed appointments) should be actively addressed and the patient's feelings about such deviations explored in the therapy hours.

2. *Increased activity of the therapist.* Compared to the treatment of a neurotic patient, work with borderlines requires that the therapist literally say more within the treatment hours. The value of these comments to the patient lies not only in their content but also in the fact that they serve to emphasize the therapist's presence, to anchor the patient in reality, and, most particularly, to prevent the transference distortions that borderline patients are prone to develop in unstructured situations.

3. *Tolerance of negative transference.* The therapist must be able to withstand the borderline's verbal assaults without either retaliating or withdrawing. By this process, the patient's hostility can be examined and understood as part of a more general pattern of relating to important others.

4. *Establishing a connection between the patient's actions and feelings in the present.* For borderline patients, action is a primary defense against the awareness of uncomfortable affects. Since such awareness is considered essential to autonomy and self-control, the patient must be helped to see that he or she communicates via action and that this serves a defensive function.

5. *Making self-destructive behaviors ungratifying.* Borderline patients have a great investment in remaining unaware of the self-destructive nature of actions that gratify certain wishes and allay anxiety. The therapist must consistently and repeatedly draw the patient's attention to the adverse consequences of behaviors such as drug use, promiscuity, manipulative behavior, and inappropriate outbursts of rage—focusing not on the patient's stated motives for such activities but on the results.

6. *Blocking acting-out behaviors.* The therapist must set limits on behaviors that threaten the safety of the patient, the therapist, or the therapy. In contrast to the neurotic patient, who may at times act out transference feelings and in doing so gain new insight into unconscious motives and fantasies, the borderline uses acting out as a major form of resistance to the awareness of transference and thus to the progress of treatment.

7. *Focusing clarifications and interpretations on the here and now.* Genetic interpretations or attempts at genetic reconstructions early in treatment are likely to be counterproductive, as they divert attention from the immediate and often dangerous pathologic behaviors that disrupt the patient's life.

8. *Paying careful attention to countertransference feelings.* Persistent monitoring of countertransference reactions is necessary to minimize the very real danger of acting out on the part of the therapist. Most authors agree that the therapist's own experience as a patient in dynamic psychotherapy facilitates this process by helping the therapist to better understand and use his or her emotional reactions in the treatment.

Etiology and Pathology

Beyond these basic principles of technique, the literature reveals numerous differences in the types, timing, and effects of interventions that are aimed at fostering therapeutic change in borderline patients. Often these differences are linked to differing concepts of what causes and what constitutes borderline psychopathology.

The primacy of conflict. Kernberg (1975) sees the borderline patient as being incapable of synthesizing positive and negative introjects into coherent self- and object images.* This is due to the danger posed by an overabundance of poorly modulated aggressive strivings that may be either primary (inborn) or secondary (reactive to the environment). That is, the child is either born with a reduced capacity to tolerate normal aggressive strivings and the anxiety that accompanies aggressive feelings toward a loved one, or develops unusually intense aggressive impulses and feelings due to excessive frustration of instinctual needs and wishes by early caretakers.

In either case, the predisposed child is ill-equipped to bring together aggressive and loving images of the self or others, lest images of a good self and a good other be subjected to an onslaught of aggression and hatred, which would put the survival of such good images at risk. The anxiety resulting from this synthesis is therefore intolerable. According to Kernberg, the child relies on the defense of splitting, along with other primitive defenses, most notably primitive idealization, projection, projective identification, denial, omnipotence, and devaluation, to prevent this catastrophic event. In concrete terms, the infant

---

*"Introjection" is defined by Kernberg (1976) as "the earliest, most primitive, and basic level in the organization of internalization processes. It is the reproduction and fixation of an interaction with the environment by means of an organized cluster of memory traces implying at least three components: (i) the image of an object, (ii) the image of the self in interaction with that object, and (iii) the affective coloring of both the object-image and the self-image under the influence of the drive representative present at the time of the interaction."

can protect the internalized "good mother" by using primitive defenses to avoid the recognition that this mother is the same as the dangerous, frustrating "bad mother." According to Kernberg, this process is *active*, requiring psychic energy to keep apart contradictory images in the attempt to master a seemingly unresolvable *conflict*. Splitting is seen as adaptive, but the price that the borderline individual must pay for this reliance on primitive defenses is a severely weakened ego, vulnerable reality testing, and a tendency to lapse into primary process thinking.

Kernberg's model of primitive defenses mobilized in the service of conflict resolution implies that the individual who faces such a dilemma already possesses a minimal capacity for object permanence and self–other differentiation—in other words, a consolidated representational world. Otherwise, there could be no experience of conflict between oppositely valenced images, and thus no experience of danger and the need for a defensive retreat (Stolorow and Lachmann, 1980).

The primacy of deficits. Buie and Adler (1982), by contrast, emphasize *deficit* rather than conflict at the core of borderline psychopathology. They posit a deficit of holding-soothing introjects that leaves the patient unable to evoke soothing images independently in times of stress, leaving him or her vulnerable to painful experiences of aloneness, panic, and abandonment. This developmental failure appears to result from mothering that is not good enough during the phases of separation-individuation. The early parenting experience is sufficiently out of synchrony with the child's needs that the child internalizes introjects that are primarily negative and fails to develop the kinds of self-soothing resources that might help to modulate his or her rageful reaction to bad mothering.

In contrast to Kernberg's notion that both good and bad images of the self and others have been introjected but that primitive defenses are used actively to keep them apart and stave off intrapsychic conflict, Buie and Adler state that good images have never been integrated in the first place, and that the borderline patient simply cannot conceive of a holding and soothing mother in times of stress.

Giovacchini (1979) sees the borderline state as stemming from deficits in ego structure. He sees the borderline patient as never having been gratified early in life and thus as incapable of forming stable mental representations of helpful experiences. This he terms a state of "privation," which is distinct from deprivation in that deprived people know what it means to be gratified; they have been able to integrate memories of gratifying experiences, and they are thus capable of feeling frustrated when they are deprived of such experiences. Giovacchini states that borderlines have not achieved the stable mental representations of external objects that would be required to experience frustration in response to deprivation. In this respect, he, too, posits a less structured psychological apparatus for many borderlines than does Kernberg.

The concept of abandonment depression. Masterson (1972) looks at borderline psychopathology as rooted in developmental problems emanating from specific mother–child interactions during the separation-individuation phase of infant development. Specifically, Masterson states that "the mother of every borderline is herself a borderline" (1972, p. 22). She is unable to tolerate what Mahler (1971) describes as the natural process of separation and individuation by which the growing infant is propelled toward increased autonomy and mastery of the environment. The mother's message to the child, overt and/or covert, is that efforts at separation will result in the withdrawal of emotional supplies (Masterson and Rinsley, 1975). Faced with an unresolvable conflict between the drive toward autonomy and the need for the mother's continued care and support, the infant resorts to the use of primitive defenses of splitting, denial, avoidance, projection, and acting out in order to preserve the illusion of symbiotic union with the mother. Concomitantly, the infant internalizes the mother's pathologic self and object representations, which remain split into what Masterson terms the "withdrawing object relations unit (WORU)" and the "rewarding object relations unit (RORU)." The infant then experiences both self and primary objects as alternatively all good (rewarding) and all bad (withdrawing). Masterson's model is, in essence, one of conflict in which the borderline individual mobilizes primitive defenses to protect against the seemingly intolerable abandonment depression that results from perceived object loss, and against the fear of symbiotic fusion when the object is perceived as engulfing.

Treatment Strategies

What relevance do these concepts of the etiology of the borderline syndrome have for clinical work? In many respects, the theorists cited above have very similar views on what constitutes the work of intensive psychotherapy. Many of their differences are not over how they ought to intervene in treatment but over what it is about those interventions that is therapeutic.

In particular, Masterson, Kernberg, Adler, Buie, Gunderson, Chessick, and Volkan all write of a "testing" phase early in the treatment of borderline patients in which the patient barrages the therapist with numerous challenges to the therapist's competence, caring, and ability to set limits on behaviors that threaten the treatment and the well-being of the patient. The major task for the therapist is to "survive" and curtail the storms of acting out, the intense negative affects, and the regressive and self-destructive behaviors that ensue whenever a borderline patient struggles with interpersonal closeness.

All of these writers agree that it is necessary to clarify the self-destructive nature of the patient's maladaptive behaviors and to confront the patient with the reality of his or her self-defeating actions that are used to manage seemingly intolerable affects. All agree that interpretation and confrontation alone do not suffice to control acting out effectively as they might in a healthier patient. Thus, they all advocate behavioral as well as verbal limit setting. That is, they assert that the therapist must *show* as well as *tell* the patient that self-destructive behaviors (such as wrist cutting and substance abuse), inappropriate expressions of rage toward the therapist (e.g., destroying property in the therapist's office), and intrusions into the therapist's private life are neither acceptable to the therapist nor in the patient's best interest. But while they agree in essence about the need for here-and-now clarifications and setting limits on acting out, they see these interventions as serving different purposes. It is here that differing notions of etiology come into play.

Interpretation: The usefulness of content. Kernberg emphasizes the need to interpret negative transference vigorously and to clarify contradictory ego states early in treatment, as well as the need to interpret other maladaptive defenses in order to demonstrate to the patient the ego-weakening effects of these defensive maneuvers. He notes that interpretations can be "heard" by the patient only when (1) the treatment is structured so as to prevent the gratification of primitive instinctual wishes by means of gross acting out and (2) the patient's distorted perceptions of these interpretations are systematically examined and clarified at the time that the interpretations are made, so that distortions do not prevent the patient from integrating what is said.

Kernberg believes that patients with severe ego weakness are capable of responding to the actual meaning of interpretive comments by the therapist, but only when the magical transference meanings of such comments (e.g., "the therapist loves me" or "the therapist is my sadistic father") have been interpreted. For example, a patient who projects his sadism onto others may hear every interpretation made by the therapist as an attack, and may therefore be unable to make use of its content. Kernberg argues that only by clarifying such misperceptions immediately, in the therapy hour, can primitive defenses be replaced by higher-level ones, resulting in a stronger ego and less distortion of interpersonal relationships, as well as the capacity to use the therapist's interventions. Boyer (1977) employs an interpretive strategy much like Kernberg's.

Masterson (1976) emphasizes that it is the therapist's repeated clarifications of the patient's destructive maladaptive behavior that eventually make such behavior ego dystonic. Like Kernberg, he assumes that borderline patients can make use of interpretive content; in contrast to Kernberg, he does not emphasize the patient's tendency to distort the therapist's comments and thereby remain unable to hear that content.

The holding environment: The importance of process. Since Buie and Adler view the core of borderline pathology as a failure in the development of holding and soothing introjects, their goal is not to undo what is already there and malformed but to create what never existed: "to promote intrapsychic structural development to redress this developmental failure" (Buie and Adler, 1982, p. 54). This requires that the patient use the therapist as a holding self-object, that is, as someone who can perform the holding and soothing functions for the patient that the patient cannot perform on his or her own.

The provision of a holding environment for the patient is a concept that is consistent with classical psychoanalytic technique insofar as the interpretive process and the stability of the psychoanalytic framework are seen as holding (Eissler, 1953; Modell, 1976). But Buie and Adler extend this concept beyond classical technique, so that the therapist functions *in reality* as a stable holding self-object for the borderline patient. This may involve offering considerable support, including the use of hospitalization, extra appointments, telephone calls between therapy hours, the giving of vacation addresses, and even sending the patient postcards during the therapist's absences (Buie and Adler, 1982; Adler and Buie, 1979a,b). It is not so much the interpretive content per se that is healing, but the fact that the therapist is a stable, consistent, caring, nonpunitive person who survives the patient's rage and destructive impulses and continues to perform for the patient those holding and soothing functions that the patient cannot perform for himself or herself.

Buie and Adler illustrate this stance with a case example: In responding to a patient's self-destructive behavior in the initial phases of treatment, the therapist not only comments upon the patient's transient incapacity to know that the therapist existed during the self-destructive act, but also suggests that when similar situations occur in the future, the patient might call or make an extra appointment rather than behave self-destructively. Through repeated experiences of this sort, the patient learns that the therapist continues to exist, remembers the patient, and is available regardless of the patient's ego state. The mode by which the patient learns in this example is primarily *experiential*, and what is interpreted are the patient's *ego defects* rather than conflict. Kernberg, by contrast, would be more likely to view such an incident as the patient's angry effort to assert control over the therapist.

The view that experiential factors are more important than the content of interpretations for borderline patients in the early phases of treatment is one that is shared by Volkan (in press) and Chessick (1982), who both write about the importance of alliance building early in treatment, as well as the provision of a holding environment. Gunderson, too, stresses the importance of the holding environment, especially in the beginning phases of treatment, as necessary to address the borderline patient's state of objectlessness (Gunderson, 1984).

Working with Transference

Borderline patients develop transference feelings for the therapist that are typically intense, unstable, and shifting. Some of the most salient differences among clinicians concern the nature of the transference and techniques for its management. It is here that ideas about the etiology of the borderline syndrome are of particular importance in determining what the therapist expects to see clinically and how he or she deals with it.

The origins of transference. Kernberg writes that the borderline patient's transference to the therapist originates largely in the fantasy distortions that accompany early object relationships. Small children mobilize primitive defenses to extricate themselves from threatening interpersonal relationships, and thus create "monsters" where in reality only imperfect parents existed (Kernberg, 1975).

Whereas Kernberg emphasizes the fantasy basis of the borderline patient's transference, Masterson emphasizes the reality basis, asserting that the mother of every borderline is herself a borderline. While he claims not to blame the mother for whatever goes wrong in the borderline's development, in his many case examples he makes few distinctions between real and fantasied aspects of early object relationships. In similar fashion, Chessick (1977) traces the roots of borderline psychopathology to interactions with the mother, but allows that social change and a breakdown in stable social networks contribute to the disruption of the calm, secure maternal environment.

These differences in emphasis have important implications for how these writers see the development of transference and how they work with it in psychotherapy. Masterson treats transference as the reflection of the patient's primary relationships (i.e., as based on real experience), and he works with it as such. Once acting out is controlled, the patient is thought to be able to use interpretations to differentiate between the current reality of the therapy situation and transference distortions based on real past experiences. Interpretation thus suffices to bring about insight and change.

Kernberg, by contrast, sees transference as existing at two levels in the borderline patient: a primitive type that is the product of gross distortions of childhood experiences by primitive defenses and a higher-level transference based on real childhood experiences. Kernberg actually sees a shift in the transference from more primitive to more realistic as therapy proceeds and the patient's ego functioning becomes more mature and less distorting (Kernberg, 1975).

According to Kernberg, interpretation alone cannot suffice to bring about insight, because the interpretations themselves are bound to be distorted in the way that early experiences with parents and other caretakers were misperceived (Kernberg, 1982). He argues that the therapist needs to supplement interpretations of the relationship between past and present experience with relentless here-and-now interpretations of the patient's distortions of the therapist's comments. Gunderson (1984) is in agreement with Kernberg on this point. He emphasizes the importance of understanding and clarifying the borderline patient's distortions not simply as a reaction to inadequate parenting, but as a defensive adaptation made by the child to parenting experiences.

While Masterson describes a gradual shift in the patient's perception of the mother from someone who is all bad to someone with both positive and negative attributes, he notes only that this is the result of growth in therapy (Masterson, 1976). Kernberg states quite specifically that the transference shifts between primitive and neurotic levels, and that the development of more realistic views of primary caretakers comes about along with the development of a more realistic picture of the therapist. This he attributes to the systematic analysis of primitive defenses that are given up and replaced by more adaptive ones (Kernberg, 1975). While giving less emphasis to defense analysis, Gunderson, too, feels that the patient must come to terms not only with the ways in which he or she distorts the relationship with the therapist, but also with his or her contributions to the pathologic aspects of primary relationships.

Buie and Adler see the patient's mistrust of and rage at the therapist primarily as reactions to inadequate mothering. In other words, negative transference is based on real past experience. In this respect, their views are more in accord with Masterson's than with Kernberg's.

Positive and negative transference. Buie and Adler differ from Kernberg in the relative importance they attach to working with negative and positive transference. Buie and Adler maintain that manifestations of negative transference are not simply to be worked through for their own sake, but also to make room for the idealizing self-object transference that the borderline must be allowed to experience with the therapist and subsequently work through. They write that positive transference is ameliorated via what Kohut (1971) termed "optimal disillusionment," a process by which patients gradually notice discrepancies between the idealized holding introject and the actual holding qualities of the therapist. Each disappointment (e.g., the therapist's vacation or absence due to illness), if it is "optimal" and not overwhelming, prompts the patient to develop insight into the unrealistic aspects of his or her positive feelings for the therapist. The therapist is ultimately accepted as he or she is, and the patient's holding introjects are modified accordingly. The therapist's job during this phase is to stay with the patient empathically, to provide clarifications and interpretations of the dynamic and genetic bases of these disappointments, and to avoid any confrontations that would intensify these disappointments (Buie and Adler, 1982).

Kernberg does not assign positive transference the central place afforded it in the treatment strategies of Buie and Adler. He allows that some patients deny their positive feelings for the therapist throughout much of the treatment and states that such denial need not always be interpreted. He most often describes positive transference as defensive idealization used to protect borderline patients from their negative transferences and as an avoidance of more mature object relations.

One might liken the contrast between these two views to a figure-ground problem in drawing. While Buie and Adler see the patient's positive feelings as the background upon which negative transference is the overlay, Kernberg sees the reverse. What results are divergent views of what constitutes the core of treatment: the interpretation of negative transference (Kernberg) or the progressive disillusionment of idealizing transference (Buie and Adler). These divergent views imply different ways of understanding the patient's behavior and material within the therapy hours. For example, Kernberg might be inclined to see the patient's idealization of the therapist as a defense against deeply rooted hostility. Buie and Adler, on the other hand, might be more likely to see the idealization as primary and the patient's hostility as secondary to disappointment.

Early interpretation of transference. This debate about whether the borderline patient's hostility is primary or reactive gives rise to widely divergent treatment recommendations, particularly with respect to the early phases of psychotherapy. Kernberg cautions that unless the therapist interprets the borderline patient's hostility and shows that he or she can tolerate it from the outset of treatment, negative transference feelings will be forced underground and will secretly undermine the therapeutic endeavor. Thus, for Kernberg, the way to maintain a working relationship with a borderline patient is to focus on and analyze the transferential roots of the patient's anger from the beginning.

By contrast, therapists who see the patient's problem in terms of deficits of holding and soothing introjects focus on the narcissistic vulnerabilities of the borderline personality and have introduced the technical modification of accepting the patient's idealization without interpretation for a long time. Adler (1979) writes that this idealized self-object transference and the patient's longing for a perfect caregiver are what hold the borderline in treatment. He believes that no true working alliance is possible with borderline patients, and that early interpretation of negative transference would simply disrupt the patient's sense of being empathically held by the therapist and would thus be likely to destroy the patient's motivation for treatment. Giovacchini (1979) notes a similar hazard and advises against early interpretation.

Chessick (1977) sees the borderline as needing to internalize an idealized image of the therapist in order to develop a more stable self-view. While he acknowledges that the borderline's idealization of the therapist can serve as a defense against rage, he believes that it is best not to confront this idealized image early in treatment unless the patient's affect is so intense (e.g., so eroticized) that the work of therapy becomes disrupted by it (Chessick, 1979).

Grotstein (1982) writes that deeply regressed borderline patients may be incapable of using the content of transference interpretations, because they need the therapist to function as a "container" for their fragmented psyches, and cannot hear interpretations about their projections until they have gained sufficient ego strength to tolerate the warded-off aspects of themselves. Searles (1980) cautions the therapist against early interpretation of transference for similar reasons. He argues that borderline patients need to be able to find some aspect of their transference in the therapist (e.g., sadism), and that the therapist needs to be comfortable with these transference characteristics before the patient can be comfortable with them. This cannot occur if the therapist interprets transference early in the therapy.

Gunderson (1984) recommends that the therapist avoid vigorous confrontation and interpretation of positive or negative transference early in treatment. He cautions the therapist against either colluding with the patient in legitimizing his or her anger or pointing out too quickly that this anger is disproportionate and unrealistic. Rather, he feels that the borderline patient's rageful reactions should be limited in their expression (often requiring considerable activity on the part of the therapist) and that the circumstances in the environment that trigger these reactions should be explored. While Gunderson believes that the borderline's excessive aggression probably reflects a mixture of reaction to the environment and drive factors, he deems it most useful for the therapist to treat such rage as reactive in order to encourage the patient to identify angry outbursts as symptomatic—that is, as maladaptive and potentially modifiable responses to specific sets of circumstances and perceptions.

The Role of Corrective Emotional Experiences

The concept of corrective emotional experience was most extensively developed by Alexander (Alexander and French, 1946). Subsequently, psychoanalytic theorists recoiled from stereotyped notions of the therapist as someone who provides the love and good parenting that the patient never had and in this way effects a cure. Such strategies are thought to be overly simplistic and to demean the intellectual rigor of the therapeutic endeavor by implying that psychotherapy amounts to hand holding. One thus treads on perilous ground in writing about corrective experiences in psychotherapy. Yet few dynamically oriented therapists would deny the value of providing borderline patients with growth-enhancing experiences that they have not previously had.

Kernberg's view of treatment is most classical and least concerned with corrective experiences. Yet even he writes of the importance of the therapist "holding" the patient, that is, tolerating the patient's expressions of intense ambivalence. As the patient sees that the therapist does not crumble under the patient's aggressive onslaughts, the patient's fears about his or her own impulses diminish and integrative ego functions are strengthened (Kernberg, 1982). Boyer agrees with Kernberg. He cautions that the therapist's role should *not* include the provision of real good parental caretaking to substitute for presumed poor past life experience. For example, he questions the need for the therapist to be available to borderline patients for emergency contacts between interviews. Rather, he states that "the best substitute parenting one can afford the patient is to hew as closely as possible to the classical analytic model" (1977, p. 418).

By contrast, Masterson, Buie, and Adler place considerable emphasis on actively providing the patient with corrective experiences, especially in the later phases of treatment when testing and acting out have diminished. Buie and Adler maintain that "the capacities to know, esteem, and love oneself can be developed only when there is adequate experience of being known, esteemed, and loved by significant others" (Buie and Adler, 1982, p. 77). In treatment this translates into a process that they call "validation." The therapist works to establish the full reality of the patient's positive qualities by reacting with "appropriate subtle expressions of esteem" (Buie and Adler, 1982, pp. 80–81) to the patient's accounts of positive experiences, conveying that these qualities have registered in the therapist's mind as realities. This allows the patient not only to feel the realness of these qualities but also to gain, through introjection and identification, the capacity for self-validation and a greater capacity for autonomous self-esteem. Buie and Adler caution that in order for this validation process to be effective, the therapist must genuinely esteem (and even love) the patient. While most therapists would agree that treatment must be based on mutual respect, few writers so explicitly weave countertransference elements into their theories of therapy with borderlines.

Masterson likewise advises the therapist to be a "real person" and to support the patient's individuation actively by maintaining and communicating the consistent expectation that the patient will act in a realistic, healthy, mature fashion. He writes, "This extends as far as congratulating the patient for realistic achievements, empathizing with his realistic defeats and disappointments" (Masterson, 1976, pp. 90–91).

Masterson also writes of a process that Mahler has termed "communicative matching" and that Masterson sees as an essential part of the working-through phase of treatment. According to Mahler's description of the separation-individuation process in infants, the toddler in the rapprochement phase insistently returns to the mother for "supplies" after wandering off to explore the world. The mother who provides these supplies by responding to the child's activities in such a way as to approve of his or her further individuation is engaging in communicative matching. Masterson posits that this developmental experience has been minimal in the borderline patient and that it is the therapist's job in the latter part of treatment to provide such an experience. This is done, for example, by discussing with patients their new interests or feelings, such as sports, the stock market, or dating. In this way, the therapist supports the patient's newly emerging self and furthers the process of differentiation (Masterson, 1976, pp. 103–104).

Gunderson's stance on this issue is similar to Masterson's and Buie and Adler's. He writes that the borderline patient's identity disturbance is best modified by noninterpretive work, which involves providing support for the importance and validity of new ideas and feelings that emerge in treatment, as well as for the patient's growing awareness of the complexity of his or her personality (Gunderson, 1984).

Chessick (1977) attaches the most importance to experiential factors in the treatment of borderlines. He notes that much more is internalized by the patient than the healthy experience of a correct interpretation. The patient comes to identify with many of the therapist's characteristics, including a nonanxious observing attitude, refusal to be manipulated, and a sense of taking active responsibility for his or her own actions and emotions. Chessick notes that at the height of the transference, it matters little what the therapist says: "The patient is not interested in the *words* at all, any more than when the mother picks up the baby, the baby cares which lullaby the mother is singing" (1977, p. 179).

Discussion

While an effort has been made to differentiate the views of a number of writers, these clinicians are probably more similar in their approaches to the borderline patient than they are different, and their differences are probably more salient on paper than they are in the consulting room. Nevertheless, certain distinctions are worth highlighting, for they raise important practical and philosophical issues for those who treat severely disturbed patients.

The problem of etiology. A common theme in the literature on the treatment of borderlines is that the therapist must redress the failures, real or fantasied, of primary caretakers. Masterson, Chessick, and Buie and Adler maintain that the syndrome results from mothering (caretaking) that was not "good enough," in Winnicott's sense of the term (1958, 1965). Only Kernberg and Gunderson explicitly leave open the extent to which factors within the patient (inborn or otherwise) contribute to the borderline syndrome, and structure their treatment so that persistent attention is paid to the patient's contribution to his or her distortions of primary relationships. Giovacchini's notion that the borderline patient is not capable of being gratified is a model that could encompass inborn factors that contribute to the patient's illness. However, in his published clinical material, Giovacchini is primarily concerned with failures in the patient's early environment.

The issue of blame and the distinction between blame and responsibility are knotty problems for all therapists engaged in treatment that relies heavily on self-understanding and insight into past relationships and experiences. Certainly, a "not good enough mothering" theory of borderline psychopathology can subtly provide support for many patients' belief that they are not responsible for their current predicament and are entitled to reparations from the cruel world that caused their problems. Such a deterministic theory can also promote countertransference difficulties. For example, therapists who see the patient as a victim are likely to see themselves as needing to be "better than" the parents who failed so miserably and caused their child so much injury. Carried to its extreme, this view leaves the therapist vulnerable to unmanageable countertransference hate when patients find him or her in some way inadequate, uncaring, or unhelpful (as is bound to happen). Similarly, therapists who view the borderline's problems as the result of poor parenting may find it difficult to help the patient see the ways in which he or she distorts and disrupts these and other relationships.

In fact, a variety of sources fail to confirm the theory that borderline psychopathology is invariably induced by parents. Clinical experience does not support Masterson's notion that the mother of every borderline is herself a borderline, and studies have described considerable diversity among the families of borderline patients (Shapiro et al., 1975; Gunderson and Englund, 1981). Shapiro (1982) notes that families of borderline adolescents undergo a group regression during the adolescence of the identified patient. Treaters in mental health care settings see families in times of crisis, when family members may function at more primitive levels than they would under other circumstances. Hence, some parents may appear to be borderline only in hospital settings such as the one in which Masterson did much of his pioneering work with adolescents.

Developmental data are equally unsupportive of the "borderlines beget borderlines" hypothesis. Work on temperamental differences in infants suggests that inborn factors exert a profound influence on the infant's patterns of receiving, processing, and reacting to environmental stimuli. And the work of Thomas and Chess (1984) suggests that the child's inborn temperament and the goodness of fit between the child and the environment have much to do with the way in which children develop styles of relating to their world. Andrulonis et al. (1982) have studied a sizable subgroup of borderline patients with histories of minimal brain dysfunction and other minor neurologic abnormalities, conditions that might cause them to process environmental stimuli aberrantly. In light of these data, the possible effects of inborn factors and parent–child fit on the development of serious character pathology must not be overlooked either in theory or in practice.

The models of conflict and deficit. Those who emphasize the centrality of intrapsychic conflict in the borderline's psychopathology see interpretation as the most powerful tool available to the therapist for bringing about basic and lasting change. By contrast, those who see the borderline's fundamental problem as one of deficits in intrapsychic structure argue that experiential learning is most important in helping the patient to form such structures, and that interpretations cannot be heard until the necessary structures are in place.

It is widely acknowledged that the term "borderline" is often employed in the literature on psychodynamic therapy to describe a broad range of patients who vary in the type and severity of psychopathology (Chessick, 1977; Adler, 1981; Andrulonis et al., 1982; Meissner, 1983). It may be that the models of conflict and deficit are not opposing or mutually exclusive but rather are applicable to different degrees with different patients, or even to the same patients at different points in time. This would be consonant with the observation that a large number of borderline patients are treated with a mixture of interpretive and supportive therapeutic techniques. Frosch (1971) subscribes to this view of borderline pathology. Thus, he is comfortable in recommending a therapeutic approach that employs supportive techniques in helping the patient to overcome ego defects (particularly early in treatment) and interpretive techniques to elucidate conflicts and pathologic defenses.

Similarly, the differing views that have been presented regarding work with positive and negative transference may reflect differences in the patient populations studied. For example, those patients whose pathology involves a considerable amount of paranoia and hostility might be more likely to respond to an approach that highlights these feelings interpretively than to an approach that emphasizes the patient's longing for holding and soothing. Similarly, patients whose ego structures are less well defined and who initially rely more heavily on the therapist to support adaptive ego functioning might be more inclined to respond to interventions that emphasize experiential learning and role modeling than those that are primarily verbal and centered on conflict. The case reports in this book allow us to explore whether such relationships between psychopathology and technique are to be found.

Most of those who write about the treatment of borderlines acknowledge that these patients fluctuate in their levels of object relatedness, sometimes from one session to the next and sometimes from one minute to the next. For example, the patient who, in a session prior to his therapist's vacation, experiences conflict between the wish to murder the therapist and the longing to be taken care of by him may undergo a psychotic regression in the face of the therapist's actual departure. Yet few writers incorporate these fluctuations into their strategies for therapeutic interventions with the borderline patient. Only Gunderson and Chessick deal specifically with the shifts in object relatedness and ego integration that borderlines undergo with such rapidity in the course of psychotherapy. They point to the possibility that these fluctuations stem not from conflict or deficit alone, but from both, and from the patient's shifts between different levels of ego integration and object relatedness.

The personality of the therapist. Classical psychoanalytic writings minimize the importance of the therapist's personality type in the treatment process. More recently, writers have acknowledged the importance of the therapist's personal style in setting the tone of therapy and in creating a therapeutic alliance. Yet few write explicitly about the ways in which the therapist's characteristic mode of relating to others affects the course and outcome of treatment. Such character traits obviously cannot be taught, and so represent a problem for those who try to formulate methods of treatment that any properly trained professional can use. The idea that the therapist's psychological makeup plays a crucial role in treatment militates against the notion of psychotherapy as an acquired skill rather than an art.

Even more troublesome is the issue of the extent to which the psychotherapist's own psychological makeup determines his or her view of the nature of psychopathology. The idea that highly personal intrapsychic determinants influence a psychodynamic theorist's concepts of mental health and illness is logical (Guntrip, 1975) but also threatening, for it calls into question the belief held by many psychodynamic therapists that they are engaged in the formulation and practice of a science.

Yet one cannot read the work of writers like Kernberg, Masterson, or Buie and Adler without noticing the striking correspondence between their theories and personal styles. Kernberg's tone is confrontive; his style is intellectual and incisive, and he seems personally eager to meet the challenges of his patients' hostility and paranoid projections. His emphasis on the need to focus on negative transference and conflict pervades the treatments about which he writes. By con-

TABLE 2-1

Controversies in the Technique of Intensive Therapy with Borderline Patients

	Buie and Adler	Chessick	Giovacchini	Gunderson	Kernberg	Masterson
Etiology of the Syndrome	Environment	Environment	Environment + (?) constitution	Constitution + environment	Constitution + environment	Environment
Nature of the Pathology	Deficit	Deficit	Deficit	Conflict/deficit	Conflict	Conflict
Early Interpretation of Transference	No	No	No	No	Yes	No
Essential Early in Treatment	Provide a holding environment	Provide a holding environment	Provide a holding environment	Explore negative transference	Interpret primitive defenses used in sessions	Interpret acting out as related to affect
Origins of Transference	Real disturbance in primary relationships	Real disturbance in primary relationships	Real disturbance in primary relationships	Real disturbance plus patient's distortions of primary relationships	Real disturbance plus patient's distortions of primary relationships	Real disturbance in primary relationships
Therapist's Role in Patient's Experiential Learning	Active structuring Validation of the patient's positive qualities	Inherent in framework Therapist is object for internalizations	Inherent in framework Soothing qualities of therapist and setting	Active structuring Validation of patient's new feelings and perceptions	Inherent in framework Therapist does not retaliate or withdraw	Active structuring Communicative matching

trast, Masterson's tone is parental, and his technique involves a certain amount of coaching. He sees his task in part as creating a better parenting experience for his patient and providing the patient with a role model on which the patient can base new, healthier introjects. Buie and Adler are less confrontive, their styles might generally be described as more warm and giving than that of either Kernberg or Masterson, and they emphasize their patients' longings for a perfect caregiver and the need to allow positive feelings for the therapist to emerge and flower. It seems likely that these approaches would resonate differently with different patients, depending on their levels of object relatedness and their specific defensive styles.

How can we reconcile the fact that these writers, who hold such different views of borderline pathology and treatment, claim to be able to treat borderline patients successfully using divergent techniques? It may be that they achieve success by these different means because the therapeutic action of their interventions is based on factors other than those that they believe to effect change—factors that are common to all of their techniques and that have not yet been identified.

Another possibility is that patients simply select themselves out, and that each writer ultimately establishes working relationships with different subgroups of borderlines with whom there is a good fit. This would be consonant with the empirical finding that the vast majority of borderline patients do not complete psychotherapeutic treatment, and that those who complete treatment successfully are likely to have had previous contacts with other psychotherapists in treatments that did not last (Waldinger and Gunderson, 1984).

The case reports and the analyses that follow represent an attempt to examine the processes of change that occur in the psychotherapy of borderline patients, using detailed clinical material as a data base. This review has focused on the questions of the relative importance of process versus content in the therapeutic work, the primacy of positive versus negative transference, the origins of transference, the usefulness of early interpretation of negative transference, and the therapist's role in providing corrective experiences for borderline patients (for a summary of these issues, see Table 2–1). We do not claim to be able to answer any of these difficult questions based on our analysis of five cases, but we hope to generate hypotheses that will inform further research in this area. Our aim is to look at different patients' baseline psychopathology, different therapists' treatment techniques, and the match between therapist and patient to see if we can determine any relationship between these factors and the outcome of intensive psychotherapy.

3

Martha
Case Report

Martha entered psychotherapy in the fall of 1976. Her chief complaint was: "I am very depressed and think a lot of killing myself." She was a single woman in her late twenties who had taught music to handicapped children. However, she was essentially incapacitated at the time she began her treatment, unable to function at her job consistently, spending her days in her apartment with a bottle of vodka, which she used as a home remedy for the anxiety and depression that kept her immobilized.

For our first meeting, Martha was brought to my office by her mother. Martha was alert, cooperative, and pleasant-looking, with a quiet, self-effacing style. She sat passively while her mother peremptorily offered her "two cents worth," which consisted of a host of complaints about such matters as Martha's use of alcohol, her poor eating habits, and her ambivalence about working. After her mother left the office, Martha sat and smoked disconsolately. She was reserved and moderately anxious, preferring to respond rather than to initiate dialogue. In response to questions, she described feelings of inadequacy, a sense of hopelessness about her life, and continual suicidal ideation.

She told me that her mother had picked her up from Rhode Island and brought her to Boston, where her mother found her a roommate, an apartment, and a job. Her mother's caretaking extended to setting the patient's hair, making her meals, and driving her around, so that the patient could not even find her way from her apartment to my office on her own.

This dependence was all the more remarkable because of her report of prior estrangement from her mother. She quickly came to feel that she could not be apart from her mother. Her general sense of helplessness led her to opt for a job as an aide, even though she had been hired as a therapist and had functioned in that capacity before. She felt that she would kill herself if she couldn't succeed at the job, and so scaled down her responsibilities as an act of self-preservation. Her mother had expressed disappointment at this move.

When the patient's mother announced that she needed to depart in order to negotiate a business deal, they both cried. Martha felt "somewhat abandoned but not angry." The patient's roomate resented the mother's bossy interference and taunted the patient about her submissiveness. Martha had no friends in the Boston area, and would return from orientation sessions at her workplace to take Stelazine (from an old prescription) and drink three glasses of vodka to numb herself into somnolence.

Over the three weeks subsequent to her mother's departure, Martha described feeling bored, stupid, and inadequate in all ways, apparently inviting me to take over for her mother. When I presented this assessment to her, she seemed unmoved by it.

She became unable to work, spent most of her days in bed, lost her appetite, began to lose a significant amount of weight, and maintained poor fluid intake. She saw her life as hopeless, without pleasure, and found it impossible to believe that it could be otherwise. I prescribed a small number of tricyclic antidepressant tablets at each of the next few sessions, but it soon became clear that circumstances and time would not permit a therapeutic trial of this modality on an outpatient basis. Martha was virtually immobilized. Her suicidal rumination was nearly continuous; she fantasized about taking an overdose of drugs or running her car into a tree. She believed that death would lead to relief from suffering and to burial next to her father, but she regretted that her sister would get all of her clothes if she died. Thus, three weeks after she began treatment, there seemed no alternative to hospitalization. Martha readily agreed to this plan. Her hospitalization at McLean provided me with the opportunity to learn more about her in a setting where I was less apprehensive about her safety.

Background Information

The patient was the second of two daughters born to a prodigal alcoholic heir to an industrial fortune and his alcohol-abusing wife. The parents were divorced within a year of the patient's birth, and the mother, sister, and patient moved to another city. The patient resumed contact with her father when she was three or four years old by spending the summers with him, a practice that continued up to and including her teenage years.

Her mother embarked on a string of unsuccessful marriages. Martha recalled being cared for by a series of nurses. Her father sent money. Her mother entertained lavishly but had little to do with the children. Martha felt guilty that she could not recall much about her mother in that period. One "good nurse" remained for 5 years but was dismissed when Martha's mother accused her of stealing (something that the patient doubts the nurse ever did). Martha began to attend small private schools, where she felt popular with the other children. Her overall academic performance was average, but she had superior reading skills.

She idealized her mother and blamed her stepfathers for her mother's unhappiness. When Martha was 12, against the advice of a counselor to whom the mother brought the patient, she was sent to live with her father while her mother moved to another state. The patient remembers badly wanting to go with her and finding the separation extraordinarily painful and inexplicable. She could not recall feeling any anger at that time. Upon moving into her father's home, she quickly felt at odds with her stepmother and had behavior problems at school. She felt fat and unattractive, and had few friends. Her schoolwork deteriorated, and she was eventually expelled for truancy, drinking, and disrespectful behavior. A year after their separation, her mother invited Martha to rejoin her. However, the patient refused, saying that she had begun to find friends. She recalled feeling alienated from her mother at that time, if not specifically angry.

She was unprepared for her menarche at age 13 and kept it a secret. Her adolescence became increasingly stormy. She fought with her father, who was continually drunk, and began to engage in overt self-destructive behaviors, including cutting her wrists, drinking alone, and allowing herself to be used sexually, with subsequent feelings of guilt. On one occasion, she cut the side of her face with a razor and noted that it felt good and did not hurt. Her somewhat secretive self-mutilation continued throughout high school and college. She also engaged in significant drug abuse.

During high school the patient had several boyfriends, but characteristically lost sexual interest in them after a time. She had not been orgasmic in any of her relationships and was never involved exclusively with one man. Typically, she became jealous and controlling in relationships. During one such episode, she began scratching her legs and threatened to jump out of her boyfriend's moving vehicle.

She managed to be accepted at a small woman's college in the West, but toward the end of her freshman year she began to run a fever, feeling tired and unwell. A chest x-ray during the summer break revealed a mediastinal tumor, which proved to be malignant. The patient then had major surgery followed by a successful course of radiation therapy. These treatments delayed the start of her sophomore year at college. The delay was the only thing that disturbed the patient, who never believed she might die. She thought at the time that her bout with cancer would "pay back my father, who deserved to have to worry about me." During her treatments, she interrupted all self-destructive activities.

The patient returned to school one year later, and during that year her father became moribund with end-stage cirrhosis. She guiltily recalled that he had asked her to kiss him, but that she was repelled by his appearance and did not do so. He died that evening after she left.

The patient then made her home with her father's sister's family in Rhode Island. Reportedly she was taken advantage of by this aunt, who called her "Cinderella" and made her do menial errands. Martha was able to complete college and, after working for two years as an aide with disabled children, returned to school for a master's degree in music therapy.

She ostensibly lived in her own apartment during this period, but in fact always stayed at her aunt and uncle's house or at the home of a boyfriend's parents. She would have frequent fights with this boyfriend, get drunk, and go off to stay with another boyfriend. She was also abusing alcohol and a variety of medications. This pattern was intensified as she found herself torn between her aunt and uncle in their martial discord. The patient felt tied by her blood relation to her aunt, whom she experienced as mean, but also felt devoted to her uncle. Her uncle rewarded her loyalty with increasing confidences, including details of his sexual frustration and his wife's infidelity. Her aunt retaliated for the patient's lack of allegiance with harassment, humiliation, and ridicule.

Martha's paternal great-grandfather had founded a major industrial concern, and a substantial amount of money remained within the family. However, her father had squandered much of this wealth, and the funds held for Martha and her sister in trust funds were controlled by an aged aunt. Martha thus had the sense that she was well-to-do but had no access to her money. Her uncle provided funds for her first psychotherapy and continued to pay for subsequent treatments after he and Martha's aunt were divorced. In this first treatment prior to her move to Boston, Martha was seen once a week and was treated with consecutive six-month trials of amitriptyline and perphenazine, without a noteworthy response to either medication.

The patient managed to complete her masters degree, but was functioning poorly at school and in her daily life. When her estranged mother visited her in Rhode Island, she decided that Martha needed protection from her aunt. It was then that her mother transferred her daughter to Boston so that she might be closer to her older sister, who had recently relocated there. The sister has had an actively rivalrous relationship with Martha and a series of unhappy relationships with men.

First Year of Therapy

In the hospital milieu, Martha's activity and involvement with people increased. She developed friendships with patients that followed the rules of gang loyalty; they played "cops and robbers" against the established community rules. This involved importing and consuming alcohol and drugs, as well as abusing privileges. The patient "supported" her friends with misleading comments in denial of their illnesses and allowed herself to be similarly misled by them. Frustrations were attributed to hypocritical and insensitive staff, inexperienced and sadistic administrators, or irrationally jealous parents. She was a passive victim. She continued to be preoccupied with suicidal ideation and impulsivity, but her actions were not serious.

I was idealized as perfect and yet remote. My observations of the shallowness of Martha's interpersonal relationships led to a deepening dysphoria and embryonic awareness that she was recreating with the hospital staff the rivalrous and passively controlling involvements with her sister, aunt, and mother. Martha described herself as "the queen of the inpatient unit," a reference to her prominence and acceptance as the acknowledged leader of the acting-out group of patients on the ward. She interpreted my visiting her for our meetings on the inpatient unit as an indication of her specialness. (Actually, she lacked the privilege to come to my office on the grounds.) She had fantasies of being adopted by me, of living with me as a sister or daughter or as the nanny for my children.

In those first few months of psychotherapy, conducted four times per week, basic themes emerged that were to become elaborated, repeated, and intertwined thereafter. There seemed to be an inverse relationship between the intensity of her self-destructive acting out and the extent to which she was aware of depressive or anxious affects. Prior to her self-destructive actions, she frequently experienced a tormenting feeling of tension in her lower back that was associated with intense anxiety and an apparently irresistible urge for self-mutilatory action that seemed to be the only source of relief. She spoke of her attachment to me and her sense that I was perfect and all-powerful in her life, and used passive means of attempting to control me (e.g., through presents, superficial compliance, flattery, and coercive dependence). Martha described a recurrent dream of a shark: She is on an inner tube, her mother is on a party boat out of her reach, and sharks circle ominously in the waters. I spoke of her fear that she would lose control of her voraciousness. In response, the patient reported seeing sharks everywhere in the room approaching her with open mouths, which led her to associate to her habit of drinking everyone's drink at parties.

When Martha's uncle voiced his reluctance to underwrite her hospital expenses, she responded with a Christmas gift to him and his new wife that expressed her profound ambivalence toward them: She had knitted a pin cushion with their pictures secretly enclosed within, so that, when used, it would result in their unwitting symbolic self-destruction. This disappointment by her uncle intensified her idealization of me. She wanted consciously to be my child. But she was also angry with me. "A lot of good you've done me—you made me know how miserable I am. I prefer to get drunk and do anything I want. I hate you . . . sort of."

Her splitting and acting out escalated. She played off her aunt against her uncle and his new wife by making inflammatory comments to one about the other. She incited her mother against the hospital and then, after her mother accused the hospital of cheating her, she told her mother about her drug abuse and wrist slashing since the age of 15. I pointed out that to the hospital she was a victim of her family, and to her family she was a victim of the hospital. She repeatedly manipulated would-be rescuers to try to outdo themselves in coming to her aid, but their efforts always disappointed her and left her with the sense of being a passive victim, "a volleyball" who, despite all the string pulling, was essentially helpless and powerless. Martha observed these patterns but then became angry with me for "taking away [her] defenses." She involved herself increasingly with alcohol, marijuana, and what she called "sleazy sex." She insisted that this was "having fun" despite my interpretation that such activity expressed her poor self-regard and anger at those who tried to control her.

In the hospital she associated primarily with male adolescents, and tended to relate masochistically to them and to set herself up as a victim of their exploits. For instance, she loaned her car to a young boy, who then used it for an armed robbery and completely destroyed it. She responded by giving him a blank check to pay for the damages. I interpreted this as another form of self-mutilation. In fact, she felt less need to harm herself within the context of such masochistic relationships.

After a staff conference at which her hospital treatment was reviewed, Martha pressed me: "Do they like me?" "Will they keep me?" "Can I be helped?" To the last question, I answered, "Yes, but not with certainty or quickly."

Martha recognized her dependence on me with alarm. She continued to view me as all good on a conscious level in the apparent hope that I would protect her (against her loneliness and rage), much as she had elevated hopes for protection by her mother and uncle. Her depression persisted, and she wondered whether others (her uncle, her sister, and me) would love her enough to stop her from killing herself. When I announced my vacation 2 weeks in advance, the patient became enraged (at her uncle!) and then depressed. She was easily persuaded to look at her feelings toward me: "I depend on you too much; if you leave, or if I can't afford to see you, I'll kill myself."

A week later, I changed the time of an appointment. She came in 15 minutes late ("I forgot") and obviously had been drinking. She related having seen me in the coffee shop during part of the regularly scheduled time and wondered "Why you weren't meeting with me then." She denied any relationship between this incident and the drinking. I interpreted her wish to be loved and her expectation of either a jealous exclusive possession or rejection. She responded by angrily recalling three minor tidbits of affection that, in her opinion, she had received over the previous 9 months of treatment (these consisted of my noticing a change in her hair style or a new dress, etc).

The impending exhaustion of Martha's trust fund made the financial support for her continued psychotherapy an obvious issue. Although she and her administrator were negotiating with the hospital for a fee reduction, she could not ask me for the same consideration. Even when I raised the subject, her attachment and fear of rejection prevented her from making such a forward request. Finally, prior to my vacation, I unilaterally set a lower fee. This seemed to hold little pleasure for Martha, who felt guilty and unworthy.

She was distinctly depressed upon my return. She feared that "you know that I'm evil and must hate me for it." I contrasted this opinion with her compulsive presentation of the false self of "a good little girl, underneath which you hide your secret impulsivity." She was given increased privileges by her administrator, and promptly used them to drink and have sex. She said, "I am incurable. Do you still feel hopeful about me?" I remarked that this was a test of my commitment to her, and carried with it the hope that I would save her and assert my claim over that of her male suitors. Shortly thereafter, she escaped from the hospital, was placed on escape status, and returned after another sex/drug-taking/alcohol excursion, losing her privileges again.

Administratively, the staff faced a dilemma: When given the privilege to leave the inpatient unit, Martha acted self-destructively; but when confined to the unit, her dependence on the hospital grew. As her trust fund dwindled and discharge from the hospital became imminent, Martha's difficulty in handling autonomy became more severe. Martha was presented with the staff's dilemma, thereby giving her more opportunity to collaborate on an adult level with the treatment team. However, she clung to the hope that her desperation would compel her uncle to pay for her continued hospitalization, and she did not cooperate with efforts to give her increased privileges and thereby wean her from the inpatient unit.

Although Martha felt better on some occasions, she could not imagine life after her hospitalization. She saw no alternative to dependence upon her uncle or suicide. Additionally, she was afraid of getting well, consciously fearing that this would mean giving up her tie to me. I assured her that "We have much work still ahead of us." Nonetheless, her acting out continued as she sought "thrills" and again escaped from the hospital, using drugs, alcohol, sex, and privilege abuse to provide the desired elements of danger and discharge of tension. After one more hazardous escapade, she asked me how I would feel if she killed herself. I replied that I would be sad. She became overtly tearful, as she had not been previously in therapy. She went on to say, "No one else knows how depressed I am." She also spoke of feeling angry that I wouldn't rescue her "by taking me home to your house with the picket fence."

The theme of rescue from her self-destructive impulses gave way, in the face of dwindling resources to support her hospitalization, to a picture of frozen panic. While recognizing that she had overidealized me in a way that replicated her view of her uncle and her mother before that, she remained immobilized and miserable, burning herself, looking frightened and overwhelmed. Facing the prospect of my leaving for another vacation, she invited her mother to return to the area, thereby recreating the initial contact that had occurred when her mother deposited her in my office.

Just prior to her discharge, she rallied briefly by locating a job for herself, finding an inexpensive halfway house, and agreeing to decrease the frequency of therapy from four to three times per week. She came to her appointments feeling miserable, complaining that she could talk about her feelings only with me, but felt noticeably better as the hour progressed. On the unit, she continued to burn herself with cigarettes and felt tense and helpless, with continual suicidal ideation. She asked for my home phone number, and I gave it to her. She responded facetiously, "I'm a shark—I want your address too," but was much relieved by my giving her access to me by telephone. Her final inpatient hour of this nine-month hospitalization period found her feeling somewhat better but fiercely dependent, sharing a fantasy of slashing the tires on my car if I had canceled this appointment.

She was discharged with a diagnosis of borderline personality and a guarded prognosis. She was extraordinarily anxious during her first few days in the halfway house, taking oxycodone (unprescribed) "to feel strong" and to block her rage. She was "good" in the therapist's office (i.e., she wouldn't cry or smoke and offered me gifts), but outside the office, she was provocative with a potentially violent male friend. As my summer vacation approached, she was filled with sadness, helplessness, depression, and anxiety, which she consciously related to my upcoming departure. She refused the option of interim therapy but was relieved when offered scheduled weekly telephone calls with me. She acknowledged fearing that I would not return because of the intensity of her rage.

Thus, after a year of therapy, the clinical picture was bleak, frightening to Martha, to Martha's administrator, and to me. The therapy itself was jeopardized by her lack of access to a containing environment; by her mother's pressure to undermine the therapy and again "rescue" Martha; by my own unspoken anxiety and uncertainty about the prospects for successful treatment under these circumstances; and, not least, by Martha's unrelenting needs and the pressure for their immediate gratification. My technical approach emphasized relentless and sometimes somber reflection to Martha of her self-deceptive attempts to control those she counted on to rescue her from her own impulses. I pointed to her reliance on overidealization and passive-appearing manipulation as the means of exerting this control. While she frequently complained of being shown things in therapy that she did not want to see and of being more unhappy as a result, she was always on time and even avid in her attendance, and had developed, this frustration notwithstanding, a profound and desperate attachment to me.

For example, she expressed much bitterness and despair regarding her uncle's refusal to underwrite her treatment. She was "hurt" when I observed that she was not really her uncle's child, but only hoped to be, and that his tangible support was equated with her value in his eyes. The parallel situation in the transference was explicitly clarified, and the meagerness of my offerings compared to her longings was underscored.

Second Year of Therapy

My summer vacation was punctuated by four telephone calls from Martha; two had been scheduled, and two were initiated by her when she felt pressured by her mother to leave the halfway house and return home to Atlanta. Upon my return, her mother accompanied her to the first appointment, entered my office with her, and delivered a barrage of complaints about Martha, her progress, and the treatment she had received. Martha remained very passive throughout, only commenting after her mother left, "She depresses me—here we go again." Her mother went home and wrote a letter to the director of the hospital, expressing many of the same feelings and emphasizing her alarm at the patient's dependence on me. She believed that I should either "sell" Martha on a transfer to a community mental health center, or failing that, forcibly compel her to return to Atlanta with herself.

In the days after her mother's departure, Martha mused aloud to me, "Does mother want to destroy me?" I suggested that this uncertainty made leave-taking especially hard. Martha recalled that, when she was 12, her mother had ignored advice to keep Martha with her, no matter what happened. Martha went on to say that her mother "took a vacation from mothering for 15 years" and added, "You're more important to me now than she is, but you may not be important enough" (to prevent suicide). For the remainder of that month, she floundered along in the halfway house and at her job, feeling depressed, stupid, ineffective, inadequate, and enraged. She spoke of her fantasies of suicide, of her wish to throw my clock at me, and to pour soft drinks over my head. My interventions emphasized the importance of this rage, of the need to speak of these feelings rather than act them out in one disguise or another. She responded, "You believe me."

In subsequent sessions, Martha described an overdose with 15 pain pills of unknown type that remained undetected by the staff at the halfway house. I confronted her with the implications of this act, but she refused the option of hospitalization and rejected her mother's plea to return to Atlanta as unthinkable, the equivalent of death. I contacted the halfway house to notify them, insisted that Martha bring in the balance of her pills, and arranged for telephone contact before the next appointment. However, an hour before the appointment, she ingested seven or eight additional pain pills and announced this upon entry. I said that I felt the situation was out of control and insisted upon hospitalization at that point. She was readmitted to McLean for 13 days, during which time transfer to the Day Hospital Program of a community mental health center was arranged.

I underscored the seriousness of Martha's suicidal behavior and emphasized that the therapy could not proceed usefully if it was a hostage to her threat of suicide. Martha was characteristically passive, offering no serious objections to her hospitalization but implicitly reserving the right to exercise her self-destructive means of protest.

Martha readily exploited the opportunity for splitting between a therapist unaffiliated with the Day Hospital and the Day Hospital staff. It was as if she had heard the admitting resident's question to me upon his review of the case: "Doctor, exactly what is it that you feel your 14 months of therapy with the patient has accomplished?" Just as she had held herself above interactions at the halfway house, she disdained interaction with the less advantaged patients of the Day Program, and felt entitled to mislead her treatment team about her feelings and to hide her ongoing low-level self-destructiveness (cigarette burns on her forearm, etc.). She tried to provoke me to fight with her administrator at the Day Hospital Program and to oppose her mother's continuing effort to have her return to Atlanta.

Furious as Martha was, it was hard for her to connect this feeling directly with me. She said that she loved me but could not talk to me. She seemed to try to surrender her fate to me, and I commented upon this consistently. I also addressed her difficulty in giving voice to her rage, noting that it was "easier to write it in blood than to speak it and feel it here."

Just prior to one of our sessions during this period, a telephone call came from the halfway house, indicating that Martha had again burned herself with a cigarette. She entered with the comment, "Now I have something to remember you by." She emphasized how hurt she was and how she felt compelled to take this action, but couldn't say that it was I who had hurt her or who had forced her into this position. I remarked, "It's frightening to need someone so much and not to be able to control them." She was moved and continued this thought, saying, "It's frightening because you can kill me with what you say" or by "not caring or leaving." I commented, "We can see why you need for me to be perfect."

In the following weeks, I raised the issue of eventually decreasing Martha's therapy from three to two visits per week because of her dwindling funds. She became tearful and described feeling "numbness, total loss." She called me three times over the following weekend but could not acknowledge feeling angry, abandoned, or misled. However, her cutting and burning increased, and when I notified her administrator at the Day Hospital Program, Martha became angry at this apparent act of disloyalty. I reiterated my need to inform the treatment team and not participate in a coverup that would undermine them in their attempts to protect her.

Martha became increasingly passive, experiencing herself as a victim. I commented that she acted as though I needed to draw things out of her because she felt that she could not speak about her concerns and saw herself again as a volleyball bounced about by an uncaring therapist and others. She spoke of feeling terrible, of crying all day on the weekends. When I noted that it was "a long time between hours," she nodded.

She moved into an apartment with a young man from the halfway house who slavishly adored her. Like her mother, the young man paid for her food, rent, and cigarettes, prepared the meals, and waited upon her. Her passivity increased, and I confronted her with her being "spoon-fed" and with how good she was at eliciting such "feeding" and its destructive effect on her self-esteem. She said, "I don't like your saying that I can't relinquish the security and pleasure of lining up rescuers." She experienced pleasure in recognizing the degree of skill involved in recruiting all of these caretakers.

During this period, Martha continued to drink excessively, cut and burned herself, and even tried to jump from a moving car. After reporting that she felt hurt about not getting a birthday present from me, she repeated the cutting and burning, but was now consciously aware of her rage toward me. At the next appointment, she shared a 3-week-old fantasy of shooting heself in the head. "It makes me mad that you don't get frustrated and angry with me. But I suppose that would be spoon feeding," she said, grinning, "and that doesn't work in here." I noted the difference in seriousness between cigarettes and guns, and also the hostility involved in the fantasy, emphasizing the need to separate fantasy from action. I alluded to her pleasure in speaking of the fantasy and remarked that she seemed insufficiently concerned about the danger. I also notified her that I would be sharing this information with her administrator at the Day Hospital. The following hour, she revealed that she had taken an overdose of five trifluoperazine 5-mg tablets with alcohol. She agreed to notify her administrator herself (I later confirmed that she had done this).

When I was late for the following hour, Martha was directly angry with me. I commented that she felt entitled to have her shoes literally tied by her devoted boyfriend/caretaker and became enraged when a relied-upon rescuer let her down (i.e., my lateness). That weekend was the first one in recent memory in which she did not cut or burn herself. The next hour, she related her sadistic fantasy of locking me out of my office, telling this in a teasing manner with clear enjoyment.

In the following hours, Martha complained that I was not sympathetic anymore, that I blamed her for everything and was trying to get rid of her, that my image intruded on her relationships with others and disrupted things. I spoke of her fear of being abandoned again, but also of her wish to be rid of me. "You have many negative feelings toward me that need to be spoken of, but I will still be here, good and bad."

At an appointment shortly thereafter, Martha entered, having had several drinks prior to the meeting. Her "demon" was tormenting her. She was able to recognize and acknowledge her anger at me, agreeing that she would like to punch me in the nose but couldn't tolerate that feeling. At the end of the hour, I reminded her that acting out her anger worked against our common purpose. The next hour, I remarked, "This demon is your anger, your screaming. You've tried to knock it out with alcohol or buy it off with a few cuts or burns." Martha became sad and said, "I don't believe I'll be able to love anyone. Will I get better?" I answered, "You're asking me to promise you more than I can guarantee." Her sadness deepened, and I noted this along with her increased capacity to tolerate that affect. In the succeeding hour, Martha said that she felt she didn't deserve anything, that she tricked people into their positive actions toward her. At the same time, she lamented that I used to be kind and giving, but was so no longer.

In an hour that followed, Martha agreed that she was always aiming at others when she hurt herself, and a week later announced that she would no longer cut or burn herself anymore: "It doesn't work; yet I feel I'm losing something." I agreed. "Yes, you're losing the illusion that you can control your mother, your uncle, or me this way." She went through the next couple of weeks without feeling like killing herself, but said she did not want to tell me for fear that I would stop caring about her. When I refused to exaggerate her disability on a claim form, Martha remarked, "You're not going to rescue me, but I know that you care." However, after I canceled and rescheduled an appointment, she again drank and burned herself for the first time in several weeks. She reported that her anger, as well as her fear of progress, had clouded her mind. I described this as a regression that did not erase her achievement; it showed that she could still use these means of self-expression if she felt she needed to do so.

When I took a vacation the following month, Martha felt tortured by herself and others. She experienced me as not sympathetic enough because I did not schedule a telephone call, but rather insisted that she initiate it (which she did after her car was stolen). She said that this was not as satisfying as it would have been if I had sensed her needs and had "spoon-fed" her. She acknowledged feeling suicidal but was reassured by the structure of therapy: "I know we'll be meeting after Memorial Day."

She viewed her relationships at this time as exploitive; she felt guilty about that and wished to be independent. Though she despised those whom she could control, she could not tolerate independent objects.

At about this time, she began to ask that I and others address her as Martha rather than "Marnie." She associated the name Marnie, she later said, with a period of impulsivity and helpless ploys aimed at vengeance. Over the next months and years she maintained this preference and came to be referred to as Martha by everyone. In retrospect, it struck me that a repudiation of her mother may also have been involved in this decision, not only because her mother called her Marnie (even after she requested the change) also because her mother herself was referred to as Maggie.

The next month, her mother urged her to discontinue therapy and return to Atlanta. Martha rejected the offer and felt better after doing so. During the following weeks, she took two small overdoses, but quickly recognized the hostility and the wish to kill the frustrating objects in her life that motivated these gestures. She pictured her mother and uncle as the villains but could agree that her own manipulation and passive-aggressiveness had set up the disappointments and ensuing depression, rage, and self-destructive attempts at retaliation. I commented, "Nothing you do at those times increases the chance that they will care for you; you experience their responses as either total neglect or successful exploitation on your part; there is no middle ground. And, of course, they seem to tempt you with promises of rescue, but you invite that and are always disappointed and enraged." She responded, "Yes, I'm sure of it; it's a setup."

Later that month, her mother was in town and joined Martha for a meeting with me. She expressed optimism over Martha's increased energy level and her beginning to work in a clerical position arranged through the Day Hospital's vocational rehabilitation department. Speaking with the two of them, I emphasized the probability of future ups and downs, Martha's remaining problems with dependency, and the substantial backlog of misunderstanding that remained with the mother and others in the family.

The next month, Martha moved into her own apartment and began working full time. When she spoke of her anxiety and misgivings, I asked, "Why shouldn't you feel burdened and unsure?"

Martha had been losing weight and at this point had reached 98 lb,

largely voluntarily and in order to improve her appearance—not, however, without a dimension of provocation ("starving before everyone's
eyes"), which she acknowledged with a smile. In the weeks before
she made her break with the Day Hospital, she had had her wallet
stolen, was nearly raped, and made telephone contact with me over
the weekend on a couple of occasions. The last week before her termination, she cut her wrist superficially. She told me that I must agree
to call her during my vacation in August. I refused, but offered the
name of an interim therapist and his telephone number in case she
felt that she needed to speak to him. She insisted that I did not understand, sympathize, or care about her, that I must wish her dead.
She then took out a camera and, over my objections, took a picture of
me that she felt she needed and was entitled to have in order to get
through the vacation.

Third Year of Therapy

During my absence, Martha got around to obtaining a psychophar-
macology consultation that had been recommended earlier. The consultant noted the family history of alcoholism and depression, and recommended a trial of lithium for her unstable mood. She refused.

She called me once during my vacation and had been drinking. She
was remorseful about having called. In succeeding meetings, her masochism was explored in terms of inviting "accidents" (e.g., giving her
car to a stranger, giving a blank check to her former slave/boyfriend,
leaving her wallet on a bar stool from which it disappeared). Her weight
had dropped to 91 lb. I pointed out her aggression and her wish to
have others take control. It was as if she were saying, "Watch me slip
away." I stated that she was making her life an issue between herself
and other people, including me, as opposed to accepting responsibility
for taking reasonable care of herself.

At this time, Martha had her first evaluation after 3 months at work
and received a good rating. She also made it a point to have her new
associates refer to her as Martha rather than Marnie. She told me,
"Marnie clings, while Martha is cool, distant, and desired by men."
In fact, her appearance was greatly changed at this time, in part as a
result of the weight loss, but also because she devoted much more
attention to her hair and her selection of clothing, which tended to be
tasteful and expensive but also sexually provocative and attention
seeking.

Martha was involved with a man who was unreliable, devaluing,
and exploitive, and who subsequently robbed her apartment. After an
incident of his abuse of her, she cut her wrist superficially for the first
time in 6 months. She described her rage and hopelessness, and agreed
that it was worsened by the sense that she had invited his assault. She

then described a plan to go "stoned" that night to a party, knowing that her former boyfriend/quasi-rapist/apartment robber would be there with his new girlfriend. I pointed out her recurrent invitation of this misery: "You haven't had enough. You're going back for more, and you have to drug yourself to hide how it makes you feel." Martha's weight then fell to 88 lb, and I observed that the weight loss began to replicate her malignancy in its effect on her appearance, in its use as a test of love, and in providing her with an opportunity for vengeance. I noted that she might again require hospitalization if there was no improvement. The next month she weighed 84 lb. I described her thinness as a continuation of her cutting and burning and said, "It's not clear if we can understand it sufficiently before you starve yourself to death." She became quite anxious and pressed me with questions on a variety of subjects that appeared to need immediate answers. However, the following hour she related that she had begun to eat and take vitamins.

The next months witnessed a sustained rise in Martha's feeling of well-being. She said that she felt "alive again" and began keeping plants in her apartment (all her old ones had died from neglect). She began to clean her apartment, painted it, expressed pleasure at her accomplishments at work, and started dating in a more self-respecting mode. She confessed that she had long held a secret "stash" of phenobarbital ("my security blanket") that she had set aside from an earlier source as a guaranteed means of self-destruction.

Martha spoke of an increasing awareness of her own role in the continuing rivalry with her sister. This was quite a different perspective from her earlier insistence upon herself as the victim of a mean and hypocritical older sibling. She also reported feeling much more capable, less afraid to socialize, to drive, and to go to work. She felt afraid of her anger, specifically mentioning her rage at her uncle, and feared that this feeling could get out of control.

She raised the issue of the future of therapy. Her mother and family urged her to decrease her attendance from twice a week, but she said that she did not agree. She asked me for a recommendation. I said that therapy was more elective at this time but that she could certainly benefit from treatment for a long time to come. She said she was no longer "a cancer patient needing radiation."

After Martha received the news of a friend's suicide, she furiously blamed the hospital, but with encouragement went on to explore her relationship to her illness; she saw herself as its victim, but could also see how she used it to extort "supplies."

In the succeeding months, aspects of Martha's character structure came increasingly into focus in her therapy. I was able to comment on her use of her sexual attractiveness (through dresses with slits, makeup, and dramatic jewelry) as a prominent way of gaining admiration and attention. She had little money but lived like royalty with her inherited silver, china, and an anticipated legacy. Her relatives provided her with these gifts and with her impressive wardrobe because they still competed for the position of her retainer. She felt special and became anxious if this status with me or with another important object appeared to be in jeopardy.

Her tendency to seek out sadistic boyfriends was scrutinized. She agreed that she was fascinated by their unpredictability and attempted to master this projected threat.

As the third year of therapy ended, Martha was working in a valued and resilient psychotherapeutic alliance, confiding in it and enjoying her connection with me. Before my vacation, she wondered, "How much do you worry about me? How much do you remember and care about me?" She expressed the fear that her increased health meant that I would be less available and that this would mean less affection for her. I asked, "So worrying is the same as caring?" she responded, "Yeah. That's the way people are—they worry when you're sick." The character of the therapeutic interaction had shifted from its earlier imperative attempts to contain her primitive impulses to the more usual outpatient relationship.

Fourth Year of Therapy

Work on character issues continued in the fourth year. Martha observed that she had always aspired to be "pretty, witty, and charming," but that this was a limiting role. I asked her whether she was growing out of her "party girl" stance, yet feared exposure of deeper emotional needs. When her self-esteem was damaged (such as when a boyfriend distanced himself), she fell back on her persecutor/victim role. When I called attention to her fluctuating estimates of how highly I valued her, she became increasingly aware of the pressure of her longing to be loved and of her ready experience of worthlessness. In the fall of that year, looking back on her self-mutilation, she said, "Ugh, I can't believe I lived that way." Her previous recklessness gave way to an inhibition about making changes. She associated change with the frequent moves, the parade of stepfathers, and the general instability of her youth.

To bring the sessions into conformance with the rest of my practice, I announced a decrease in the length of the sessions from 50 to 45 minutes (an announcement that I had deferred until I felt she was on sufficiently solid ground). Martha wondered about her specialness but was able to speak of this, verbalizing her fear that this decrease represented a rejection and a lessening of her importance to me.

She still could not speak of sexual issues with me; she found them "too disturbing—it doesn't go with my Victorian lady image." Shortly thereafter, she wondered if I had been angry or frustrated with her. With some prodding, she went on to ask how therapy would stop, who would decide, and whether I would announce it (as with the shortened meetings). I asked, "After three years, are you asking if I would unilaterally throw you out? Your father left, and you didn't understand he was going, or say goodbye; it won't happen that way here." Martha cried and felt relieved.

Her taste in boyfriends had by now changed substantially. She found herself in a longer-term relationship with two professional men who appeared to be drawn to her attractiveness and hysteroid charm but who did not seem to be looking for marriage. She was able to recognize the emergence of her "Marnie" side, with its clinging demands for closeness and for an intimacy that neither these men nor she could tolerate. As if to confirm this analysis, she eliminated one boyfriend by a conspicuous use of alcohol, amphetamines, and cocaine, accompanied by vivid stories of her previous hospitalization. When this behavior frightened him off, she managed to become separated from her purse and camera, and had a second apartment break-in, in a repetition of her posture as "a potential victim waiting for a crime." She retaliated against men who disappointed her with sexual teasing, which she recognized as sadistic and they confirmed as hurtful. I said, "You've turned yourself into a weapon, but you can't solve your depression from the outside by coercing them to provide reassurance, hedges against loneliness, and a sense of self-worth."

A few weeks later, just prior to a planned skiing vacation with her remaining boyfriend, Jack, she overdosed with alcohol and five or six of his Quaaludes in his apartment. He took her to a local emergency room, where she was released in a few hours. When she came in for her next hour, I reclarified her regressive attempts to extort love and to express rage through the use of alcohol and pills. She responded, "It doesn't work."

Indeed, after they returned from skiing, the boyfriend withdrew. Martha felt sad and angry, but reported that she did not feel wholly bad or responsible. She noted that this was the first time she had not been self-destructive in response to a major loss. I acknowledged that she had indeed had something to do with the man's withdrawal but that she was not the sole cause. She said, "I told Jack not to worry— I always have you." In fact, she was maintaining and availing herself of many sources of support for her self-esteem: She turned to friends, she continued her running (a reasonable sublimation that she had developed in lieu of the prior cutting, burning, and starving), and followed through on an appointment with her internist. At the end of a poignant hour, in which I was moved by her courage, I said, "You're handling this like a woman. It's as though you know that you're still worth something after Jack."

Martha continued to do well, and in her telephone contact with Jack dealt humorously with him, his evasiveness, and her responsibility in frightening him off with her demands. She acknowledged loving him still, and told me that she felt okay, and found this strange. She said that she felt this was possible as a result of our joint work. She said, "We can both love." Indeed, I felt that I did love her in that hour, her courage and tenacity in the search for love and self-respect. She continued to work through her loss in the following weeks, knowing that she was angry with Jack and fearing a return of "Marnieism," but told me, "The worst is over."

Martha reviewed the relationship and could see how Jack's distancing had fed into her self-doubts and self-loathing and increased her frantic selling of herself, which in turn had increased his anxiety and distancing, creating a vicious cycle. She took pride in this exploration and seemed visibly to divert her residual masochism into long-distance running and cycling.

She asked again what my feelings were toward her. She said she felt that "You made me a person," but did I care for her as a person or just as a case? I asked, "Do you think you could feel so connected and vulnerable with a machine, a technician?" She said, "No, but it's hard to say that in here; outside it's easier."

Later that spring, Martha heard that her mother had accidentally stepped on and killed her pet bird (which she had entrusted to her mother's care). Disturbed as she was by this, Martha was also impressed with the humor of this incident and how it captured the smothering, the inconsistencies, and the hazards of her mother's caregiving.

As the summer break approached, more work was done on Martha's "hyperfeminine" appearance. She understood how her style belied her career goals, her seriousness, and even her commitment to running. It seemed to be successful in attracting men, but that in itself had its problems—who she attracted and for what reason.

Fifth Year of Therapy

Martha asked for my telephone number prior to my vacation but did not use it. On my return, she began to speak of her sexual frustrations ("I can't believe I'm saying this") and struggled through feeling "bad, dirty, and wrong" in her "Victorian woman attitude." She found that she enjoyed her sexual encounters and was even orgasmic at the outset, but eventually lost interest and then experienced the man as unattractive and contact with him as "repulsive."

At times, Martha would briefly feel her "demon" return. But on a few occasions, this feeling was dispelled dramatically during the course of the hour when some blocked affect (usually rage) was identified and expressed. This experience was sufficiently impressive that she began this type of introspection on her own, with recognizable success.

She had been working as a ward clerk at a local hospital and had broadened her role substantially by presenting a proposal to her superiors to work as a patient advocate and explainer of the frequently strange and sometimes painful diagnostic studies she scheduled. She was assigned to an oncology unit, and her empathic understanding as a former cancer patient was enormously useful.

Over the course of the next 6 months, Martha twice ingested several drinks and a few tranquilizers while she was angry. They were identified as overdoses by me because of their dynamic meaning: They followed an abortion (which terminated an unwanted pregnancy) and her uncle's announcement that he was withdrawing the remaining modest financial assistance that he had continued to provide. Interestingly, before the latter overdose, Martha visited the uncle and dealt with him directly about her anger and disappointment. She had prepared for this visit by speaking in therapy about her fears that disabling anxiety and depression would recur, and by recognizing her latent desire to be the special daughter of a powerful father who would take care of her and rescue her.

The fifth year of therapy ended with additional work on narcissistic issues. Martha's talent for living like a monied person despite her actual meager circumstances was likened to the fable of "stone soup." Without any significant income, she managed to dress expensively, eat in the finest restaurants, and vacation in Europe. She could entertain the possibility, advanced by me, that the ostracism and envy that she felt from co-workers (the "hate-Martha group," as she called them) was perhaps related to her entitlement and her special carriage. She took these observations to heart, and appeared to gain some perspective on and objectivity toward her sometimes thorny involvement with her colleagues. Also, her "soap opera" entanglements with her family began to wane. Concurrently, she found herself able to pass up opportunities to revenge herself on men who, in the past, she might have tempted to exploit her.

Sixth Year of Therapy

Martha raised the issue of obtaining plastic surgical repair of the burn scars (from cigarettes) along her forearms, saying that it was "safe now" and that the scars were embarrassing and unpleasant reminders to her. In her relationships with men, she could see how she needed to have two in progress at any given time and to press each man in his own particular area of vulnerability, a process that served to contain her own anxiety about closeness.

She acknowledged her difficulty in expressing herself about her sexual feelings toward me but began to do this: "If you touched me, I'd fall to the floor. I can't imagine you that way." I linked this attitude to her compartmentalization and her "Victorian woman" squeamishness, which impeded her pleasure in sex. The following month she met a serious young man, and for the first time deferred sexual intimacy until she felt she knew him better.

Her circle of friends broadened and became more stable, with fewer bitter breaks following intense attachments to sister surrogates. She began to have a number of close woman friends (these had been conspicuously absent during the early years of her therapy), and these ties became more enduring and mutual.

During that winter, Martha reported feeling for the first time that her uncle and his new wife "really like me." She avoided invitations to conspire against or with the varying factions of her family. She expressed a sincere appreciation of her uncle and was authentically compassionate when he experienced difficulties. She found him to be less defensive and more emotionally available to her even as he provided less material support. Indeed, she began to view his new wife as a friend who was troubled herself, and not as an intrusive, manipulative witch who had preempted her claims on her uncle.

Obsessive defenses appeared more commonly in the therapy, such as the reaction formation embodied in Martha's notifying me that she would "try to keep her appointment next Friday, but I want you to charge me if I don't make it." She had difficulty in parting with her sick image, but consciously recognized it as a source of entitlement to passive gratification from me, as it had also been with her uncle, with Jack, and with her mother.

By the spring, Martha had narrowed her interests to this one young man and decided to turn down invitations from new and old boyfriends in order to give this one relationship an honest try. She had difficulty in relaxing, accepting sexual pleasure, and being passive in that sphere. Though she told me that she could not imagine asking for or refusing to give sexual pleasure, the following month she reported being able to talk with the boyfriend about her sexual needs, despite their mutual embarrassment.

At around this time, she was able to get angry with me for my "unfair charge" for an hour in which she had been delayed in traffic.

When Martha's boyfriend said a series of rejecting things to her during my vacation, she reported feeling very sad: "I wished you were here, but it was all right because this time I knew you were coming back." Sometime thereafter in the midst of a quarrel with her boyfriend, she was able to get some perspective on her anger and tell him, "I'm just saying these things because I'm feeling hurt."

Toward the end of the sixth year of therapy, Martha prepared for her mother's annual summer visit. She had kept her mother at a great distance in recent years, not calling her although she had a toll-free number, not allowing her mother to stay with her in her apartment, and barely seeing her over the course of her mother's month-long visit to Boston. Martha was obviously irritated with her mother. She complained that she drank too much and embarrassed Martha in front of her boyfriend and his parents. "Everything she does annoys me." She noticed that her mother was looking older, and she felt bad for her. I asked her if she felt secure enough about her longings to be taken care of and about her past disappointments to be able to allow herself to be closer to her mother. She was doubtful.

Seventh Year of Therapy

Four areas merit brief comment to bring the reader up to date in this ongoing treatment.

First, responding to Martha's request, I proposed a reduction to once-weekly meetings. I said that she tended to second-guess herself, and that reliance on therapy sessions twice a week to review and scrutinize her reactions compounded this habit. She acknowledged her dependency and could see how it might be counterproductive, but she valued the contact and wanted to postpone any decrease. After several weeks of sometimes poignant, sometimes angry exploration (including a review of past fears of abandonment), once-weekly meetings were agreed upon. There were no incidents connected with this change.

Second, while Martha felt she was overqualified for her present position, had several job interviews, and received some offers, she has not taken a new job. "I don't like changes," she said apologetically.

Third, when her relationship with her boyfriend foundered, she persisted and tried to sort matters out. In fact, she remained long past the point where any real hope of reconciliation seemed likely. Then, somewhat abruptly, she concluded the relationship and began another in a matter of days. That relationship has lasted for nearly a year and has permitted the resolution of many of her residual sexual conflicts. Specifically, she remains erotically interested after the "honeymoon" phase, is able to say "no" to her boyfriend's sexual overtures when she is not interested, and can speak with me and her boyfriend about her sexual wishes. Most recently, she has worked on separating her pressure to have an orgasm for him from her own enjoyment.

Finally, she still has little contact with her mother and still worries that her mother is aging. "When I'm ready, I want to do something about us. I'm afraid to have her die with us so distant."

Case Discussion

Martha fulfills the DSM III criteria for the diagnosis of Borderline Personality Disorder. In fact, she presented at the outset of treatment with seven of the eight characteristics of borderline personality listed in DSM III: impulsivity, unstable intense interpersonal relationships, identity disturbance, affective instability, intolerance of being alone, physically self-damaging acts, and chronic feelings of emptiness and boredom. By the time she came to treatment, these traits were long-standing and had impaired both her social and occupational functioning. Martha did not show evidence of psychosis at any time during the treatment, except in the context of an anticholinergic crisis secondary to medication.

Differential diagnosis in this case centers on the patient's narcissism and her disturbances of mood. While narcissistic traits such as entitlement and interpersonal exploitativeness play a prominent role in this woman's disorder, she does not demonstrate the grandiosity, lack of empathy, or extreme sensitivity to criticism that are commonly seen in Narcissistic Personality Disorder. She also demonstrates considerable masochism, but this is not the central feature of her disorder, as it might be in those who warrant the older diagnosis of masochistic personality. Her affective instability is characteristic of Borderline Personality Disorder, but she presented to the hospital at the time of her first admission with a full-blown depressive syndrome that included vegetative signs and symptoms. While this would meet the DSM III criteria for a Major Depressive Episode, its resolution occurred in the context of hospital treatment and psychotherapy without an adequate trial of antidepressant medication. This suggests that Martha's depressive episode was secondary to her character pathology.

Martha brought considerable *strengths* to her psychotherapy. She was motivated for treatment and persistent in her efforts to get help, although it may be argued that this persistence was initially based more on transference distortions than on a realistic perception of her need for therapy. She was capable of reasonable reality testing in the therapy hours, so that her primitive defenses were not mobilized to distort the therapist–patient interactions. She did not show much paranoia in the treatment and was capable of putting some measure of trust in her therapist (based in part on a rather primitive idealizing transference). Unlike many borderline patients, she did not defensively and rigidly deny her dependence on the therapist. She was engaging, sensitive to others' reactions, and seductive, all of which undoubtedly contributed to the ease with which her male therapist was able to sustain his interest in her through some very stormy periods.

Martha's *ego functioning* at the start of treatment was severely impaired, and her level of object relatedness fluctuated dramatically. She used predominantly primitive defenses, including splitting (e.g., with her treatment team and her family), denial (of her self-destructiveness and manipulativeness), primitive idealization (of her therapist), projection and projective identification (of her aggressive impulses), and acting out. She demonstrated a marked incapacity to soothe herself in times of stress when important others (such as her therapist of her mother) were not present.

Martha's amenability to analytically oriented therapy was rated by the authors on the scale in Figure 3–1. She was seen as relatively intelligent but poorly motivated, and she scored quite low on self-discipline, impulse control, and the capacity for empathy. We rated her as tending to externalize her problems and as prone to vengefulness and deceit. She had social supports that were below average among patients in our group. The overall picture was certainly mixed, and she appeared less amenable to psychodynamic therapy than other patients in this study.

Martha's therapist was a man whose personal style in certain respects provided a reasonable fit with his patient's needs. He was comfortable with dependency in others, and he described himself as "parental" in the context of this treatment. He was by nature a patient man and capable of tolerating a fair amount of anxiety, so that he was able to sit with Martha despite her frequent self-mutilatory acts and the constant threat of self-destruction.

Martha's *transference* to her therapist was predominantly pre-oedipal. She saw the therapist as a parent and protector who would save her from her mother's and her own voraciousness. In this respect, the therapist played a role in her fantasy life similar to that played by her uncle. She needed to see the therapist as perfect throughout much of the beginning of treatment, and to maintain this primitive idealization she had to project hostile and aggressive impulses onto other members of her treatment team. She manifested intense wishes to fuse with the therapist. She felt vulnerable when she believed that she could not control him, and so could not tolerate evidence of his independence from her. This was shown by the degree of her distress at times of separation and by her inappropriate rageful responses to the therapist's lateness or changes of appointments.

Within the transference relationship, Martha's sense of herself fluctuated. On the one hand, she felt that she was special to the therapist and even that he would one day write her up as an interesting case. On the other hand, she believed she was a disgusting person whom the therapist wished to be rid of. Her self-view vacillated with her sense of empathic connection to the therapist and with the extent to which she believed she could control him.

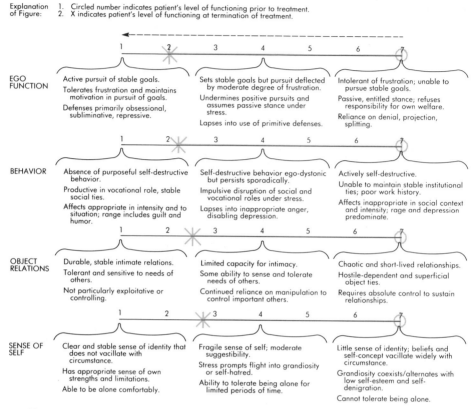

Explanation   1. Circled number indicates patient's level of functioning prior to treatment.
of Figure: 2. X indicates patient's level of functioning at termination of treatment.

EGO FUNCTION

Active pursuit of stable goals.
Tolerates frustration and maintains motivation in pursuit of goals.
Defenses primarily obsessional, subliminative, repressive.

Sets stable goals but pursuit deflected by moderate degree of frustration.
Undermines positive pursuits and assumes passive stance under stress.
Lapses into use of primitive defenses.

Intolerant of frustration; unable to pursue stable goals.
Passive, entitled stance; refuses responsibility for own welfare.
Reliance on denial, projection, splitting.

BEHAVIOR

Absence of purposeful self-destructive behavior.
Productive in vocational role, stable social ties.
Affects appropriate in intensity and to situation; range includes guilt and humor.

Self-destructive behavior ego-dystonic but persists sporadically.
Impulsive disruption of social and vocational roles under stress.
Lapses into inappropriate anger, disabling depression.

Actively self-destructive.
Unable to maintain stable institutional ties; poor work history.
Affects inappropriate in social context and intensity; rage and depression predominate.

OBJECT RELATIONS

Durable, stable intimate relations.
Tolerant and sensitive to needs of others.
Not particularly exploitative or controlling.

Limited capacity for intimacy.
Some ability to sense and tolerate needs of others.
Continued reliance on manipulation to control important others.

Chaotic and short-lived relationships.
Hostile-dependent and superficial object ties.
Requires absolute control to sustain relationships.

SENSE OF SELF

Clear and stable sense of identity that does not vacillate with circumstance.
Has appropriate sense of own strengths and limitations.
Able to be alone comfortably.

Fragile sense of self; moderate suggestibility.
Stress prompts flight into grandiosity or self-hatred.
Ability to tolerate being alone for limited periods of time.

Little sense of identity; beliefs and self-concept vacillate widely with circumstance.
Grandiosity coexists/alternates with low self-esteem and self-denigration.
Cannot tolerate being alone.

FIGURE 3–1.   Standards for assessing levels of functioning—baseline and outcome: Martha.

Her sadomasochism was strikingly evident in her relationships with lovers but was less obvious in her relationship with the therapist. Certainly, she saw herself as a victim, at the mercy of her therapist's power to leave her at will, and her self-destructiveness had a decidedly sadistic component. She was not, however, overtly hostile or sadistic in therapy sessions and did not, in the therapist's experience, invite his attack (a factor that undoubtedly made treatment more bearable for both parties).

Elements of the therapist's *countertransference* (used here in the broad sense of the term) played a significant role in determining the therapeutic technique and setting the tone of treatment. The therapist noted, "There have been very few human beings in my life with whom I have been as intensely involved as I was with this woman." He felt that this degree of involvement was mutual, that he was the most important person in his patient's life.

His involvement was matched by the extent of his concern for Martha's well-being. He worried about her safety and feared that she might die at some point in the treatment. He described feeling helpless in the face of Martha's self-destructiveness and worried about his ability to keep her safe without keeping her locked up on an inpatient unit. At the same time, he recognized the limits of his ability to protect her from her self-destructiveness. He described reconciling himself to the possibility that she might die during the course of treatment. Yet despite the therapist's concerns about her prognosis, he managed to preserve hope about her ability to benefit from treatment and to communicate this hope to her.

He believed that Martha was, *in reality,* poorly parented, and he saw himself as the better parent who would bring her from a more primitive to a more developed state. Given this view, it is not surprising that the therapist did not do extensive work with the patient's distortions of her relationships with primary caretakers (as Kernberg would advocate).

The therapist's parental countertransference probably diminished the extent to which he experienced sexual feelings for the patient, as well as the extent to which he focused on the erotic elements of her transference. It also contributed to his self-sacrificing stance in the treatment, which prompted him unilaterally to lower the patient's fee at one point and to offer her a variety of contacts with him outside of regularly scheduled sessions.

The influence of the hospital milieu on the treatment cannot be underestimated. The lengthy inpatient stay at the start of therapy freed the therapist from major responsibility for the Martha's safety and her overall management, since hospitalization occurred in a setting in which therapy and administration are not done by the same person. Martha's therapist acknowledged that it was a great relief to be free to focus on establishing a positive therapeutic relationship while others took charge of her privileges and her inpatient treatment program. Had Martha not been in the hospital, where acting out could be contained during the early months of treatment, it is not clear that she could have established a lasting therapeutic relationship.

The therapist demonstrated enormous patience in the face of Martha's self-destructive behaviors in the early years of therapy. In retrospect, he wondered whether he had more tolerance than was in the patient's best interest, and whether more vigorous confrontation and limit setting could have curtailed some of her acting out. Both the therapist and the inpatient unit staff used less confrontation than they might have in the face of Martha's almost continual self-destructive behavior. One important ground rule of treatment was that confidentiality did not apply where Martha's safety was concerned, so staff and therapist routinely exchanged information about Martha's self-destructive threats and actions.

The therapist's *technique* in this case might best be characterized as a constantly changing mixture of empathy and limit setting. Both of these elements seemed essential to the work. The therapist spent a great deal of time focusing on the self-destructive aspects of Martha's behavior, which she vigorously disavowed during much of the early phase of treatment. Similarly, he emphasized the manipulativeness of her relationships with others. He interpreted her manipulations and exploitiveness as arising from her longing to be cared for and loved (a view of borderline psychopathology advocated by Buie and Adler), rather than as moves to control, to hurt, or to gain power over others. His interpretations and clarifications were focused primarily on the present—that is, on her life in and out of treatment—and particularly on linking Martha's behavior to affects. He spent relatively little time exploring childhood memories or linking the past to the present.

The management of separations was a fundamental part of the treatment. Over several years, the therapist engaged in a very gradual weaning process. He began with interventions around times of separation that were heavily supportive, such as offering extra appointments, scheduling telephone calls, and sending Martha post cards. Eventually, scheduled telephone calls during the therapist's vacation ceased to be offered, and Martha was given the therapist's telephone number but was responsible for taking the initiative to call if she felt that this was necessary. Slowly, the therapist moved to a position of less availability during vacations, and Martha was offered interim therapy with someone else. Finally, the therapist offered no special arrangements during his absences: This weaning process was designed to emphasize the therapist's separateness and to take Martha to the limit of what she could tolerate during times of separation from him. It eventually culminated in the *therapist's* suggestion that the frequency of therapy sessions be reduced from twice to once a week.

A similar strategy underlay the therapist's announcement, at one point in treatment, that Martha's continued participation in therapy was elective. This seemed to underscore the separateness of therapist and patient at a time when Martha remained heavily invested in denying that fact. In addition, this move was aimed at getting the patient to assume greater responsibility for her own treatment and to foster a firmer alliance.

Martha's therapist was actively involved with her other treaters even after she left the hospital. He was in communication with her administrator when she was affiliated with a day treatment center, and he attended a conference there. This was done in an attempt to heal the splits that pervaded Martha's treatment. Similarly, the therapist met with Martha's mother, and this, too, diminished some of the distortions that resulted from splitting. However, the therapist did not actively interpret Martha's splitting. Involvement with her family served another important function in that the therapist modeled a way of tolerating her mother's anger and anxiety without caving in or being punitive.

The therapist found that the use of consultants was an important factor in maintaining the treatment. In particular, at a time when other members of Martha's treatment team were demoralized and skeptical of Martha's ability to use long-term psychotherapy, a senior consultant strongly encouraged the continuation of intensive treatment. On another occasion, Martha's family sought consultation from a psychiatrist because they were concerned about whether Martha was making progress in treatment. Here, too, the consultant urged the continuation of the therapy, and this helped to restore the family's confidence in Martha's therapist.

The therapist made it clear to Martha that he was committed to continuing with her treatment. This was conveyed verbally as well as in action. He stated directly and indirectly the importance of protecting the treatment (e.g., from her wish to undermine it through self-destructive behavior). Moreover, his unilateral decision to lower Martha's fee was a sign of his unwillingness to abandon the work. This decision had many ramifications, including the fact that it was undoubtedly seen by Martha as an effort to rescue her. Her increased agitation after the announcement of the reduced fee may have been due in part to her increased fear that she could in fact control the therapist and that she might be capable of overpowering him.

The therapist openly encouraged Martha's efforts to increase her autonomy and improve her social and occupational functioning. He was explicitly congratulatory when she handled situations in ways that he deemed appropriate, and he actively acknowledged her new feelings and growing awareness of the complexity of her personality as these emerged in treatment. He functioned to a considerable extent as a self-object, in Kohut's sense of the term. His approbation was also made clear when she attained goals that he deemed desirable.

Martha changed considerably during her psychotherapy. Most obviously, she transformed herself from the depressed, overweight, and rather unattractive person who presented for treatment into an attractive, well-groomed, and more poised young woman. Her persistent self-mutilatory and self-destructive behavior has virtually ceased. In interpersonal relationships she is markedly less manipulative, and she is more capable of maintaining a sense of connectedness to important others in times of separation and in the face of frustration. Her occupational and social functioning have thus improved dramatically.

The intrapsychic changes in Martha are less visible but clearly underlie the outward improvements in her life noted above. She now relies much less heavily on primitive defenses (splitting, devaluation, primitive idealization, and projection) than she did at the outset of

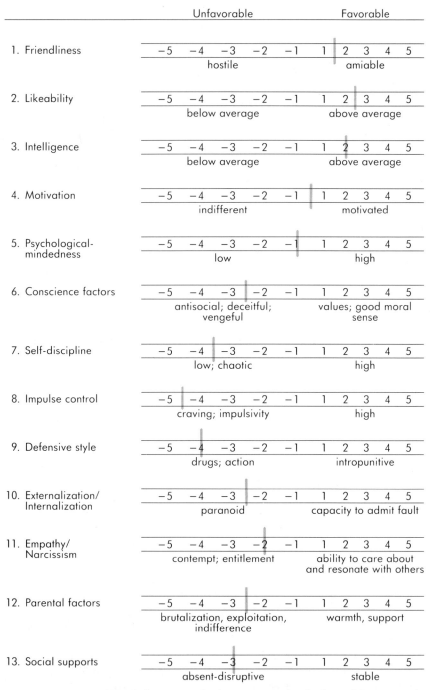

FIGURE 3–2.   Amenability to psychotherapy: Martha. [Adapted from Stone's Amenability for Analytically Oriented Therapy Scale (Stone, 1985)].

treatment. Her self-view is more stable, and she possesses the capacity for ambivalence regarding herself as well as others. She has develoepd strong identifications with her therapist, particularly in regard to phallic activities (e.g., in her work) and in her ability to persist at a task despite frustration. She has managed to sublimate some of her masochism into more constructive behaviors such as running.

Figure 3–2 shows the authors' ratings of Martha's level of functioning before treatment and at the end of year 5 on four scales: ego functioning, behavior, object relations, and sense of self. Martha received the lowest possible ratings on the four scales at the start of treatment. She was assessed as having made substantial gains in all four areas by the end of her fifth year of therapy, with the best outcome in ego functioning and with more limited gains in object relations and sense of self.

From the therapist's description of the work, it is not clear how much Martha has mastered her difficulty in tolerating the experience of being alone. Martha continues to see her therapist once weekly, and no termination date has been set at the time of this writing. Thus, the extent to which she can maintain the gains of treatment in the absence of an ongoing psychotherapeutic relationship remains to be seen.

4

Ann
Case Report

I first met Ann when she was 22 years old. At that time she was unmarried, unemployed, and living with her parents. She was referred to me several weeks after the psychiatrist whom she had seen for 13 years died after a long illness.

Actually, Ann knew me before I knew her. Her psychiatrist, Dr. Brightman, was a former teacher and friend of mine, and I stood with tears in my eyes at his funeral, unaware that Ann was watching me intently. She had, in fact, watched me for some years as our paths crossed in Dr. Brightman's waiting room. Everything that happened in the office and in Dr. Brightman's waiting room was of great importance and interest to her, and I am sure that she asked him about the young doctor who waited outside. Ann was remarkably knowledgeable about everyone connected with the psychiatric community, including the identities and occupations of all of Dr. Brightman's patients and colleagues.

The day after the funeral, I received a phone call from Dr. Marshall, a referring psychiatrist, who was trying to place the patients who had been left by the death of our colleague. He asked me if I would see Ann. I did not know until much later that Ann had explicitly asked to see me because I seemed to care about Dr. Brightman. Within 15 minutes of my conversation with Dr. Marshall, Ann called me to make our first appointment.

She arrived at my office the following day at the appointed hour, marched in, and announced with some fanfare: "I am Ann." She promptly held up her car keys, dropped them on the floor, and sat down next to them with her dress carelessly draped about her. I asked if she would like to sit on a chair, stating that I would prefer that. She shook her head and looked at the rug. Then she raised her eyes, made a squinting grimace, and took her glasses off as if to show me her eyes. She shook her head from side to side in a rather stereotyped manner and exercised her jaw, but said nothing.

With this auspicious beginning, she spent our first hour trying to extract from me a promise that I would be her doctor. She had no interest in giving me any information about the symptoms or problems that had brought her to psychiatric treatment in the first place. In fact, she seemed reluctant to be pinned down to any communication about specific complaints or to give any facts about her life. She did tell me, however, that she felt she was socially superficial and unstable, that she had trouble being alone, and that she frequently became so tense that she lost touch with reality.

We set up subsequent appointments, which she kept faithfully. She spent most of the time quizzing me about whether I was acquainted with the many psychiatrists whose lives she followed from afar, and she attempted to extract from me intimate details of their lives. She informed me that Dr. Brightman had written her up as a case report in a journal and gave me the reference if I wanted to look at it. She revealed her belief that she had kept Dr. Brightman alive during the long illness that plagued him in the last years of his life.

My efforts to secure her history were met by Ann with smiles, grimaces, evasions, and non sequiturs. She would recite lists of "important" schools she had visited or attended and prominent people whom she had known. She would also protest constantly that she was sick and had always needed treatment, and that her life had been saved by psychotherapy. She considered herself a friend of Dr. Brightman's family and seemed to have difficulty tolerating the ordinary degree of privacy that exists in professional relationships. She believed that Dr. Brightman was more of a parent to her than her own parents had been. In a rare moment of genuine sadness, she said that after her last appointment with Dr. Brightman, she had gone into the bathroom and cut her wrist superficially, bled into the sink, and then cleaned up before she left.

She spoke about her family with little interest or feeling. She told me that she and her parents were civil to each other at home but were not close. What little I could piece together about her current life from these interviews was that she found it difficult to make friends, experienced periods of profound anxiety accompanied by gastrointestinal distress, and lived what amounted to a lonely and empty existence outside of treatment. She had been maintained on low doses of diazepam (Valium) to deal with her periods of anxiety, and gave vague hints of being out of touch with reality at times, but had no history of any frankly psychotic symptoms. Her indirectness and illogical manner of speaking were present intermittently.

Background Information

Information about Ann's background came slowly and over many years, since history gathering in the traditional sense was impossible in our early interviews. What follows, then, is a condensation of information that took several years to learn.

Ann was the second of two children born to middle-class nonpracticing Catholic parents. Her father, an engineer, was moderately successful in his career and was a leader in local church activities. He was described by others as a pillar of the community, competent and conscientious, but "not a mover and a shaker." Ann saw him as fairly passive, as someone to whom she related very little, and as easily manipulatable ("unable to control me").

Ann described her mother with contempt, picturing her as an aloof woman whose reactions were unpredictable and toward whom she usually felt angry. Ann related many stories about how her mother had been neglected by her own parents. When I met her mother at several family meetings held during the treatment, I, too, found her to be coolly detached. She clearly felt used and abused by her daughter, and while she seemed concerned about Ann's future, she showed little affection for her and little concern about the family's possible role in Ann's difficulties.

The family meetings held later in Ann's treatment were remarkable in that the mother clearly pushed the father aside. While the father appeared to be a personable man who seemed interested in participating in our discussions, the family stance was that he did not count for very much. The mother was less affable than the father, and seemed to have made peace with her environment by withdrawing into herself and refusing to discuss any difficult or unpleasant issues.

Ann's brother was 3 years older than she, and was described as a strong-willed and often volatile child. In particular, he argued violently with his mother and had a generally hostile relationship with his father as well. He had difficulties at school that eventually prompted the family to seek a psychological evaluation for him. Ann seldom mentioned her brother in treatment, since the two of them appeared to relate to each other very little. The rest of Ann's family was reported to be free of major psychiatric illnesses, including depression, alcoholism, psychosis, or suicide. No relatives were known to be under psychiatric care, and none had been hospitalized for mental illness.

I gleaned little information about Ann's infancy and early childhood. In grammar school, she was described as clever, but she had difficulty in following directions. She did very poorly on tests, and she became so anxious that she found it difficult to pay attention in class and to learn what was required of her. She recalled feeling physically uncoordinated and stated that she had little sense of where her body was in space. She also recalled intense homesickness when away from home, particularly at summer camp. In fact, at camp she experienced such severe nausea and vomiting that she lost weight and received a great deal of attention from the camp's medical staff.

When Ann was 9 years old, her maternal grandmother died. Her mother became depressed at that time and entered psychotherapy, which continued for 2 years. Ann recalls her mother being even less emotionally available at that time than previously: "She was really out of the picture for a while." At this time, Ann developed fairly persistent bouts of vomiting and stomach pain. She often feigned sickness, since she had become increasingly fearful of attending school. Both she and her brother were having significant problems in school, and because of these difficulties they were both referred to a psychologist for testing and evaluation.

Psychological testing characterized Ann as "borderline" at age 9, highlighting her poor reality sense and her tendency to distort perceptions. She was noted to have a grossly disturbed relationship with her mother, whom she saw on the Thematic Apperception Test as cold, unreliable, and unpredictable. After this evaluation, Ann was referred to a psychiatrist for therapy, but she reported never liking this doctor and ended treatment with him after 1 year. She was then referred to Dr. Brightman for further psychotherapy.

She began seeing Dr. Brightman regularly at age 10 and continued with him (usually two times per week) for the next 13 years. While her difficulties in school and with peers persisted, she managed to graduate from a good elementary school. She described her relationship with Dr. Brightman as one of open access to him. She felt that he loved her and that they had a "mutual admiration society." She felt that he watched over her and recalled that he liked to watch her play tennis on occasion. He was, in fact, a very giving individual, and my impression was that he indulged many of her requests for extra time and loving attention.

Ann reported that her adolescence was quite troubled, with periods of feeling extremely paranoid and cut off from people; at such times, she was afraid of having anyone come near her. She described feeling for days at a time "like my senses were all off." She originally thought that these feelings were due to a virus but later realized that her thinking was "not like the other kids'," and during these periods she began to have severe suicidal ideation. She felt unsafe during these periods but on no occasion made any significant attempts at suicide. She described her high school years as a constant struggle to stay out of a psychiatric hospital. She was successful, but described prolonged periods during which she felt tense, angry, and frustrated, longing to be someplace where she could be taken care of. During such times she picked compulsively at her skin. When her self-destructive impulses threatened to overwhelm her, she told Dr. Brightman, "I really believe in you, and as long as you believe in me, I won't hurt myself."

She continued to be plagued by a variety of hypochondriacal complaints, most notably gastrointestinal problems, and as a young adult spent time working in medical settings in an effort to get information that would reassure her that she was not seriously ill.

Upon finishing high school, she was accepted at a good college that was half a day's drive from her home. Dr. Brightman referred her for psychological testing again (at age 18), in part because he and her family were concerned about her current mental state and her ability to function away from home and from psychotherapy. This second battery of tests revealed perceptual distortions but a fairly good intellectual endowment, and again the diagnosis of borderline personality was made. Ann went off to college and did reasonably well there, seeing Dr. Brightman in therapy during vacations and completing a bachelor's degree in 4 years.

Dr. Brightman began to suffer from a chronic debilitating illness during Ann's last years of college, and she became increasingly concerned about his health. She began to believe that she was keeping him alive. Her mother described Ann as being locked with Dr. Brightman in a "dance of death." As his health deteriorated, Ann became increasingly out of touch with reality and began to cut her wrists superficially. Her parents worried about the intensity of her relationship with the dying psychiatrist and wondered if continuing in this therapy was in her best interest. Ann insisted that if her parents stopped paying for her therapy with Dr. Brightman, she would have to be hospitalized.

Despite Ann's increasing distress and self-destructive activity around the time of Dr. Brightman's death, she managed to avert hospitalization by immediately contacting Dr. Marshall, not only for a referral but also for her interim therapy.

First Year of Therapy

Ann and I began meeting three times per week, and she immediately asked for more frequent sessions. I told her that I thought it best to keep to this schedule and see how things went. Our work in the beginning centered almost entirely on her demand that our relationship be something other than a professional one. She asked for special treatment and violated almost every conventional boundary that existed between us. For example, she would walk into my office swinging her arms so that I had to duck to avoid being hit in the head as she entered. From the start of treatment, she would call me at home at night following our sessions. During the therapy sessions, we struggled over innumerable parameters of treatment, such as whether or not she could lie on the analytic couch, whether she would have to sit in a chair or be allowed to sit on the floor and grab my legs, and whether or not she could call me at home between sessions.

I responded to her many demands by asking why such measures were necessary. I openly expressed the opinion that many of her wishes (e.g., to clutch my legs) were inappropriate, stating that she would have to abide by certain rules in therapy and learn to be more independent if we were to continue working together. I made it plain that

I did not want to hear from her by telephone every night (a statement she diligently ignored). My experience during these interactions was of being a parent who was firmly setting limits for a demanding young child. I did not feel her demands to be hostile but simply predatory; she wanted *more* of me.

Ann made it clear in the first weeks of treatment that she feared she would not get enough of me. Several weeks into our work, I discovered that she was continuing to see Dr. Marshall regularly, having told him that she was unsure of her commitment to working with me. She told me that Dr. Marshall was "shocked" that I was not seeing Ann five times per week. When Dr. Marshall learned from me that Ann and I were in fact engaged in treatment, he immediately discontinued his sessions with her.

However, during the subsequent 4 months, Ann periodically went off in search of another psychotherapist when she became angry at me and felt I was not giving her what she wanted. She saw other therapists briefly and eventually let me know about it, at which point I insisted that she decide which one of us would be her therapist. Her "doctor shopping" finally ceased, but she continued to try to extract a promise that I would *really* be her doctor, that is, that I would always be there for her and would not disappear from her life.

Ann's demands for more frequent sessions included some rather grandiose threats about what her parents and Dr. Marshall would do if I did not comply with her wishes. She also insisted that without more frequent meetings she would need to be hospitalized, and informed me that the director of nursing at McLean Hospital was a family friend who had a bed waiting for her at any time "just in case." She made many references to cutting her wrists and taking overdoses of drugs if I did not do as she wished. I responded by saying that I hoped she would not act self-destructively, but I did not think that my seeing her more often would protect her. I interpreted her threats as efforts to exert control over me. While this interpretation calmed things down somewhat, her compliance seemed to stem more from a wish to appease me than from any genuine understanding of her own manipulative motives.

Ann's telephone calls to me at home came in an easily recognizable pattern: She phoned in the evening immediately following each of our sessions, and on no other occasions. During these calls, she would typically argue with me over something I had said during our session that day, insist that I had not said the right things to her, and state that she was unable to wait until our next appointment, that she could not carry on alone until then. I routinely attempted to explore with her the reasons for her calls and what she hoped to gain from them. In response, she claimed that her former therapist welcomed her calls, and she wondered why I did not. It seemed to me that our meetings stimulated her wish to merge with me, and that, facing the pain of separation after the hour, she needed to hear my voice. In fact, I felt that these phone calls supported her until the subsequent session.

Ann's knowledge of the personal lives of local psychiatrists and their families was quite unusual. She gathered this information by incessantly questioning the many people within her family's social sphere who knew these psychiatrists. Many of her childhood friends were the children of psychiatrists, and she systematically pried information from them as well.

She was curious about the ages of my children, their names, where they went to school, where I was born, whether my parents were alive, my father's occupation, and innumerable other details of my personal life. Finding me unwilling to indulge in this kind of autobiographical sketching, she went to the library of my alma mater to find these facts for herself. As our relationship stabilized, she was able to talk about this behavior. She said that she insisted on knowing all about me because she felt that, by being in psychotherapy, she was the one who was being treated as a specimen, "like a butterfly pinned down by a collector to be scrutinized." She felt that her only escape from such painful exploitation was to turn the tables on me and do to me what she feared psychotherapy was doing to her.

It seemed that this intrusiveness and fear of exploitation were based on some prior life experience. While Ann said little about it, she eventually claimed that she had been sexually abused by the family's housekeeper when she was 9 or 10 years old. Sexual contact with this woman consisted of Ann rubbing her legs and buttocks with some accompanying arousal, while the house-keeper masturbated. This reportedly went on for several months, but Ann said that it stopped, perhaps because both parties felt ashamed of the practice.

By this time, we had reached the eighth month of treatment, and it became clear to me that Ann's insistence on keeping the details of her own life secret left me at a major disadvantage in our work. She strictly limited what she let me know about her parents, her brother, her interactions with peers, and her activities outside of the therapy hours. In doing so, she left me unable to use this data to confront her with the maladaptive and repetitive nature of her manipulative behaviors. In essence, I had no view of her activities except her own to compare with my experience of her in the office. My repeated inquiries into the reasons for her secrecy were met with grimaces and evasions, while her "acting in" during treatment hours continued unabated. She refused to sit in a chair and happily played the role of the preschool-age child in the face of my obvious displeasure with this behavior. Moreover, she continued to idealize Dr. Brightman and made it clear that I did not compare with him in terms of warmth, caring, or personal interest in her.

Feeling that we were at an impasse, I reversed my initial decision about contact with Ann's parents and met with them on several occasions. (We had spoken on the telephone briefly prior to this time, but had had no discussions about Ann beyond making the practical arrangements for her treatment.) Their description of Ann's behavior at home was certainly consistent with what I saw in the office. She was reported to be willful, childish, and disorganized. She did, however, have a number of friends who were drawn to her rather pleasant and appealing social manner. She was entertaining in company and an enjoyable guest. Her outside activities consisted mostly of socializing with girlfriends, spending time at the local country club, and attending occasional parties.

Ann's mother described her relationship with Dr. Brightman as a "dance of death." Ann firmly believed that she was keeping him alive during his long illness. Before Dr. Brightman's death, she often spoke of him as tied to her, and believed that when he died, she would die with him in spirit. Her parents were alarmed at Ann's inability to think of herself as separate from Dr. Brightman. Nevertheless, they believed that she had benefitted from the relationship with him in that he was always available to her and, whenever he saw her, she would leave feeling better. They noticed that after Dr. Brightman's death, Ann's behavior had become increasingly child-like and willful at home, and remained so for a year after the event. Yet despite these complaints, her parents admitted that there were no overt disagreements at home, that Ann got along reasonably well with everyone, and that the situation was not intolerable.

My meetings with Ann's parents had a remarkable effect on the treatment. The very fact that I had refused to accept Ann's "rules" for our work and had gone to other sources for information seemed to sober her. Moreover, my discussions with her parents reinforced my own view of Ann's manipulativeness and bolstered my confidence in confronting her willful behavior in my office. I began to insist that she sit in a chair, that she speak to me in a mature fashion, and that she use the hours more productively, making it clear that otherwise we would be wasting our time. She reacted by dealing with me in a more straightforward and responsive manner. Limit setting became easier for me and seemed to work well. I began to think that she would have acted out less in the beginning phase of treatment had I spoken with her family earlier and used this information as part of a general strategy of gentle confrontation from the beginning.

Toward the end of the first year of treatment, Ann got a job as a researcher in a mental health facility. Her work involved searching old records, and to some degree this gratified her appetite for psychiatric knowledge about the mental health community. She enjoyed her work and functioned well. This was a major achievement, since she had not been previously employed, despite having been out of college for 2 years. She soon found another research position that was more to her liking, and she held this job up to the time our treatment terminated 4 years later.

Second Year of Therapy

As we entered the second year of treatment, Ann's life seemed to be increasingly filled with age-appropriate activities. In addition to her job, she spent more and more time with friends. Initially, she had associated mostly with the children of psychiatrists, but her social network gradually expanded to include other young women of her age. Much of her social life centered on the country club to which her family belonged. She also began to date, although she did not become particularly close to any young men during this time. I attributed these gains in her level of functioning to her feeling held and supported in her relationship with me.

Not surprisingly, while Ann's life outside of treatment improved, therapy centered exclusively on her relationship to me. She spoke constantly about her dependence on me, her wish to be closer to me and even to be one with me. She was acutely aware of separations; weekends caused her considerable pain, as did the separation from me in the evenings following our sessions. My repeated refusal to tell her the details of my personal life was a source of pain, since it constituted evidence of our separateness. She greeted any indication of differences in our interests or status with distress or denial. My work during this phase consisted almost entirely of setting limits on my involvement with her and of helping her to verbalize her sense of frustration and her feeling of low self-esteem. We also addressed her confusion about who she was and the difference between her own thoughts and feelings and those of others.

In the middle of the second year of treatment, an incident occurred that I feared would undermine the therapy. From the beginning of our work, I had been seeing Ann in my home office. This situation stimulated her fantasies about my private life, particularly since she had occasional opportunities to see my wife and children entering or leaving the house. She was intensely interested in the cars in the garage, the toys in the yard, and other aspects of my home life that were in view as she came to the office.

One winter afternoon, as she came for her usual hour, the city was hit with a massive snowstorm. When we ended the hour, I expected that Ann would make her way home as usual, and I proceeded to see my last patient of the day. However, when I finished with that hour and returned to the house, I discovered that Ann had not gone home but was in fact sitting in my family's living room, waiting for dinner to be served. She told me that her parents were unable to use their car due to the inclement weather, and that she had called a taxi but none were available. She had apparently come back to the house to wait, had begun playing with my children, and had been invited by the children to stay for dinner. My wife somewhat helplessly agreed to this arrangement.

I felt embarrassed and confused about what to do. I tried to tell Ann that she needed to get a taxi or find some other means of transportation home, noting that I did not think it made sense for her to have dinner with my family. However, it was quite apparent by then that she was snowbound in our house, and that she could not leave until the blizzard subsided. I began to realize that there was nothing I could do to change what seemed to be a most awkward situation.

To my amazement, Ann was not at all self-conscious as she chatted happily with my children during dinner. She obviously enjoyed their company and seemed to relish her role as the special guest. Her wish to be a child in my family seemed clearer than ever before, and the opportunity to dine with us gratified this wish and made her feel cared for. Ann behaved with appropriate politeness and took none of the liberties with my family that I might have expected given her behavior in my office. When, several hours later, her father was able to get his car out of the driveway and come to retrieve her, she thanked us appropriately for taking care of her and giving her dinner.

My own reaction to the evening was one of shock and dismay. I was confused about the effects that such an event would have on the treatment, and felt it likely that the work would be totally disrupted or hopelessly stymied by such a gross breach of the traditional boundaries of a therapeutic relationship. However, that is not what happened. Instead, this massive dose of reality seemed to have a markedly therapeutic effect on Ann. In subsequent treatment hours, she discussed the details of my home life, noting how mundane my house seemed, how much my children were like other children she knew, and how ordinary the chicken was that my wife had cooked for dinner. In her fantasies, my house had seemed like an inner sanctum and my family like the ideal one for which she had always longed. Suddenly she was brought face to face with the fact that what she had so ardently yearned for was not very special at all. This seemed to have a calming effect on her, and she subsequently spent less and less time badgering me for personal information.

The focus of treatment gradually shifted to her life outside of therapy. She spoke of dealings with friends and the various minor narcissistic injuries she sustained at their hands in the course of social events and dating. She was also able to use friendships to help her get over these minor slights, and developed some perspective on her dealings with others.

Third Year of Therapy

In the third year of our work together, Ann became increasingly preoccupied with her need to have me always available. This need was most evident around times of separation. She grew more and more concerned about my absences and vacations, but she was not particularly bothered when it was she who did the leaving. Her own vacations with friends and relatives caused her little anxiety or distress.

Whenever I announced that I was going away for any length of time, she railed at me for frustrating her and making her life miserable. She launched into a barrage of complaints about my lack of caring and her inability to remain safe while I was away. For example, on one occasion she warned me: "I'll try to be okay during your vacation, but I don't know if I can do it. I just might have to go into the hospital." These comments were not accompanied by any overt threats of self-destructive activity. While she occasionally pushed a fingernail into her palm and grimaced to show me how much distress she was in, she did nothing more serious than that while she was in treatment with me. Moreover, she made no such manipulative threats to her family; her acting out seemed to have become focused entirely on the treatment.

In reaction to upcoming vacations, she actually mounted a campaign to keep me at home. She called me almost nightly to reiterate her claim that she would not be able to function without me. It was as though, by persistent pleading, she might persuade me to stay at home. Her infantile demands and transparent attempts to control me seemed largely ego syntonic.

Toward the end of the third year, her distress reached its peak when I took my yearly summer vacation. I went with my family to the seashore for 2 weeks. Since we had vacationed at the same place for several years in a row, it was not difficult for Ann to learn, through her many social contacts, the location of our summer house.

Much to my surprise, she began calling me frantically at my vacation home, insisting that she could not cope on her own, that something needed to be done to help her, and that I needed to see her before my vacation was over. Her complaints were vague, she continued to function well at work, and she did not seem to be in any real danger. I told her that I thought she could hold on and take care of herself until I returned. My reassurances were met by more insistent demands that I do something for her.

After several days of such banter on the telephone, Ann said that she simply had to see me. I reiterated that there was no need for us to meet, and she hung up. The next day, she arrived at my summer house, ready for an appointment with me. There seemed to be little I could do but have an interview with her. I asked my family to clear out of the living room, and Ann and I met for an hour.

After our meeting, I assumed that she would return to the city. In fact, she left the house and disappeared. A few hours later, I discovered that she had been out with my children, playing with them on the beach and enjoying a game of tennis. They were delighted to have a playmate and, during their afternoon together, invited her to have dinner with us and to spend the night. I decided to allow her to stay, and again she spent a quiet evening with us *en famille*. She joined us for dinner and then we all went to a drive-in movie. After spending the night in our guest bedroom, Ann thanked my wife politely for her kind hospitality and drove back to the city.

This second major intrusion into my family life seemed to be a turning point in the treatment. Again Ann was forced to compare her idealized image of domestic bliss with the mundane reality of my family's summertime existence at the beach. Her more detailed knowledge of what my children were like, of how I interacted with them, and of what I did with them when I was away from her demystified my home life. She had been convinced throughout the treatment that becoming a child in my family held the key to her survival and well-being. Yet in the sessions following my vacation, she spoke of her dawning realization that mine was a family like any other. And while she had had a taste of what it would be like to join that family, her stay with us brought home the painful fact that no matter what she did, she could never be my child.

After this incident, Ann's attitude toward me and the treatment shifted. Her incessant demands for extra time and attention subsided, and she took a serious interest in her own problems and what she might do about them. She began to speak of herself in much more affectively genuine terms, and wished to look more intently at where she was in her life and where she wished to go.

Fourth Year of Therapy

The visit to my summer house became a major theme in Ann's treatment during the next year. She was struck by the extent to which she had idealized me and wished to become one with me. She began to point out the many other relationships in which she had similarly created idealized pictures of others and then found these people to be ungiving and disappointing because they failed to live up to her image. For the first time, she was able to look at her relationship with Dr. Brightman from this vantage point and to see the unrealistic expectations she had of him.

Concurrently, she began to explore her grandiose notions of who she was and what she was entitled to from others. She realized that she often withdrew haughtily from social situations rather than risk the realization that she was not of central importance to everyone in her life. She also acknowledged that her intrusive information gathering allowed her to distance herself from those upon whom she felt too dependent. She seemed genuinely confused by these different images of herself and by what she saw as her fuzzy sense of who she was.

Sobered by the events of the previous summer, I was concerned that further interruptions in the treatment would be met with more acting out by Ann. To my surprise, she was less rageful toward me in anticipation of my next vacation and more curious about her own way of dealing with separations. For some time, she had been in the habit of writing me occasional letters between therapy hours, and these became increasingly articulate and insightful about her relationship with me. Prior to my yearly long vacation, she wrote:

> What strikes me about this letter, other than that it is manipulative and innocent-yet-guilty, is that it indicates on one hand my ability and need to relate to you (post facto) and on the other, my almost total inability to relate to you when threatened by separation from you. It's almost as if your presence is blinding to me, or utterly distracting, or tempting. I don't know whether to hit you or hug you when I won't see you for a while.

Subtle shifts in her ability to look at herself coincided with a change in her social interests. While Ann was an attractive and engaging woman, she had previously spent most of her leisure time with girlfriends, and dating had been relatively unimportant in her life. However, she now began to go out more often with a variety of eligible young men and seemed to take genuine pleasure in getting to know them. Within a few months she met James, a lawyer, who immediately captured her interest. He was an avid and accomplished golfer, and she found herself taking genuine pride in his achievements both in his athletic endeavors and in his career. He, too, enjoyed social activities and liked to surround himself with friends, and Ann began to realize that they had many interests in common. He seemed to enjoy her company a great deal and appreciated her admiration of his accomplishments.

Ann quickly decided that she would date James exclusively. They spent a great deal of time with other couples, developing what appeared to be a relatively stable social network of mutual friends. Although Ann was still living in her parents' home and remained in treatment three times per week, her life came to be centered more and more outside of her family and outside of therapy. She continued to work full time at a responsible job and spent increasing amounts of time with James.

During this year of treatment, the affective tone of our sessions changed. Ann was no longer willful and demanding, but worked collaboratively with me out of a genuine curiosity about herself and how she lived her life outside of treatment. She became more involved with James, more appreciative of his good qualities, and less concerned about what she might or might not get from me.

Yet, near the end of the fourth year of treatment, she underwent a minor regression. Not surprisingly, this had some connection with Dr. Brightman. Ann discovered from her many sources in the local psychiatric community that his son was getting married. She also discovered that I had been invited to the wedding. She became enraged at the fact that her name was not on the guest list and made it clear that she was jealous of what she saw as my privileged position in the Brightman family.

After the wedding, she badgered me to tell her who was there, what the food was like, and whether I enjoyed myself. Her tone was far angrier than it had ever been in her sessions with me, and her demands for information were made with the same childish insistence that had characterized the first 3 years of our work together. I was surprised and dismayed to see this manner reappear after more than a year of collaborative work. Her anger at me persisted for several weeks after the wedding. I was unable to understand its resurgence.

Finally, Ann admitted that when she thought of me at the wedding, what made her most angry was her idea that I must have gone to the ceremony feeling very superior. I thought she meant that I must have felt superior to her, because she was not invited. However, she made it clear that this was not her concern. Rather, she assumed that I viewed everything at the wedding with a critical eye, that I was disdainful of the food, the guest list, and all the details of the wedding plans. It became clear that she had projected onto me her angry and arrogant feelings, and then proceeded to excoriate me for this unacceptable attitude.

We did considerable work on this issue over the next few months. Once I pointed out to her that she had made a most peculiar assumption about my feelings at the wedding, she was quickly able to recognize the extent of her projection and was somewhat taken aback by her own behavior. She worked long and hard on her confusion about the boundaries between herself and me, between herself and former therapist, and between herself and members of her family. She was concerned that she had so obviously lost all sense of who was feeling what, and realized that this was a common occurrence in her relationships. Moreover, she began to understand that others did not share her intrusive and devaluing approach to the world, that her own defensively haughty attitude toward important people was not necessarily reciprocated, as she had imagined. From this point on, Ann was much more interested in trying to recognize and examine the source of her projections.

Fifth Year of Therapy

As we started our last year of work together, Ann received a proposal of marriage from James. She was flattered and spoke with considerable warmth and pleasure about what it meant to her that he wanted to marry her. She realized that she liked him and felt quite certain that he would be good for her. Yet, for all of these positive feelings, she seemed uncertain about whether or not she would marry him.

One day she came to her appointment and seemed obviously uncomfortable, as though there was something on her mind that she was reluctant to bring up. Finally she paused, looked at me very seriously, and said that she wanted to ask me a very important question. With great hesitation, she said, "I've had a proposal from James and I want to know one thing: Do you intend to ever get divorced and possibly marry me? If this is a possibility, I would not want to get married to him." I was moved by her obvious earnestness. With as much gentleness as I could muster, I told her that I did not intend to marry her, that such an event would be absolutely impossible as far as I was concerned, and that her fantasy of being my wife was an integral part of the problems that had plagued her up to this point in her life. She thanked me for being frank with her. She said that, as far as she could tell, she loved James. And since I was not available, she wanted to marry him.

I went to the wedding, and at that time both she and her parents treated me as an honored guest. The marriage has now lasted for more than 10 years and has gone relatively smoothly.

During the rest of that year, it was clear that Ann thought of herself as living a life that was independent of mine, and she began to review the work we had done together. She noted that I spent a lot of time saying no to her, and had "trained" her by setting limits and prescribing realistic expectations for her conduct during the therapy hours. She felt that most of my work with her consisted of modeling appropriate behavior and of shaping her behavior by my expectations. In addition to her letters, she often wrote poems about our sessions. One day brought a poem in which I was described as a dog trainer and she was the unruly dog who needed to be taught to behave:

D.T. for dog trainer
D.T. for delirium tremens
D.T. for doctor therapist
Ah, A for analyst
big boy, and I'm
your playful pet

Stay with me, big boy,
tolerate me with all
your might. Don't
give up and don't let
me. You can train me,
d.t., you have the
strong hand and

strong mind, just
make a less
mixed-up me,
a less depleted
Pluto, a more
deplutoed me.

Ann noted that part of my training consisted of constantly reminding her of our therapeutic contract and making it clear that the real purpose of our relationship was not for me to take care of her but to support her independent life and growth. She spoke with sadness about her persistent wishes to be a child and not to assume adult responsibilities. In one of her letters written in the last year of treatment, she summarized her growing sense of responsibility for her own fate:

> If I want to be able to make responsible decisions then I have to both understand myself and accept myself. At this point I am capable of neither. Somehow to verbalize this is painful. I am becoming extremely aware that you are not going to sit there telling me that everything will be fine. Neither of us has any proof that it will be (or won't be). You are not going to put me under your magic wing and carry me through life. I've got to accept myself for better or for worse, make my own decisions—about life and death, having babies or not—and use you as a doctor rather than as a fairy godmother.

We began to talk about termination. Ann felt that she would never be able to stop seeing me, and made some mild protests when I entertained the possibility that she could continue our work on her own. Nevertheless, she began to think about her own wish to get on with her life. We set a termination date several months in the future. There was some mild regression at around this time, which took the form of a resurgence of her phone calls to me on the nights following our sessions. Occasionally James would be the one who called, saying that Ann felt I hated her and did not want to see her. I would ask to speak to Ann, and was easily able to calm both of them down and to reflect with Ann on her anxieties about our upcoming termination.

She wanted me to have a picture of her, and brought in a photograph along with numerous poems she had written. She explained that she wanted me to have a record of what she was like and how she looked. Our termination was relatively uneventful. She never explored in depth her sense of loss or her feeling of dependency on me. In retrospect, it seems that she simply transferred her more appropriate wishes to be cared for to another more available love object. Thus, ours was not a classical termination, as one might expect with a neurotic patient. Ann never completely came to terms with the limitations of our relationship.

In the last weeks of therapy, she reiterated her sense that she was not a particularly strong person. It was almost a relief to her to acknowledge that her needs were not overwhelming to others and that she could allow herself to be dependent on James. She felt that she would always need to surround herself with people who could help her, and that by doing this she would be all right. She also believed that she would be able to cope with life because of the work she had done in therapy.

She was able to say goodbye with considerable warmth. Not long after our last session, I received the following poem:

On My Leaving Someone Who Was Leaving Me

Not that I saw you when I left.
I was blinded by moisture the filaments
of my eyes and choked for you
who were my vital supply about to be
cut off.

I reached nakedly for a piece of your flesh.
I blessed a futile blade of grass.
Would that I had cried my soft storm
helplessly alone soothed only by a
damp torn kleenex. Your hand lay dormant
possessing the knowledge that it could
not quell the sadness.

The air was silent at the moment
when you faded from my greedy gaze.
And later my mind heaved, pregnant
with images trying to feed craters left empty
by the depths of our distance.

Not that I saw you when I left.
Not that I even was able to look
at you whose young vacation is a
hint of an older death. Gently,
you turned the knife in my
vulnerable back.

Follow-Up Interview

Ten years after we terminated treatment, I telephoned Ann to ask her if we might meet. I informed her of my interest in contributing to a book on intensive therapy of the sort we had done, and wanted to discuss whether she might find it acceptable for me to use her treatment as an example of this sort of work.

Although Ann and I had lived in the same city all these years, we had had almost no contact since termination, and I was eager to see how she fared. She arrived looking quite happy and well. She eagerly ly told me of her two children and a marriage that continued to be a source of pleasure and support to her. She said that she continued to have an active social life and felt generally content with her life.

She reported that the only major setbacks for her in the last 10 years came at around the time of childbirth: She experienced a brief dissociative episode after the birth of her first child, and suffered from intractable vomiting that required hospitalization during both pregnancies. Otherwise, she described taking pleasure in her children and getting satisfaction from her role as a full-time homemaker.

When I asked her about her reactions to ending treatment, she candidly informed me that as far as she was concerned, no genuine termination occurred. She said that she agreed to set a termination date because she felt it was what I wanted. If she had had her choice, she would have continued therapy with me indefinitely. She noted that although she felt she could trust me through the termination period, she could not help feeling abandoned by me, and that her fear of abandonment had never entirely disappeared. She remembered feeling angry that she had to end therapy with me but believed her feelings to be of no consequence, because the outcome would have been the same regardless of her feelings: I was bound to send her away.

Yet she felt that treatment had been of use to her in that she was more aware of her need to rely on people and found herself able to get support from her husband and from friends by relating to them in a well-intentioned way. She described herself as follows: "I can be one of the nicest people I know. I don't have a mean bone in my body, and I am basically a timid person. On the other hand, I can also get terribly angry, and I still have problems trusting myself and other people." She said that she manages to stay on good terms with friends and gets along well with her family. She does, however, shy away from competitive situations. She said that although much of her social life centers on athletics, she cannot play in formal competition, because she suffers from gastrointestinal distress whenever she signs up to play a match.

Ann told me that she feels much less impulsive than she did when we began treatment and that her life is much more stable as a result. She also finds her relationships with family and friends less superficial than before. She feels better able to tolerate being alone.

Our interview was remarkable to me. Ann appeared to be both a happily married mother who felt pleased with her life and someone with a keen awareness of significant limitations with which she felt she could live.

Case Discussion

Ann meets the DSM III criteria for Borderline Personality Disorder. At the start of this treatment* she manifested inappropriate intense anger, identity disturbance, affective instability, intolerance of being alone, and chronic feelings of emptiness and boredom. She manifested little impulsivity and only mild self-destructiveness. In the sessions with her therapist, she clearly created an intense and unstable relationship. Ann had a history of brief, ego-alien psychotic episodes. She experienced altered sense perception with paranoid ideation as a schoolgirl. At such times she felt cut off from others, believing that her thinking was not like other people's. She also had a history of a major regressive reaction in her previous therapy that included false beliefs of delusional proportions.

The *differential diagnosis* is confined to Axis II of DSM III, since Ann did not show any significant affective disturbance or other symptomatology suggestive of an Axis I disorder. The three personality disorders that must be considered most seriously are Narcissistic Personality Disorder, Dependent Personality Disorder, and Histrionic Personality Disorder.

Ann manifested many narcissistic features, including interpersonal exploitiveness, lack of sensitivity to the needs of others, and a need for constant attention and admiration. She also began, near the close of treatment, to reveal more fully her grandiose sense of self. However, Ann's struggles centered less on her maintenance of self-esteem than on her ability to survive (emotionally and physically) in the absence of an important other. The grandiosity, haughtiness, and interpersonal aloofness that are characteristic of Narcissistic Personality Disorder were not prominent features in her presentation, and the profundity of her identity disturbance was more suggestive of a borderline than a narcissistic disorder. Nevertheless, her relatively mild impairment in superficial social functioning and her almost total lack of self-destructive behavior might suggest a diagnosis of less severity than the borderline diagnosis.

Ann's manifest dependency and willingness to give others the responsibility for her life are consistent with a diagnosis of Dependent Personality Disorder. Moreover, her poorly formed identity and her sense of herself as helpless are typical of this personality type. As an adult, Ann manipulated her situation so as to preserve the fantasy that her parents and a succession of therapists managed her life for her.

*For the purposes of this discussion, Ann's psychotherapy denotes the treatment described in this case report, as opposed to the psychotherapy she had previously undergone.

In this respect, she meets DSM III criteria for Dependent Personality Disorder.

The diagnosis of Histrionic Personality Disorder is suggested by Ann's overly dramatic, reactive, and intensely expressive behaviors. She was perceived by others as superficially charming but shallow. She lost function in ways that demanded that others take responsibility for her welfare and saw herself as a helpless person who needed constant reassurance. In fact, Ann fulfills the diagnostic criteria for Histrionic Personality Disorder. However, Ann's history of dissociative episodes, her devaluation of those who were important to her, her hostility, and her mild self-destructiveness are all more typical of a borderline disorder.

Ann brought many *strengths* to her treatment. She was an engaging woman who not only charmed acquaintances but also endeared herself to her therapist through her warmth and childlike naiveté. Unlike several of the other patients in our group, Ann openly acknowledged her intense dependency needs. When she came to treatment, Ann functioned well in social situations on a superficial level, having a circle of female friends with whom she was not emotionally close but who provided her with companionship and social activity. She also completed college in 4 years, an achievement that was unique in our group of patients. Ann was not engaged in steady work when she entered treatment, but she found a full-time job soon after she began therapy and worked steadily from that time on.

Ann's psychological deficits at the start of treatment were considerable. Her childlike manner belied a striking capacity for regression to juvenile modes of functioning, as demonstrated by the immediacy with which she reverted to such behaviors in the therapist's office as grabbing his legs and refusing to sit in a chair. Moreover, she demonstrated considerable interpersonal boundary confusion, having difficulty differentiating her own thoughts and feelings from those of her therapist and of Dr. Brightman.

At the start of this treatment, Ann was not particularly curious about herself or how her mind worked. She had little awareness of affect and little inclination or capacity to look inward. She relied primarily on primitive defenses, most notably primitive idealization, denial, projection, and acting out. She confined most of her acting out to prying into her therapist's private life. She made many suicide threats during the course of treatment, but she never acted on them. It is remarkable that, despite considerable psychological impairment, Ann was capable of confining most of her regressed behavior to the treatment situation.

Ann's amenability to analytically oriented therapy was rated by the authors and is shown in Figure 4–1. She was scored as being of above-average intelligence, but she was rated very low (relative to the other patients in our group) with respect to psychological mindedness. She

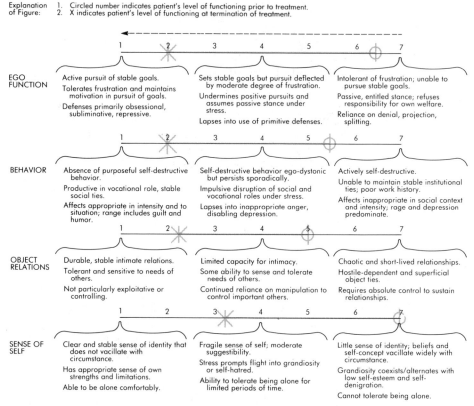

F I G U R E 4–1.   Standards for assessing levels of functioning—baseline and outcome: Ann.

also had little self-discipline; but she was not seen as being as impulsive, action oriented, or externalizing, as were some of the others in our group. Finally, she was rated as having good parental and social supports from the start of treatment.

Ann's therapist was a particularly patient and fatherly man who was himself warm and engaging. This, no doubt, contributed to the fit between the two of them. At the time of this psychotherapy, the therapist was very involved in parenting his own young children. For all of his distress about her intrusiveness and inappropriate behavior toward him, he nevertheless seemed basically comfortable working with Ann's intense dependency and her insistence that he be a parent to her. His work involved broad contacts within the local mental health community, and this, combined with his gregariousness, may have made it easier for him to accept Ann's unending curiosity about his life.

Ann's *transference* to her therapist was predominantly idealizing. She wanted a substitute for her previous therapist, in part so as not to have to experience fully Dr. Brightman's loss. Thus, she chose someone whom she saw as closely connected with Dr. Brightman. Her primitive idealization of the therapist was but a continuation of her previous therapeutic relationship. She could not tolerate recognition of any differences with her therapist in taste or personal interests, and her idealization extended to the therapist's family life, which she saw as perfect. Her predominant transference wish was to become part of the therapist's family and in this way to be united with him.

Ann wanted her therapist to function as an extension of herself and to perform functions for her that she could not perform on her own. For example, she found it difficult to experience genuine sadness at Dr. Brightman's death, but she chose a therapist whom she saw with tears in his eyes at Dr. Brightman's funeral. Ann presented her most dysfunctional side to her therapist, presumably because she felt she needed to be a regressed child who could not take care of herself in order to keep the therapist engaged. In return for his caretaking, she promised to be an adoring patient. However, when she was frustrated by her therapist's failure to live up to her idealized image (e.g., when he expected her to participate in sessions, when he took vacations), she saw him as an inadequate parent who had failed her, as her own parents had. She reacted to such frustrations with suicide threats and other efforts to control him and to deny their separateness. This fantasy of a symbiotic relationship was fraught with the danger of fusion and loss of self, so Ann's compliance with the therapist's limits may indicate her relief at his maintaining clear boundaries between them.

Ann's negative transference was initially buried beneath a facade of childlike adoration. Her early evasiveness and chaotic manner of relating to the therapist eventually came to be understood as a maneuver designed to protect Ann from her image of the therapist as a frightening predator who would pin her down and use her for his own ends. Not surprisingly, he saw her insatiable curiosity about his personal life and her intrusiveness as an identification with the aggressor— she was going to do to the therapist what she feared he would do to her. This transference image is likely to have evolved in part from her experiences as the victim of sexual abuse as a child. Overt sexual feelings for the therapist were acted out sporadically but did not become a prominent part of her transference to him.

The therapist's *countertransference* was, as noted above, primarily parental. He saw her as a "needy kid" who required better parenting than that which she had received. He remarked that there was little sexual feeling in the treatment. He also mentioned that he felt uncomfortable when her behavior did evoke sexual feelings in him (e.g., when she grabbed his legs). He also experienced difficulty in setting limits with Ann, as, for example, when he found it impossible to prevent her from spending the night with his family at their vacation home.

The therapist's *technique* seemed to be based on a deficit model of psychopathology. He saw her as childlike and viewed her difficulties more as the result of developmental failures (as described by Buie and Adler) than as stemming from conflict between positive and negative introjects (à la Kernberg). He tended to view her provocativeness and refusal to cooperate in treatment (e.g., refusing to give him any historical information) as predatory in an infantile and orally needy sense rather than as hostile. Thus, he rarely interpreted the aggressive and controlling aspects of these behaviors even after limits proved successful in curtailing them. He did interpret her suicide threats as efforts to control him, but he did not address the hostility contained in these threats.

Particularly in the early years of treatment, the therapist's work consisted primarily of providing a stable, consistent holding environment and exercising gentle but persistent limit setting in order to preserve the treatment. Few genetic roots of Ann's difficulties were traced. The therapist did not emphasize the relationship of Ann's present to her past, but instead focused primarily on the here-and-now of her relationships in and out of therapy. Overall, this therapy made the least use of interpretation.

The therapist began to establish limits at the outset of the therapy (e.g., resisting Ann's pressure to see him more than three times per week). He made it clear that she would have to observe a certain amount of decorum appropriate to a professional relationship (e.g., she would have to sit in a chair during therapy hours) if they were to continue to work together. However, it was only after the family meetings occurred several months into treatment that limit setting began in earnest. The parents' descriptions of Ann's behavior at home gave the therapist confirmation of his sense that she manipulated those around her in an effort to control them and to keep them at a distance. Thereafter, he insisted that Ann's secrecy was a form of resistance to treatment and emphasized her need to collaborate in her treatment if therapy was to succeed. Limit setting was partially successful in that she was able to comply with many of the rules laid down by her therapist and thereby protect the treatment.

The therapist balanced limit setting with the provision of a holding environment. He saw Ann as needing frequent reassurance of his continued existence outside of the treatment setting. Thus, he viewed her constant telephone calls to him as necessary to sustain her between psychotherapy sessions. While he told her that he did not want to be called every night at home, there were periods when she virtually ignored this wish and called him with considerable regularity. The therapist questioned her motives for calling, and on some occasions interpreted this activity as intrusive and controlling. He also interpreted her wish for and her fear of fusion with the therapist, but these interventions did not constitute the primary thrust of the treatment.

The therapist did make considerable use of clarifications in the therapy. In particular, he spent a great deal of time helping Ann to verbalize feelings of frustration and low self-esteem that she had heretofore expressed only in action. These clarifications served to emphasize Ann's separateness from the therapist and to help her achieve a new appreciation of the complexity of her personality.

In considering what helped to bring about a therapeutic effect in this treatment, it is important to emphasize the extent to which Ann's therapist served as a role model with whom she could identify. She watched him struggle with his own intense affects in the therapy without resorting to action. Moreover, he was able to remain emotionally involved with her in the face of frustration, neither withdrawing nor retaliating in response to her intrusiveness and her manipulative behaviors.

It may be argued that Ann's ability to push the therapist out of a professional stance and to see him outside of the therapy setting were crucial in bringing about a shift in her object relations. While limit setting improved Ann's behavior, it did little to ameliorate her unrealistic wish to join the therapist's family. Yet seeing him at home at the dinner table and going with his family to a drive-in movie somehow served to reduce her primitive idealization of him and his personal life. This gratification of her wish did not result in regression (as it does with so many borderline patients), but rather in a diminution of the intensity of her transference demands. In this respect, her forays into the therapist's private life resulted in a progressive disillusionment of her idealizing transference (to use Kohut's concept). Her idealization did not give way to devaluation of the therapist as a "bad object." Rather, her disillusionment allowed her to see the therapist as more differentiated from herself than had previously been the case. Nevertheless, her fantasy of marrying the therapist persisted until very late in the treatment.

Ann's occupational functioning improved early in treatment and remained improved throughout; she found and held a responsible full-time job by the second year of therapy. She also developed a fuller social life, which included dating soon thereafter. It was not until relatively late in treatment (year 4) that Ann became truly curious about herself and began to wonder at the way in which she had created similarly pathological relationships with her therapist, Dr. Brightman, and other important people in her life. It was also at this late date that she began to work on her boundary confusion and to collaborate actively in exploring her difficulties in differentiating her own thoughts and feelings from those of others. She began to experience her affects more fully (as is evident in her poetry), and needed to rely less on the therapist and others to experience affects for her.

The authors rated Ann's level of functioning before and after treatment on the four scales shown in Figure 4–2. She was assessed as

Effective Psychotherapy with Borderline Patients

	Unfavorable					Favorable				
1. Friendliness	−5	−4	−3	−2	−1	1	2	3	4	5
			hostile				amiable			
2. Likeability	−5	−4	−3	−2	−1	1	2	3	4	5
			below average				above average			
3. Intelligence	−5	−4	−3	−2	−1	1	2	3	4	5
			below average				above average			
4. Motivation	−5	−4	−3	−2	−1	1	2	3	4	5
			indifferent				motivated			
5. Psychological-mindedness	−5	−4	−3	−2	−1	1	2	3	4	5
			low				high			
6. Conscience factors	−5	−4	−3	−2	−1	1	2	3	4	5
			antisocial; deceitful; vengeful				values; good moral sense			
7. Self-discipline	−5	−4	−3	−2	−1	1	2	3	4	5
			low; chaotic				high			
8. Impulse control	−5	−4	−3	−2	−1	1	2	3	4	5
			craving; impulsivity				high			
9. Defensive style	−5	−4	−3	−2	−1	1	2	3	4	5
			drugs; action				intropunitive			
10. Externalization/Internalization	−5	−4	−3	−2	−1	1	2	3	4	5
			paranoid				capacity to admit fault			
11. Empathy/Narcissism	−5	−4	−3	−2	−1	1	2	3	4	5
			contempt; entitlement				ability to care about and resonate with others			
12. Parental factors	−5	−4	−3	−2	−1	1	2	3	4	5
			brutalization, exploitation, indifference				warmth, support			
13. Social supports	−5	−4	−3	−2	−1	1	2	3	4	5
			absent-disruptive				stable			

FIGURE 4–2. Amenability to psychotherapy: Ann. [Adapted from Stone's Amenability for Analytically Oriented Therapy Scale (Stone, 1985)].

having made substantial gains in all four areas of ego functioning, behavior, object relations, and sense of self. She was rated as having
made the greatest gains in ego functioning. Although she made considerable progress toward developing a more stable identity, she scored
lowest on sense of self at the end of treatment. Her improvement in
object relations was judged to be less than that on other scales, but
this in part reflects a higher pretreatment score in this area.

Both Ann and her therapist saw the results of treatment as significant
but limited. Her difficulties in the direct expression of aggression persisted at the end of treatment, as evidenced by her difficulty in engaging in competitive sports despite her wish to do so. Termination
occurred with little working through of the experience of loss, and in
this respect the termination process recapitulated the end of her treatment with Dr. Brightman. She was compliant but essentially saw herself as being abandoned by her therapist and as having no choice in
the matter. One wonders, too, about the extent to which her attachment
to the therapist was simply replaced by her attachment to her husband,
so that the husband came to serve as a self-object for her in the way
that the therapist had done. Certainly, the loss of the therapeutic relationship was softened considerably by the presence of Ann's husband.

Yet despite these qualifiers, Ann's functioning and quality of life
were significantly improved at the end of treatment. She was working
full time, involved in a satisfying marital relationship, and engaged
in a variety of social activities from which she derived pleasure. Ten-
year follow-up suggests that these gains were lasting.

CHAPTER 5

Stewart
Case Report

Stewart's treatment began with his first admission to McLean Hospital. At that time he was 20 years old, single, and working as a short-order cook. Upon entering the hospital, he stated that he was there because "I am a bad person." He had been referred by the hospital's outpatient clinic, where he had sought an evaluation because of persistent loneliness and self-loathing and because of intrusive and bizarre thoughts that had recurred over the preceding several months. While preparing a meal, associations with the bodily elements of a dead cousin led him to run outdoors. Stewart had also beaten himself and burned himself repeatedly with a candle. A third problem was his preoccupation with ideas of influence; he felt that he was somehow being thwarted by a local business and feared that he was being watched over by their representatives. In addition, he had thoughts of throwing himself in front of a train, along with murderous impulses that twice, on visits home, had led to the violent destruction of objects.

Background Information

Stewart was the youngest of four children raised in a middle-class suburban household. His father, a corporate attorney, was a distant, intellectual, socially awkward man with a sarcastic sense of humor. His mother was described as a colorless, soft-spoken, perpetually worried-looking woman. She had begun work as a shopkeeper when Stewart went to college. His siblings included two brothers, 8 and 6 years older, who were both married, with successful careers, and whom Stewart looked up to and admired. His sister was 4 years older than he and worked as a nurse. There was no known psychiatric illness in the family except for some alleged eccentricity among the father's relatives. The family unit remained intact in the same suburban home throughout Stewart's development.

Throughout grade school, Stewart was the smallest child in his class. He was a quiet boy who avoided conflict and also avoided opportunities for praise for his achievements in school and in sports. At home, however, he could be tyrannical with his mother and constantly fought with his sister, who teased him until he lost his temper. He tended to brood over injustices and longed for happier times, which he believed characterized his family prior to his birth. He developed a small group of friends in grade school with whom he maintained stable friendships that continued through the time of our first meeting. These relationships often involved elaborate games, intellectual interests, and outdoor activities. Stewart was often intolerant and withdrew from this group of friends when submissiveness was required. When he was 13 he developed a fantasy about a utopian society that increasingly preoccupied him during the next few years, to the extent that he sometimes believed in its existence. He was a good student with diverse interests and abilities, yet without special relationships to his teachers. He was demanding of himself and often did special projects. At age 14, he became so frustrated with an algebra problem that he stabbed his book with a knife. He graduated near the top of his class in high school and subsequently attended a prestigious university in the Midwest.

Stewart's sexual history is sketchy. In elementary school, he tied himself to his bed and hit himself with a belt while wearing a dresslike robe. In high school, masturbation was accompanied by fantasies of being tied up. He continued to have fantasies of being beaten up to the time of his hospitalization. His actual relationships with girls were quite limited. He had his first sexual relationship during his second year of college, and the breakup of that relationship was one of the factors that led him to withdraw near the end of his second year. In addition, he left school because he believed that his mother felt neglected and needed him at home. His school performance, however, remained excellent.

In the year-long interval between leaving school and his admission to McLean, he had generally lived by himself in an apartment while working as a warehouse clerk. He prided himself on his ascetic existence and saved virtually all of his salary. A close relationship with a second young woman, this one nonsexual, led to his seeking psychiatric evaluation when she told him that he was "a cold person" and thus confirmed a fear that Stewart had long harbored about himself.

First Year of Therapy

I began working with Stewart shortly after he was admitted to McLean. I was initially impressed by his intelligence and eagerness to please. He was a good-looking young man who wore his hair very short and dressed in white so that he had the appearance of a refugee from a religious sect. We agreed to meet three times per week and continued to do so throughout his treatment.

Within the first few visits, he became openly suspicious of my motives, including my possible homosexual interest in him. I responded by asking what prompted this concern. Receiving no response, I pushed further by asking whether this question reflected a more general concern of his. He denied that it was an issue in his life but retreated from further overt suggestions about my sexual orientation and motives.

In the first few months of therapy, Stewart closed off discussion of any subject that appeared to him to arouse my interest. I was interested in getting a detailed record of the events leading up to his hospitalization, especially descriptions of his relationships with his girlfriend in college and subsequently with the young woman who had precipitated his evaluation. He was overtly concerned and interested in what motivated my inquiries and what deductions I would draw from the material he provided. The sessions were very tense. He examined the furnishings in my office and found a sinister meaning in them. I did nothing to reassure him in the face of his suspicions that the sessions were, for example, being tape recorded. Indeed, I commented that his accusations of my sadism and insensitivity were evidence of his own angry distrust.

At one point, therapy reached an impasse when he felt that it was impossible for him to use me in any helpful way because of the intense suspicion and anger he felt in my presence. On this occasion, I reluctantly agreed with his suggestion that we take a walk together. I told him that I did not expect this to be useful; it would only serve to deflect or delay us in our task of understanding the origins of his fears and anger. To my surprise, he returned to the subsequent hour agreeing that such a deflection would not be useful, but bringing along a game of backgammon, which was a compromise that he felt might serve the same function of decreasing his anxiety. He spent much of one hour teaching me to play and, in the process, displayed both his ability to beat me and his concern about doing so. During the next session, he came without a game and declared that it was not a productive way for us to spend the time. There was no further request for such activities.

As the year progressed, Stewart became increasingly involved in ward activities and in occasional family meetings. The content of his therapy hours reflected this change. As he reported his daily activities, I had the opportunity to interpret repeatedly his hostile, controlling, and manipulative motives in dealing with others. For example, I noted that his consistent failure to appear at times and places that his family or the ward staff expected him was designed to arouse considerable anxiety about his welfare. He rejected this interpretation angrily, but at the same time, these interventions led to a diminution of this behavior pattern.

In the course of our work during the first year, it became clear that Stewart was reluctant to get involved or invested in new people or situations, but, having done so, was even more reluctant to leave or give up that to which he had become attached. Associated with this pattern was the tendency to devalue bitterly and at great length people whom he felt let him down or let him go. The most persistent objects of this bitter devaluation were his parents, whom he felt had not provided sufficient care as a child to allow him to be psychologically competent as an adult. Thus, his hospitalization was an indication of both his own deficits and their failures. For this reason, he felt entitled to good nurturant experiences in the hospital and within his psychotherapy—experiences in which he need not be actively, responsibly involved.

I clarified and interpreted these patterns over and over again as they recurred in his relationships with me and all other potentially nurturing figures in the hospital environment. An effort by the hospital social worker to initiate family therapy failed after half a dozen visits due to Stewart's refusal to discuss directly with his parents the family problems that he so actively complained about elsewhere. For him, the family therapy failed because the social worker did not take an openly combative role toward his parents. He felt betrayed by this failure.

During his hospitalization, Stewart developed an interest in basketball, which was important insofar as he had previously retreated from most competitive sports. His attitude was stimulated by the interest shown in the game by an admired older man, but perhaps also because he knew me to be interested. In any event, he began practicing diligently and participating in basketball exercises with other patients, many of whom had a similar lack of prior experience. He soon developed legitimate confidence in his growing ability. As a result, he spoke increasingly of pursuing a basketball career. He envisioned himself getting a scholarship to college, becoming a star, and rising to the professional ranks. Not just a wishful fantasy, this became, for Stewart, a serious plan for his future. He was furious when I suggested that he discuss this plan with the head of the recreation program to assess his chances before taking steps in the assumption that he was likely to succeed.

After 6 months in the hospital, the ward administrator raised the issue of discharge with Stewart. His initial reaction was to harshly condemn the ward as a place he would be glad to be rid of and could not wait to leave. This was accompanied by a recurrence of much of the acting out that was characteristic of his early period in the hospital—namely, veiled suicide threats, prolonged absences, and heavy drinking during leaves from the ward. Eventually he agreed to move into a halfway house, although his original inclination had been to move home. As the transition to the halfway house began, his reactions were very similar to those that had occurred when he came to the hospital. His devaluing and testing of new staff alternated with a feeling of loss and regrets for misbehaviors.

Second Year of Therapy

That summer, Stewart saw an interim therapist during my absence, an arrangement he subsequently felt was unnecessary. Also, during the second year, he called me in a panic just prior to a vacation, but otherwise there were no intersession contacts with him throughout his therapy. With the transition to the halfway house, a shift in the psychotherapy also occurred. Stewart began to recall memories from his childhood about which he had previously claimed amnesia. From these memories emerged a picture of him as a private, isolated child who could be extremely willful and arrogant in his relationships. His recollection of this trait in childhood echoed and reflected his recognition of this willfulness as an obstacle in his current relationships. In several autobiographical accounts, he carefully described his long-standing absence of a sense of identity and his use of fantasy, often of a fantastic nature but invariably self-aggrandizing, as his substitute for the lack of security and confidence he felt in his relationships in the actual world.

At this time, Stewart began a relationship with a young woman that was largely characterized by her sexual initiatives. His anxieties about this relationship were diminished by projecting many of his self-doubts onto her. He was largely attracted to her because of his envy for an idealized relationship he imagined her to have with her parents. After several months, he abruptly stopped seeing her when he discovered that her relationship with her parents was not as ideal as he had imagined.

He continued to be intermittently resistive in sessions, for example, smoking or eating and then devaluing me when I eventually set limits on these activities. Otherwise, the sessions were filled with an unending stream of bitter complaints about his father for his failure to give him sufficient teaching, attention, and financial support. Failing to get sympathetic validation for these views from me, he sought it from his mother in private discussions, pledging her to secrecy.

Stewart's angry defiance reached a peak when he claimed that he would have to either leave the halfway house or leave therapy because of his inability to afford both. I expressed skepticism about the reality of this predicament and pointed out that he persistently refused to make inquiries of his father about financial support. In this context, at my initiation, we held several family meetings. I told his parents that it would be unfortunate if Stewart had to leave either his therapy or the halfway house. Moreover, I expressed the view that his inability or unwillingness to explore the possibility of financial assistance with them was symptomatic of broader problems with behaving responsibly on his own behalf. I urged his parents to take this issue seriously and to appreciate that it reflected a continuation of the problems that had led to his hospitalization. In this regard, I cautioned them against assuming that his recent discharge from the hospital reflected anything more than a small advance in his larger developmental needs.

These meetings opened up a new dialogue between Stewart and his father that had been almost totally lacking. In due course, he was forced to recognize his father's apparent willingness to offer financial help and to recognize the ways in which his demands for apologies made dialogues difficult. Finally, he became more aware of his father's personal shortcomings. He did not welcome these insights, but viewed them as complications that compromised his prior position—that his problems were directly caused by father's withholding resources from him. These insights supported my ongoing injunction that, independent of his parents' contributions to his disturbed personality, he had to assume responsibility for perpetuating his adaptations to them. This included the possibility that he had distorted the meaning of formative interactions with his parents in the same ways that he presently did with me and others.

The deepening of Stewart's therapy during this period was also evident in the occasional dreams he shared. In one dream, he fearfully entered an underground bunker that he had dug during his childhood. To his surprise, he found that it was clean and inhabited by others. He also found bowls and glasses of confusing shapes. His apprehension was replaced by a feeling of pride. This dream was interpreted as reflecting the sense of danger, discovery, and newfound pride he took in his recently renewed sexual functioning and in recalling childhood memories during therapy. The dream was also examined with respect to the ongoing conflicts and concerns about his sexual identity (i.e., whether he was feminine, as represented by the bowls, or masculine, as represented by the glasses).

Another dream neatly summarized several of the major themes of his therapy:

> Stewart was on the shore with his father and his brother, but left them to go out on a pier by himself. When he returned to the shore, his father and his brother were discussing Robinson Crusoe. During his absence, he had changed and now felt unable to join their conversation.

In the exploration of this dream, three major themes of the second year of therapy were outlined. The first was his active paranoid perception of people as inaccessible and hurtful, and the growing recognition that he was an active participant in determining his own fate. We noted that, in the dream, he left the company of his father and brother; and it was he, not they, who changed in ways that made communication difficult. He was finding in his real life that people could respond positively and sensitively to him, but he had to take the initiative to express his wishes and feelings. The second major theme of his therapy was his passivity and his ongoing lament that there was nothing he could do for himself. In contrast, his increasing involvement with his parents, with me, and with his girlfriend complicated his life. He had found it lonely and difficult to ignore the people around him, but being involved made it hard to justify the degree to which he blamed everyone for his isolation. Finally, the dream reflected his own belief in himself as Robinson Crusoe, the self-sufficient hero, and thus his defensive use of withdrawal into grandiose fantasies. However, like Robinson Crusoe, he was finding, upon returning to life outside the hospital, indeed to life outside himself, that it was difficult to adjust and that in fact his social skills were retarded.

In his transference, these themes were actively joined around the issue of paying his bill. His payments were repeatedly late and arrived only after reminders from me. He cited these reminders as evidence of my mercenary and uncaring attitude. At such times he became angrily accusatory, and he occasionally walked out of the session. Paying his bill was predictably accompanied by angry silences or open devaluation. I repeatedly interpreted the degree to which his own passivity and entitlement placed him in situations that both jeopardized his own welfare and led to responses that confirmed his paranoid expectations.

By late in the second year, he was occasionally able to acknowledge his wish for a special relationship with me, his wish to have me pick him up and console him, and—most especially—to see him without charging! He left me a short note expressing his appreciation for my help. On the other side of this note were detailed calculations that he had prepared to demonstrate how I had—once again—overbilled him.

This second year was marked by major adjustments in Stewart's life outside of therapy. He eventually settled into the halfway house and became attached to the people there. He took a few extension school courses and found employment as a recreation supervisor. His relationships at work were fraught with conflict, since he felt devalued and victimized by his employers and envious of his peers who seemed comfortably affable and less self-conscious. In the course of his transition from the halfway house to an apartment, there was a resurgence of his complaints about the inadequacy and failures of the halfway house staff and his parents. Nevertheless, he was able to acknowledge concerns about his ability to live on his own. He feared the growing dependence he would have on me in the absence of other forms of support. During this time, he began reading extensively about Hitler, whom he admired and envied for his enormous powers. In his dreams, he reassured himself that he could return to the safety of a bunker if he left it, reflecting the warlike atmosphere he anticipated as he moved into a less sheltered living situation.

Third Year of Therapy

Upon moving into an apartment, Stewart began for the first time to experience a longing to return home, especially when confronted with a case of stomach flu. Eventually he did return home for several weeks, and he was keenly aware of the gratification he got from his family's care. At the same time, however, he felt acutely ashamed of his wish to be nurtured, since it conflicted with his view of himself as independent and self-sufficient.

Stewart gradually approached the possibility of returning to school. Without being explicit, I think he knew that I supported this idea and felt he was ready. After making plans to resume school in Boston the next fall, he announced his decision to go on a vacation. He inquired whether he would be charged for the missed appointments. When I told him I would not charge him, he immediately rose from his chair and began to accuse a psychiatrist in a neighboring office of listening in. Then, turning to me, he accused me of having systematically overbilled him for the past 6 months. He calmed down only when I volunteered to charge him for his missed appointments, saying that he was "clearly too ill, that is, paranoid, to leave with my support." Although he failed to have a good time on this trip, it represented his first effort to seek satisfactions on his own, independent of his parents and/or the mixed parental transference to me. It is notable that up to this point he had evidenced little reaction to my absences except some anxiety about my safety.

With his return to school, Stewart's fears about his social and intellectual competence increased. His heightened interest in studying Russian became understandable as an effort to identify with strength and authority attributed to the Russian people in circumstances where he felt weak. This led to memories about childhood fantasies in which he had always played the part of a victorious military conqueror. He relied upon these fantasies most heavily under circumstances in which he experienced himself as very small in the face of explosive outbursts of temper from his father and sadism from his overbearing older sister.

Stewart was engaged in a major struggle within the transference related to his conviction that unfair authority figures kept him from advancing in every endeavor he undertook. I offered interpretations about the degree to which he was kept back by his passive longings and implicit demands for a push from the rear. I did not explicitly emphasize the homosexual aspects of this stance, but rather the experience of impotence and the wish for someone to give him a penis that would allow him to compete successfully. The material for this theme arose not only out of his historically based complaint about his father's failures to provide for him, but also in his relationships with the present school authorities, which were marked by both ingratiation and fear. A series of dreams expressed his conviction that the basketball players he admired had large penises and that if he befriended them, they would lend him their powers. In therapy he angrily waited for me to initiate the sessions, and he expressed ongoing dissatisfaction with my failure to provide direction, advice, and other explicit signs of care such as telling him how to talk to girls.

By midyear, it was clear that Stewart was performing at an excellent level academically and, despite his protests of inadequacy, was socializing with girls more comfortably. At this point, his therapy shifted toward the problems of committing himself to any single career, identity, or relationship. For example, he took a variety of courses in college but had not declared a major, and he had become promiscuous in his relationships with a series of women. By the spring term, he was feeling much more comfortable and confident. He had begun to pay his bill regularly, without evident resentment; he came to sessions ready to talk about himself; and he expressed occasional warmth and humor. He was working competently enough to consider going back to his original college for the remainder of his education.

Fourth Year of Therapy

After the successful conclusion of the school year, Stewart resumed frequent visits to his parents' home. In this context, he began to work on issues related to leaving home. The conflict concerned his wish to please his mother and his resentment of what he perceived as her need to have him around. In turn, he cited this need as further evidence of his father's failures and of his superiority to his father.

He also began to sift systematically through the things in his room, which contained all the clothes, toys, and papers belonging to him since his earliest childhood. He found going through his possessions a painful process because it involved many memories. He had to confront the fact that many of the items from his childhood were no longer of value or interest to him. Moreover, it was not possible for childhood experiences to be relived with more perfect outcomes. Hence, the issues of imperfection, separation, and letting go were directly and powerfully brought to the fore.

The process of actually throwing away some of his old possessions led him to make his first reference to eventually terminating treatment with me. When, a few sessions later, I advised him of my forthcoming vacation, he responded by setting a termination date for the fall. I replied that termination was the major issue left for him to work on in his therapy, and he quickly became enraged. He stopped visiting his house and viewing materials there, and he began to focus on reasons for cutting down his therapy. I advised him that while I felt that termination was an important process, his wish to cut down was really a defense against that possibility and an effort on his part to attenuate the therapy indefinitely. He insisted that the issues of money, convenience, and the general unpleasantness of his visits made cutting down reasonable. I pointed out that the processes of leaving home, selecting a vocation, becoming self-sufficient, and replacing his family were still incomplete, and that these problems were all tied to the issue of termination. At present, he needed to continue examining why it seemed so impossible to give up immature and unhappy attachments. I refused to cut down on his appointments, and at one point I threatened to discontinue seeing him altogether if he did not continue coming three times a week.

In the weeks prior to my vacation, there was a sullenness in Stewart's attitude and more silences, but he still, at least intermittently, participated responsibly in sessions. After my return from vacation, Stewart entered the most intense and unremitting period of rage in his therapy. The subjects of this rage were my failure to provide him with what he needed and my having "addicted him to therapy," taking all of his money so that he could have no pleasures in his life. He acted out about paying bills and about arriving at and leaving sessions at times designated by me. I spent a great deal of time interpreting these maneuvers as his efforts to regain a sense of control over me and as reactions to his recognition that I could and would let him leave. He acknowledged the former but angrily denied the latter. He spent therapy hours in angry tirades about these subjects, followed by periods of silence and a contemptuous and overtly sadistic attitude that made it difficult for me to maintain my equanimity.

At times, I was tempted to agree with Stewart's claim that the therapy had failed to do any good. It was also tempting to agree with his wish to reduce the number of sessions and accept his rationalization of the financial reason for doing so. My inner struggles were largely limited to the time within the therapy hours. The time between hours was useful to restore my objectivity and equanimity, so that Stewart had little opportunity to observe my vacillations. In this regard, he complained that I was like a rock that he washed up against year after year without apparent effect. I was pleased by this analogy but knew it was not true.

In the fall, Stewart postponed his termination date. He complained that I had created a need in him. I responded that he was afraid to acknowledge that he wanted to come to therapy. I also remarked that he clung to his anger and was postponing the work he came to therapy to do. By the winter, he began to use some of his time to resume talking about his father. Specifically, he recounted his father's temper tantrums, which, when Stewart was a child, seemed enormously out of proportion to the minor incidents that prompted them. His father's angry outbursts had frequently caused Stewart to leave the area, go to his bedroom, and slam his door. After an interval, his father would come to his room in a calm mood and plead or cajole him to "forgive and forget," as Stewart saw it. In recalling these episodes, Stewart was resistant to my suggestion that his father's motives might have been other than self-serving. This was a difficult countertransference issue insofar as I worried about the extent to which my wish to have him forgive and forget was motivated by self-interest—to deflect his unremitting accusations of my exploitiveness.

I was aware that Stewart sometimes drank heavily, but I had not been concerned about the severity of this problem or its potentially self-endangering effects. One night he got drunk and crashed his car, narrowly avoiding serious damage to himself. Earlier that day, his mother had signed the papers that made the car legally Stewart's. Although he had driven the car almost exclusively prior to this change of ownership and had referred to it as "his" for several years, he and his mother had resisted the legal transfer of responsibility.

In appointments subsequent to his accident, he expressed anger at his mother for caring more about the car than about him. I related the accident to his anger at her for being willing to let him go. Surprisingly, he recognized the truth of this interpretation and accepted it. He then remembered and described feelings he allegedly had about being weaned from his mother at the age of 14 months. During this period in the treatment, there was a dramatic decrease in the intensity and duration of his diatribes against me. His angry feelings were, for the first time, more specifically directed at his mother and to a lesser degree at his father.

As Stewart became increasingly aware of his anger at his mother, he recalled her foolish insistence upon cleanliness and tidiness. He was particularly enraged about the value she placed upon a collection of teacups that were untouchable and unused but took up a great deal of space in the kitchen cabinets. This perception of his mother was related by me to his own devotion to outmoded but highly precious possessions and relationships—especially to his parents, and his continued clinging to outmoded defensive styles including anger, paranoia, and passivity. Finally, the teacups were interpreted as a symbolic reflection of how he felt his mother had always treated him—as something precious but untouchable.

In subsequent appointments, Stewart reported having intense and urgent tingling sensations around his lips and on the inside of his mouth before his hours. These feelings would then subside during the sessions. Unlike the previous months, he began these sessions by talking without prompting. He said that talking helped to relieve the tingling in his mouth. He related the sensations to the experience of weaning in early childhood.

In one session, he reported two dreams. In the first dream, he was planting a garden. He remembered having actually done this as a child, and an old man who passed by had offered the comment, "It's a bit late to start a garden." He had reacted by thinking that the old man had no right to comment on this fact and that he—the old man—wasn't so smart himself. The second dream concerned an effort to reach some beautiful giant red apples that were hanging from the uppermost branches of an apple tree. As he reached to grab the apples, the sky suddenly got stormy with thunder and lightning. At the urging of a friend, he descended to the ground. Once on the ground, he and his friend found a burrow where they felt safe from the storm, and he felt relieved that he had not been hurt.

I related these dreams to his efforts to do something to relieve his own hunger (e.g., by talking in therapy sessions) rather than raging at me for not giving him the fruits of my garden. (The entrance to McLean is through an apple orchard). These "fruits" included my penis, my money, and all the other signs of status or power that he perceived and envied in me. We talked about his feeling of being torn between a desire to go ahead and do things for himself, even though his achievements might be imperfect, and a wish to remain angry and envious and to attempt to get me and others to do things to him or for him. He began to acknowledge the degree to which his envy and entitlement determined his long-standing anger at his father and at me. Although I interpreted the red apples as representing his mother's breasts, and although he seemed to accept this idea, he was not then aware of the full extent to which he remained invested in claiming his mother's breasts exclusively for himself. As termination began, this time in earnest, the issues of his envy and entitlement remained prominent themes.

Shortly thereafter, Stewart made a final effort to manipulate me into decreasing his appointments by claiming a schedule conflict with the classes required for him to graduate. I attempted to accommodate his schedule by changing his appointment times. When faced with my flexibility and readiness to change his long-standing appointments, his anger towards me revived. I interpreted this as reactive to his wish for absolute stability and as reactive to my apparent willingness to let him go. He then became further enraged at the possibility that I would not change his appointment times. Eventually, he was able to recognize his feelings of loss and disappointment when we adopted a new schedule.

During the next four months, Stewart imposed a new pattern on the psychotherapy hours. He generally entered sullenly and angrily, re-

maining unresponsive to my inquiries or to interpretations directed
at his procrastination. I became increasingly prepared to sit silently
with him until he decided to begin. At some point, he would sigh as
if overcoming forcefully some persisting discontent and begin to talk
about things that were troubling him. The following is the content of
one such hour that occurred prior to a vacation:

> Stewart arrived looking angry and hurt. A few minutes passed before he
> said, "I really don't have anything to say." He went on to say that he felt
> good, things were going well at work, with his friends, and he felt better
> about himself. I inquired, "Does that mean you feel you will be ok when
> I am gone?" He said, "Sure. When will you be away?" There was a silence
> and he said, "I guess you feel I can take care of myself," and he pulled out
> a piece of paper from his pocket on which the dates of my vacation were
> written. He then asked where I was going and quickly added rhetorically,
> "Why do I even bother to ask?" He then went on to give me a lecture about
> the reasons why I should be more conversational. This was followed by a
> complaint that coming to appointments was a chore, he felt he was doing
> penance, and, at the moment, he felt hungry. There was a silence. When I
> inquired about what was on his mind, he said that when his hour was over,
> he planned to go home and eat a big meal. He added that, in the meantime,
> there was nothing for him to do here. I responded by inquiring, "Does that
> mean you don't want to plant your garden? Do you see those big apples of
> mine and just feel angry that I don't give them to you?"
>
> He said, "I guess so. Somehow (silence) . . . somehow these meetings
> are important to come to. They're mysterious, intangible, but strangely vital
> . . . as if I am missing something without them. I am not sure what—it's
> just a feeling." I inquired about this feeling and he explained that it was
> in the back of his neck—a feeling that he had previously connected with
> being angry.
>
> He went on. "That's what I feel. It's like my brothers and my sister when
> they laughed at me." He then described a time when, as a child, he quit a
> game because a brother had forced him to surrender some of his winnings.
> He had left yelling, "You have no right!" I pointed out that the feeling he
> had then and that he was having now sounded similar to what he felt when
> his mother refused to buy him a toy that he wanted. He responded, "I felt
> she was being cruel, unfair, vindictive." After a thoughtful silence, he added,
> "I have mainly felt resentful towards you for a long time. I feel you have
> something that belongs to me—something I long for." He went on to de-
> scribe how eating and reading were really not satisfactory substitutes. Even
> basketball games served more to preoccupy and distract him, but he didn't
> really enter into the flow of the games. He concluded by describing how,
> late at night, he often felt like he wanted to say something and he was not
> sure what or to whom he wanted to say it.
>
> As the hour ended, I asked whether there was something he'd wish that
> he had said before we parted. He said no, followed by a silence. Then he
> inquired where I would be going. I asked him what interested him about
> that. He said, "I want to know if you're safe—to make sure there's no ac-
> cidents." I pointed out that this had concerned him frequently during my
> absences since the beginning of our work and I wondered why. Rather than

exploring that, he responded with the single statement that he didn't want me to go; and after another silence, it was because he wanted me to be with him. That was the end of the hour.

During this period, Stewart frequently described his growing awareness of the degree to which he enjoyed and felt comfortable being angry. He claimed that he neither wanted nor knew how to be attached to anyone. He would describe himself by saying, "All I am is angry. I need people to hate." He made conscious efforts to overcome the palpable resistance he felt toward giving up his vendettas toward me and his family. He was aware of the futility and the waste of time involved in his angry, silent sulkiness. This was interpreted in terms of his wish to hold on to his sickness and to the feeling that he needed me. He gradually resumed utilizing the entire hour in productive exploration of himself in a way he had not for nearly a year.

Near the end of his fourth year, Stewart planned and undertook another vacation. This was an initiative he took independent of the pressures of school, family, or his mental health, that is, it was neither in compliance nor defiance. Prior to the vacation, he expressed anxiety about how well he would function, concern over the incompleteness of the projects that he was leaving behind, and fears about unforeseen dangers. I interpreted these worries in terms of his separation anxiety, his castration anxiety with its more paranoid elaborations, and as a departure from the clinging vengefulness in his relationships with me and his parents. He went on this vacation with a friend, with whom he shared expenses and driving. It is noteworthy that, although he was recurrently anxious, he managed to have some very good times.

Fifth Year of Therapy

After he returned from vacation, Stewart once again began thinking about the possibility of a new termination date. I interpreted his push to set a termination date as aggressive, since it represented his wish to leave me in the wake of my having failed to hold on to him. Yet, I also made it clear that this was a progressive move because he had returned from his vacation with a more realistic sense of what separations were likely to entail and how this developmental step was essential for his continued growth. He then set a termination date for himself in late summer and had the following dream:

He was in a rickety elevator that took him up to the penthouse of a building. However, he needed to go two floors down in order to be on the floor where he belonged. The elevator was slipping, and there was a constant danger of his falling off it altogether.

The anxieties reflected in this dream mirrored the anxieties he felt about being too separated from "mother earth," but also his recognition that he did not belong in the penthouse, but instead at a less superior or lofty level appropriate for him. Shifts in his perfectionism were also apparent. He noted that he had received B's in some of his courses, in contrast to his usual A's. He also noted that he had read papers I had written, and that my work "wasn't that great either." He accepted his B's and reported my limitations without his prior animosity or blaming.

In a dream at that time, Stewart referred to himself as being like the roots of a tree buried beneath concrete and thought to be dead, but that were now sending up first shoots and widening the crevice in the concrete to allow for continued growth. In general, his life outside of therapy at this time showed a rapid expansion in the amount and quality of his interaction with his peers. His relationships with his roommates were deepening. He was developing more respectful and stable relationships with girls. He was given more responsibilities at work because of his improved sociability. At school, he was working productively but more selectively on the subjects that interested him. Within his therapy sessions, he continued to spend less and less time in angry, envious silences, and he paid his bill on time without complaints.

Concurrent with all these positive signs of growth, a new theme entered his therapy, wherein he repeatedly expressed concern about my welfare. He perceived me as being preoccupied and troubled or not feeling well. At times, he was resentful because he felt I was too preoccupied with myself to listen to him and to respond sensitively to what he said. Although the developmental antecedents of this attitude were not clear, his associations indicated that it related to an early perception of his mother as being troubled and his early and ongoing efforts to try to please, appease, heal, or make up for the pain he believed she was experiencing. I clarified this aspect of his transference and related it to his fear of the harmful impact that his recent move toward more independence would have on me.

Stewart recalled how he had always expected that someday I would understand everything about him and that he would have a very special role in my life—both as an informative patient and as a source of solace. We developed the analogy between this expectation and that of his being seen by his mother as a highly valued, extremely rare, but untouchable teacup.

As his summer termination date approached, he set it back to the fall. Near the end of the summer, as he made plans for another vacation and anticipated this new termination date, he had the following dream:

He had gone for a ride in a car, but as he approached his destination, the car broke down. He found that there was no engine under the hood. Fortunately, his mother arrived to help him by giving him a ride. Nevertheless, he was very upset about the failure of his own car.

I interpreted the dream as reflecting his concern about whether he had enough inside to sustain him as he prepared to leave. By this time,

Stewart was deeply aware that his view that others kept him from leaving therapy was a rationalization that hid his own doubts about his ability to function independently. He could talk movingly about having had no inner sense of purpose or direction—although he perceived himself as developing this sense. On this late summer vacation, he camped out with a friend. He had many apprehensions about his ability to live so closely with someone in a situation where compromise and collaboration were essential. In fact, he had a great time.

With the arrival of September and the return to his final term of college, Stewart was confronted by two dilemmas that provided him with a reason to postpone the termination date once again: He had procrastinated in completing an assignment; and he was afraid to declare a major and complete the credits in that area in order to graduate. These issues were clearly related to his fear of emerging from his defensive posture to take an identifiable stand and thereby risk failure. His vacillation about terminating therapy was clearly connected to his wish to take regressive comfort in a position of sickness. His dreams portrayed the dilemma he felt about pursuing his goals, which, in addition to declaring a major, included terminating therapy and completing the "packing" of his childhood memories. He perceived moving ahead as being like entering a war zone, but also felt that to do otherwise was shameful. His dreams reflected a vision of life ahead in terrifying terms: as a treacherous battlefield where there were limited reserves and no lines of retreat. I also noted that he was afraid to enter his father's world and to compete. Stewart vehemently agreed with this assessment.

He soon went ahead and chose a major that seemed appropriate. This commitment was accompanied by his exposure of heretofore unexplored goals of "learning everything" or "setting the world afire with a theory of general knowledge that unites all intellectual endeavors." These ambitions had been with him, more or less unaltered, since he was 12 years old. He struggled obsessively with the problem of how his initiatives, decisions, or other responsible positions and commitments foreclosed the more universal and perfectionistic ambitions that he entertained. But more than this, he recognized that the amount of effort he put into making exactly the right decision postponed any investment and involvement, so that life regularly passed him by. This situation implied that, although he was unsure and frightened and aware of his imperfections, he ought to get on with the business of living his life and stop studying it. This realization also had implications for his continuation in psychotherapy. He had come to recognize the regressive function that psychotherapy was serving for him. At this point, he again wanted to set a termination date.

He chose a termination date that was about 2.5 weeks away. It was close enough so that he would not lose sight of it and postpone paying attention to it, but far enough away to allow enough sessions so that he could say goodbye. Still, he was very ambivalent. In a subsequent session, he reported the following dream:

> He was sitting with a former patient from McLean, discussing a voluptuous woman who was dancing in an adjacent room. The two of them were watching her. As they talked, Stewart got sexually excited, and he ejaculated so profusely that his pants were visibly wet. He then felt acutely ashamed and woke up.

His associations with this dream reflected his concerns about issues that were still incomplete in his treatment. The dream revealed the degree to which sexual issues in his life had not been fully discussed and explored. Homosexual concerns were identified behind the shame of having an orgasm in front of a male. I pointed out that he had always felt that he had needed to come to therapy, and that further therapy at this point was more a matter of choice than of necessity. Therefore, to continue in therapy would almost certainly require deeper recognition of the positive feelings that he had toward me. In his subsequent session, the dream was explored from another viewpoint: He felt tempted to "jerk off" with me instead of going out into the world to pursue the objects of his ambitions. In this sense, his shame was related to his sense of failure and weakness.

Stewart went on to talk about the fact that he felt he had been learning things in everyday life from his interactions at school, at work, and with his family, and that this was a new experience for him. In fact, he sometimes felt so intrigued with the involvements that he had outside of therapy that the meetings with me were pale by comparison. He concluded by saying that he had decided that he really should stop therapy for now, and that he doubted it would be as traumatic as he had always imagined. It was, after all, "really just a goodbye without any great revelations at the last minute and without any unbearable grief." I pointed out that he had been preparing to leave for a long time; he had spent more than a year reconciling himself to my being willing and able to let him go. I noted that, with this recognition, he had had to wrestle with his own limitations and mine. I reminded him that he had entered therapy because he had become frightened about his ability to live up to these standards. Insofar as his standards had become more realistic and he was now better able to take responsibility for his fate, he was well prepared to try again.

He talked about how he had always searched for someone to live his life for him. Growing up, he had imagined for a long time that his older brothers would do that and that he could survive by staying within their shadows. He hastily added that he reserved the right to change his mind about terminating, and, as if to reassure himself, he brought up the issue of payment of the last bill. He made some passing inquiries about why I had decided to work with him, and commented that he had thought for a long time that it was because I had seen something special in him. Maybe, he concluded, it was just that I had time available when he came to the hospital. Therapy, he said, is not very human. After 4.5 years, he did not feel as attached to me personally as he had expected.

In the next to the last session, he said that he often imagined me to be the former patient of a senior colleague with whom he often saw me chatting in the hallway. He hoped someday to have a relationship with me that was not so formal. I told him that I felt sure he would continue to find men with whom he could develop collegial relationships, but that I would always be his therapist. He was tearful and said that he wished he could come back occasionally to see me. I said that would be nice. He said, "You could die and I wouldn't even know about it." I replied that it was like him to worry about the effects of his leaving me behind. He smiled at this and was silent. Then he said, "Still, it seems cruel to stop abruptly without knowing whether I'll see you again." He asked whether I thought so too. I considered this for a moment before I answered, and then replied that I thought it was not. I added that there was a time and a place for things, and that his decision to leave now made sense to me. The rest of the session he spent talking about how therapy could have been different with another therapist. He also spoke about some of the issues that he felt he still had not resolved, such as sex and being afraid of people. He said he might want to return to therapy to work on these problems sometime in the future.

In his last session, he began by saying, "I can't believe I'm actually here." He went on to talk about his weekend, in which he had decided to put aside completing some of his homework in order to go out with a friend. He said that this was the most obvious thing that had changed in his life—that he felt he needed and enjoyed people. He added that he was not so compulsive and did not procrastinate as much, and was less concerned with the possibility of making errors. He added that he had always done good work, but now was less concerned about criticisms and imperfections. He then talked about the various somatic complaints that he had had for a long time, and how he managed to identify a tenseness in certain muscle groups that responded to the meditation exercises he was doing. He summed this up by saying, "We have done a good piece of work, but it is over. I am pleased that I have managed to retain my belief that it is right for me to go." He then described how he felt tingling all over his body and, introducing a new issue, noted that in the past he had been unable to feel on his left side.

He mentioned that someone with whom he had formerly worked and whom he admired had killed himself. He had just learned about this and had been surprised and saddened because he had liked this man and had felt that he was "solid." He said, "It didn't freak me out. I will never kill myself because I have things I want to do." In the closing minutes, he said that he felt anxious, "like a sheet in the wind waiting to see which way the wind would blow." As he stood up to leave, he said, "I am not sure how I am going to feel about this." Then we shook hands and, looking a little grim and quite sad, he left.

In the process of getting Stewart's review and consent for this case report, he gave his views on the effects of the psychotherapy 4 years after its completion.

Stewart indicated that he subsequently completed college and had pursued an independent and personally meaningful career. His achievements were a source of pride to him, as was his independence. He reported that he had come to recognize his own authority and did not look for it outside himself. While still concerned with the inhibiting and controlling effects of outside influences, these concerns reflected sublimations congruent with larger current social realities and concerns. He had had no recurrence of bizarre thoughts, self-loathing, ideas of influence, and thoughts or impulses toward either suicide or murder. In fact, his self-destructiveness seemed confined to the relatively minor issue of sometimes smoking too much.

In other respects, his life was not as satisfying as he had hoped, nor did he see much hope of further change. He remains a relatively solitary individual with continuing unhappiness. The latter he attributes in part to a "greater tolerance of pain—a greater willingness to suffer consciously rather than to deny that anything is wrong."

In looking back on his treatment, he viewed it as a difficult period. The process of defining himself had continued after therapy. The case report reminded him of aspects of himself that now seem foreign to him and about which he feels ashamed. While clear in his appreciation for the ways in which therapy helped him, he remains somewhat distrustful about it and disappointed that his therapist was unable to know him more than the case report suggests.

Case Discussion

Stewart meets the DSM III criteria for Borderline Personality Disorder, since he presented with a history of impulsivity, grossly disturbed interpersonal relationships, inappropriate anger, identity disturbance, and physically self-damaging acts. He also complained of chronic feelings of emptiness and loneliness. These symptoms were quite characteristic of his long-term functioning, and they significantly impaired his ability to utilize his potential in social and work-related activities. He manifested transient psychotic symptoms of an ego-alien variety, and at one point his delusion that his cousin was in the food he prepared seemed real enough to prompt him to flee the restaurant in which he worked. Interestingly, he was the only member of our group who reported significant violent impulses that were sometimes acted upon (damage to property). In other respects, he presented with a less classical picture of Borderline Personality Disorder than others in our group (e.g., Susan, Martha) in that his interpersonal relationships were distorted but not particularly chaotic, and he did not demonstrate significant affective instability.

The *differential diagnosis* is not complicated in Stewart's case, since he gave no evidence of an affective or other Axis I disorder. Moreover, his symptomatology does not cover a broad range of Axis II disorders. However, it is important to consider whether his condition would be better described as a Narcissistic Personality Disorder rather than as a Borderline Personality Disorder. Certainly, he did not present with the hungry, needy quality that many borderline patients exhibit. His superficial coldness and aloof style, his guarded demeanor, and his intolerance of the wishes of others are characteristic of the narcissistic personality. Moreover, grandiosity and entitlement were prominent features of his presentation—and this, too, is more typical of narcissistic than of borderline patients. Nevertheless, Stewart's impulsivity, self-loathing, and self-destructiveness weigh heavily in favor of the borderline diagnosis. He clearly fits into Kernberg's broader category of Borderline Personality Organization (see Kernberg, 1967).

The second differential diagnosis that must be considered is Paranoid Personality Disorder. Stewart exhibited pervasive, unwarranted mistrust of people—most notably his therapist. He was guarded and hypervigilant, and was constantly suspicious of others' motives. He also manifested hypersensitivity to slights, and he exaggerated his own difficulties. While Stewart showed restricted affectivity, he did possess a sense of humor and gave evidence of passive and tender feelings (both of which are less typical of Paranoid Personality Disorder). He fulfills the criteria for Paranoid Personality Disorder, but this diagnosis does not account for Stewart's identity disturbance or for his action-oriented and impulsive traits, which are more consistent with a borderline diagnosis.

Stewart brought considerable *strengths* to psychotherapy. He was an engaging and intelligent person who managed to interest his therapist and others in working with him. He came from a relatively stable environment that included an intact and financially supportive family and a few enduring but distant friendships. He had managed to perform excellently in his academic work until he dropped out of school in order to live closer to home.

He relied very heavily on primitive defenses to manage unpleasant affect and to maintain his fragile sense of self. Most prominent was his use of projection, which allowed him to externalize all responsi-

Explanation   1. Circled number indicates patient's level of functioning prior to treatment.
of Figure: 2. X indicates patient's level of functioning at termination of treatment.

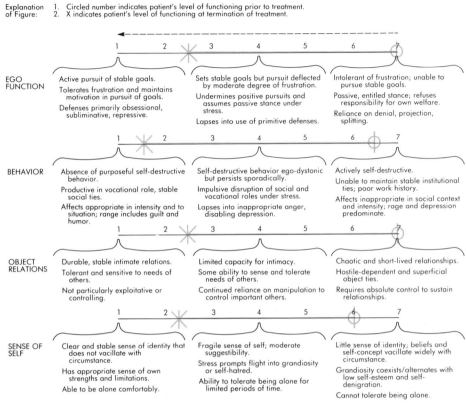

FIGURE 5–1. Standards for assessing levels of functioning—baseline and outcome: Michael.

bility for his difficulties and fostered a paranoia that was more pronounced than that of any of the other patients in our group. He found
his own dependency needs intolerable, and so assumed a counter-
dependent stance that alienated others. He routinely withdrew from
the threats and frustrations of interpersonal relationships into schizoid
fantasies of a grandiose nature. This withdrawal and grandiosity were
accompanied by harsh devaluation of others. These defenses had tre-
mendous costs in terms of his social and occupational functioning and
in terms of his ability to exercise sound judgment in situations where
his physical safety was at stake.

The authors rated Stewart's amenability to analytically oriented
therapy on the scales shown in Figure 5–1. Not surprisingly, he did
not score highly on friendliness or likability, but was rated as very
intelligent. He was of average psychological mindedness among those
in our group. He was not seen as highly impulsive, but was rated as
very paranoid and as having little capacity for empathy relative to oth-

ers in this group. His parental and social supports were rated as above average.

Stewart's therapist was an interesting match for this patient. The therapist was a man who clearly valued activity and prided himself on being active in his work and in his personal life. He was a fairly autonomous person who relied less on peer support than some of the other therapists in our group. He believed in the importance of independence and modeled this behavior in his personal style. He was not particularly comfortable with passivity or with dependency needs—his own or those of others.

Stewart almost certainly felt some measure of safety in the presence of a strong male figure who had no difficulty establishing clear boundaries in the treatment. The therapist was comfortable with the sparring that took place in the context of Stewart's paranoia and counterdependence. He remarked that he actually admired Stewart's somewhat combative and negativistic nature.

Initially, the most salient feature of Stewart's *transference* was his paranoia. Stewart saw people as hurtful and exploitive, and this view prompted him to keep the therapist at arm's length throughout much of the treatment. From the outset, he was intensely suspicious of his therapist, and found sinister meaning in everything from the therapist's interest in Stewart's current life to his choice of office furniture. This created something of a stand-off between patient and therapist in the early phases of treatment: Stewart perceived the therapist's growing interest and concern as evidence of the therapist's homosexual designs on his patient, which prompted Stewart to retreat from any subject that seemed to engage his therapist's attention. At the same time, he was ready to see his therapist as uncaring and demeaning, so that any perceived lack of attention on the therapist's part was used as evidence to support this view.

Stewart's paranoid position only partially camouflaged his intense longings for care and nurturance, and these longings gradually emerged as his attachment to the therapist deepened. He felt entitled to such nurturance as reparations from a cruel world that had deprived him of the love and support he needed as a growing child. Stewart attempted to get his therapist to validate the perception that he had in fact been traumatized by his parents and that the world owed him compensation. He took a passive stance in the therapy and tried to coerce the therapist into doing things *for* him. Slowly, Stewart's fantasy emerged that the only way for him to grow up and succeed in the adult world was to be given the supplies, the mind, and the penis of the therapist, and in this way to share the therapist's power. Stewart's oral neediness emerged most dramatically in the termination phase of treatment, when he faced the process of being "weaned" from psychotherapy.

Treatment was an intensely dysphoric experience, because Stewart did not feel that he was getting what he needed from the therapist, but he could not let go of the therapist for fear that they would both be hurt—the therapist by being abandoned and he by his persistent sense of inner deficits. As with his mother, Stewart believed that he and his therapist were locked in a symbiotic relationship in which each needed the other for survival. The automobile accident was the most vivid demonstration of the power of this belief, and much of the later phases of Stewart's therapy dealt with its elaboration and working through.

The therapist identified *countertransference* responses to Stewart that were similar to those he was having with his son at the time of this treatment. This may account in part for the intense involvement that the therapist felt with this patient. Certainly, the intensity of what transpired between himself and Stewart in the treatment caused important aspects of Stewart's life outside of therapy (e.g., his continued abuse of alcohol) to be overlooked. The therapist found himself wanting to stop Stewart's accusations of exploitiveness and somehow to ameliorate Stewart's contemptuous attitude toward him. He was even tempted to agree with Stewart that it would be best to cut down on the frequency of appointments. His persistence through these discouraging periods is a testimony to his desire to master what seemed at times to be an irresolvable situation.

The therapist's *technique* was based on a conflict model of Stewart's psychopathology. He saw Stewart's primary problems as stemming from conflict about having and expressing anger and his use of projective defenses. Later work focused on the patient's counterdependence and his projection of abandonment fears. The therapist did not conceive of Stewart's behavioral disturbances as based on ego deficits, but rather held that the patient was capable of more responsible behavior and had to take responsibility for his refusal to utilize that capability. In keeping with this view, the therapist resisted Stewart's attempts to get him to attribute Stewart's problems to bad parenting. In fact, the therapist insisted that the patient take responsibility for the poor adaptations that he made to his early environment and for his distortions of his formative interactions with his family. The therapist noted that he was explicitly supportive of Stewart at times when Stewart was despondent about some aspect of his personality—a technique that discouraged externalization and rewarded Stewart for accepting responsibility for his feelings and behavior.

The therapist's technique was predominantly interpretive, and this was the most classical psychoanalytic psychotherapy of any in our group. Where others might have been tempted to provide reassurance and reality testing early in treatment (e.g., in regard to Stewart's concerns about confidentiality), Stewart's therapist consistently withheld such reassurance and instead interpreted his patient's paranoid projections and other primitive defensive maneuvers. The therapist was particularly active in interpreting the hostile, controlling, and manipulative motives that lay behind much of Stewart's self-destructive and maladaptive behavior. He also spent a great deal of time highlighting Stewart's sense of entitlement as it manifested itself in the therapy (e.g., struggles over payment of bills).

The therapist interpreted Stewart's passivity and retreat from growth and independence in a variety of situations, both in and out of the therapy. While he clarified Stewart's longings to be given nurturance and his wish for a "push from behind," he did not explicitly explore the homosexual aspects of this stance.

The therapist's ability to maintain a primarily interpretive stance early in treatment was undoubtedly facilitated by the fact that Stewart was hospitalized throughout this phase. It might well have been necessary to use more supportive measures in building an alliance with this patient had it been easier for him to flee treatment in the early days when his attachment to the therapist was not yet well developed.

While this therapy relied heavily on interpretation, Stewart's therapist did a considerable amount of work to create and maintain a holding environment once Stewart was discharged from the hospital. The therapist was constantly working against Stewart's transference, and at times against his own countertransference, to protect the therapeutic contract from Stewart's incessant attempts to alter it. Stewart saw his therapist as a "rock" in his steadfast adherence to the work of therapy, and it was clear that this picture provided Stewart with a sense of safety. The therapist handled departures from his usual technique (e.g., playing backgammon during the hour) by clarifying them as such and suggesting that they might not be helpful to the patient. On the rare occasions when the therapist deviated from the contract without such analysis (e.g., when he offered not to charge Stewart for a vacation), Stewart became agitated and was relieved when the rules were again enforced.

The therapist's involvement of the family in Stewart's treatment was another way in which he worked to protect the boundaries of the therapy. By initiating family meetings, the therapist helped to assure the continued financial support of the treatment and enlisted the parents as allies. Given his father's willingness to pay for treatment, Stewart was confronted with the fact that he had held on to a distorted view of his father as withholding and unsupportive. He observed his therapist model a style of directly asking others for what was needed (in this case, financial support), and this intervention coincided with a reduction in Stewart's transference demand that the therapist solve all of his problems for him.

The therapist placed considerable emphasis on issues of separation—

on Stewart's difficulty in letting go of old attachments and his difficulty in allowing himself to be let go of. It is of note that the therapist highlighted the issue of termination as soon as Stewart brought it up, and well in advance of when he thought Stewart would actually be ready to terminate. The therapist rigorously maintained the frequency of appointments despite Stewart's wish to reduce therapy, but at the same time he interpreted Stewart's attachment to therapy as a regressive retreat from getting on with his life. He structured a setting in which Stewart could experience and accept the loss of his attachment to the therapist and see that such a loss could be survived.

Stewart's psychotherapy might be characterized as one of intense involvement of the patient and therapist, without a great deal of warmth. The therapist was a strong male figure with whom Stewart became increasingly identified. Stewart paid close attention to his therapist's personal attributes, including the therapist's comfort with self-assertion and his manner of dealing directly with others. Stewart used his therapist as a model for his own behavior as he searched for more adaptive ways of conducting his life.

The therapist's interpretations of Stewart's negative transference and the aggressive motives behind his maladaptive behavior coincided with a dramatic reduction in acting out over the course of the first year of psychotherapy. His functioning improved steadily after that, so that he was able to move gradually into a more autonomous living situation in the second year of treatment, and functioned increasingly well at school and at work over the subsequent years. Moreover, he developed more satisfying and more stable relationships with men and women over the course of treatment.

The change in his relationships with peers coincided with a more general shift in his object relations during therapy. His rather stereotyped and distorted view of his father did not hold up in the face of his own recovered childhood memories and the reality of his father's continued support of his treatment. His father came to be perceived as a more complex figure who could be both disappointing and gratifying. Similarly, Stewart's view of himself and his therapist shifted over the course of treatment. He was able to give up much of his reliance on withdrawal and devaluing, and to arrive at more ambivalent and accepting images of himself and the therapist. He was also able to sublimate some of his grandiosity and need for absolute control in the pursuit of more realistic interests, such as the study of Germanic culture.

Two events of Stewart's treatment stand out as pivotal points. The first was the automobile crash, which seems to have had a sobering effect on him. It dramatized the fact that the therapist could not protect him, and that he was not symbiotically tied either to his mother or to his therapist. The second pivotal event was the reconstruction of his

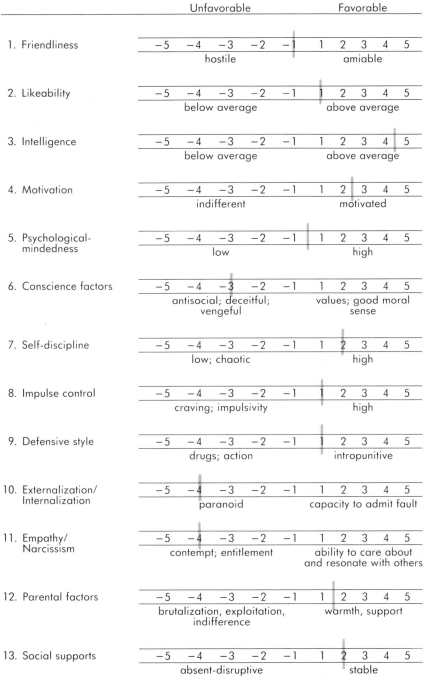

	Unfavorable	Favorable

1. Friendliness

−5 −4 −3 −2 −1 | 1 2 3 4 5
hostile | amiable

2. Likeability

−5 −4 −3 −2 −1 | 1 2 3 4 5
below average | above average

3. Intelligence

−5 −4 −3 −2 −1 | 1 2 3 4 5
below average | above average

4. Motivation

−5 −4 −3 −2 −1 | 1 2 3 4 5
indifferent | motivated

5. Psychological-mindedness

−5 −4 −3 −2 −1 | 1 2 3 4 5
low | high

6. Conscience factors

−5 −4 −3 −2 −1 | 1 2 3 4 5
antisocial; deceitful; vengeful | values; good moral sense

7. Self-discipline

−5 −4 −3 −2 −1 | 1 2 3 4 5
low; chaotic | high

8. Impulse control

−5 −4 −3 −2 −1 | 1 2 3 4 5
craving; impulsivity | high

9. Defensive style

−5 −4 −3 −2 −1 | 1 2 3 4 5
drugs; action | intropunitive

10. Externalization/Internalization

−5 −4 −3 −2 −1 | 1 2 3 4 5
paranoid | capacity to admit fault

11. Empathy/Narcissism

−5 −4 −3 −2 −1 | 1 2 3 4 5
contempt; entitlement | ability to care about and resonate with others

12. Parental factors

−5 −4 −3 −2 −1 | 1 2 3 4 5
brutalization, exploitation, indifference | warmth, support

13. Social supports

−5 −4 −3 −2 −1 | 1 2 3 4 5
absent-disruptive | stable

FIGURE 5–2. Amenability to psychotherapy: Michael. [Adapted from Stone's Amenability for Analytically Oriented Therapy Scale (Stone, 1985)].

weaning experiences as an infant. Stewart had set and retracted numerous termination dates prior to this phase of therapy. However, it was not until he became more directly aware of his wish to cling to nurturing figures and his anger and sadness at losing them that he was able to set a termination date in earnest. It is understandable that more than a year of therapy was spent on the issue of termination; the experience of separation and loss was extensively worked through by the time treatment ended.

Stewart's level of functioning before and after treatment was rated by the authors on four scales shown in Figure 5–2. He was judged to have made significant progress in all four areas of ego functioning, behavior, object relations, and sense of self. Prior to treatment, he was rated as most impaired in behavior and object relations. Of all the parameters rated, he was seen as having made the greatest gains in behavior over the course of therapy.

Certainly, there was much that remained undone when this psychotherapy was terminated after 4.5 years. Stewart's yearnings for nurturance were managed and interpreted, but perhaps were not as extensively explored as they might have been. One might predict that closeness and warmth in relationships will still be fraught with difficulties for this man. More particularly, the entire area of sexuality was left largely untouched in this treatment.

Nevertheless, at the time of this writing, Stewart lives independently and is self-sufficient. He is actively engaged in pursuing creative interests, is closer to his father, and reports a fair degree of satisfaction with his personal as well as his professional life. Now 4 years out of treatment, he shows evidence of continuing to work on intrapsychic problems on his own. Among these problems are his lack of intimate relationships and the limited degree of openness with which he is comfortable. However, these problems hamper his life considerably less than they did when he entered psychotherapy.

6

Jennifer
Case Report

Jennifer was a 24-year-old unemployed, married, white female referred by the health services of her husband's university. She complained that her husband did not protect her from her father. She had come to therapy in order to grow up, to cease looking for relationships that hurt, and to help overcome her fears of criticism and her feeling of desperate loneliness. She described periods of depression during which she would curl up in a blanket and think of jumping out of the window. She noted that she had told a prior therapist about her suicidal ideas, and when he responded that she would not do something like that, she immediately thought of jumping out of the window. She also noted that she immediately wanted to seduce him.

Jennifer was a petite, attractive woman dressed in plain casual clothes; she appeared quite depressed and angry. She cried frequently and spoke of feeling hopeless. There was no evidence of any thought disorder. She tended to speak in a rather soft, coy voice. Her seductive manner alternated with an attitude of despair, demands that she be rescued, and a voice full of fury and rage, particularly at her husband, Mark.

Because of her increasing depression and marital problems, Mark had arranged for the referral to me through his university's health service. In the initial interview, when I saw Mark and the patient together, I was struck by their appearance. Jennifer was a remarkably petite young woman, while Mark was a large, muscular man who towered over her; they appeared to be a child and an adult, respectively. He seemed passive and compliant. Jennifer was angry with him about his sexual performance; he ejaculated prematurely, and her main frustration was that he insisted that the lovemaking be primarily for his gratification. Jennifer also had difficulties; she experienced orgasm only if the relationship was illicit. Mark wanted her to be seductive in dress and actions, and this made her extremely uncomfortable. She was most distressed when she had to walk in front of men or dance. She felt that they were staring at her body.

Background Information

The patient was the oldest of six children and the only child of her mother's first marriage; she had five half-siblings, aged 13 to 20. Jennifer's mother had married at age 18 after being impregnated by the patient's father. Jennifer described him as a dark, handsome, loving man. For the first 18 months of Jennifer's life, they all lived with her maternal grandparents. Then her father left and her mother and Jennifer continued to live with her mother's parents. Her father visited often until Jennifer was 4 years old; then the grandfather told him that the visits had to stop. He reasoned that Jennifer became too upset when her father left. Jennifer's earliest memory was of her father carrying her to bed while she was asleep.

Her father continued to write the patient for a time, but all contact ceased when she was 5 years old and her mother was remarried to George. Her mother said she married Jennifer's father because she was pregnant and remained with him because she had a child and therefore needed a husband. As a result, Jennifer came to believe that neither the marriage nor the divorce was her mother's fault. Instead, she came to believe that because her mother had been pregnant with her, she had been forced to marry, and therefore she owed her mother whatever her mother wished.

Jennifer recounted that she "did not speak well" until she was 4 years old. She remembered going to speech classes and speech therapy instead of to kindergarten. Also, at age 4, Jennifer's maternal uncle, who had been "a father to her," married. Soon afterward, her mother married George, following a brief affair with him. George, a biologist, came from a poor family and had struggled to become successful. Shortly after the marriage, Jennifer and her mother moved to an apartment with him. A year later, Jennifer's last name was changed to her stepfather's name, although her biologic father did not allow him to adopt her legally. She remembered being lonely when she began grade school at age 6, but after school and on weekends she had wonderful times with George, fishing and playing. He clearly adored her.

By age 8 Jennifer had been given major caretaking responsibilities for her younger stepsiblings. At age 10, when her last half-sibling was born after a difficult delivery, George had a vasectomy without informing anyone. At about that time, too, Jennifer had her menarche. It was during this time, between her tenth and eleventh years, that George began to come into her bedroom, rub her back until she woke up, and masturbate her, telling Jennifer that her mother had asked him to teach her about sex. She said to me, "If I had been older, I would have said 'no' to him." Soon thereafter, George had intercourse with her. He later told her that an affair with another woman had just ended because of the woman's death. Soon Jennifer began to have dreams and nightmares in which her mother was portrayed as a witch. The next year, her twelfth, the entire family went to Canada so that George could pursue his scientific research. Canada was very lonely and Jennifer missed her grandparents, but George was very available and consoling, without sexual interplay. They remained in Canada for a year.

From age 14 on, Jennifer began to have intercourse regularly with George. He began to tell her about his affairs and his sexual difficulties with her mother. Jennifer began to have suicidal ideation, which she attributed to doing poorly in school despite her best efforts. George insisted that she perform well in school and prepare herself to enter graduate school in biology, his field. He promised that he would pay for everything if she were admitted to graduate school. (Later, when she was accepted into a graduate program in special education, he refused to pay.) Jennifer began to feel that she never did anything well enough, that her only talent was in seducing George. She devalued women, had few girlfriends, and perceived only men as worthwhile. The patient wondered if her mother knew about her sexual relationship with George and was only "playing the martyr" by remaining silent. When George was offered a position at a university in Illinois, it was Jennifer who went with him to visit it. She was introduced as her mother's sister. On this occasion, she refused to have sex with him and he tore off her nightgown.

At age 16, Jennifer began dating boys. She was frightened that they would realize that she knew much more about sex than they did. She knew that her relationship with George could not continue; she preferred to be with men older than herself, but they had to be more clearly in her own generation. She used dating as a means to distance herself from George. He insisted that she describe her sexual activities with her date, and she was certain it was for his own vicarious gratification. She complied.

The sexual relationship with George ended when she moved to college, though she continued to see George frequently and he usually made sexual advances. In her second year of college, George told her that her mother had been unfaithful on a number of occasions. She remembered thinking, "I wish I didn't know; I wanted my mother to be like she used to be." After several years of college she transferred to a college farther from home, and it was then that she met Mark, who was in Boston. During this period George had several manic decompensations, which were treated with lithium. This period was a tumultuous one: Jennifer left college for Boston, both because she was not doing well and because she was getting sufficiently involved with Mark to be considering marriage. Also during this period, her mother told Jennifer that George, who had been upset by the news that Jennifer intended to marry Mark, had been caught with another woman. Mark was ambivalent about marriage but consented when Jennifer threatened to leave him if he did not marry her immediately. At the wedding, both George and Mark's mother wept copiously, falling into each other's arms, overcome by sadness. The marriage was 14 months old when Jennifer's treatment began.

A month after the marriage, the patient's mother told Jennifer that George wanted a divorce because he intended to marry a woman who was Jennifer's age. The patient's reaction was a series of actions she did not understand but felt compelled to do; she began a series of extramarital affairs, and she began to try to locate her biologic father. Four months prior to our first meeting, her mother informed Jennifer that she intended to go on a vacation with a lover, and had given George the excuse that she would be visiting Jennifer. Her mother insisted that Jennifer collude with her. Jennifer became increasingly depressed and unable to sleep; she noted increasing arguments with Mark and a recurrence of her suicidal ideation. In this context, she and Mark consulted the university's health service, which referred her to me.

First Phase of Therapy

Year One. Jennifer began therapy stating that George had promised to be financially responsible for her treatment. In our second session, she told me that she had felt so distraught after the first interview that she wanted either to call me or to run away. She spoke of a difficulty in understanding herself. When I commented that it was as though she were a stranger to herself and others, that she felt she never belonged to anyone or in any situation, she replied that sex was her means of becoming attached to a man, although it also seemed a way to be hurt. From the very beginning of treatment, she was very responsive to any intervention; when she was upset about being unemployed and I suggested that it was as though she were waiting for George to rescue her, she found work by the time of the next session.

After four interviews, I asked the patient to decide whether she thought we would be able to work together in ongoing psychotherapy. In the next session, she appeared dressed very seductively in black net stockings and a brief black dress. I decided not to comment on this change. She said that she wanted to see me, and we agreed to meet once a week.

The early focus of treatment was on Jennifer's marriage, her anger with Mark's passivity, and her use of her own passivity to manipulate him. Both with Mark and with others, she could not connect external events and internal experience; she felt passive in relation to her own emotions. On one occasion, her mother called to announce that she planned to visit. The next day, Jennifer felt very angry and could not understand why. Gradually, she began to experience anger at her mother for being inattentive and untouchable and for telling them that no matter what their problems were, hers were worse. It seemed to her that only her maternal grandmother had loved her. She was convinced that if she were ever close to anyone again she would lose something of herself, yet she wished she could just curl up in Mark's lap and fall asleep.

Jennifer spoke of George, who had married her mother because he thought it was immoral to have an affair, but had not been concerned about morality with her. She remembered actively participating in their mutual seductions and wondered if her current passivity were connected with that fact. She loved to be with him because he could be so maternal and understanding, yet in rages he would call her his "tar baby." She felt possessed by him in a way that made her feel safe, yet uneasy. None of the boys she had dated had made her feel as good or as lovable. She wondered whether her belief that she could get close only through sexual intercourse originated with George.

I focused on clarifying Jennifer's conflicts rather than on answering questions. She remembered that when she told George of her plan to marry Mark, he had run out of her house, only to be discovered later by her mother in a motel with another woman. Because George seemed a more positive figure in her life and because there were no other objects currently valued, I emphasized the more positive aspects of her involvement with him, particularly the maternal aspect of their presexual relationship. Jennifer's response on these occasions was a tentative articulation of her anger at her mother for having had to do her work: cleaning the house, taking care of the children, and cooking the meals when she herself was still only a child.

As she began to feel sad, especially about her relationships with Mark and her mother, Jennifer noted a particular type of sexual arousal associated with her sadness: "When I feel bad, I want to be fucked until I'm numb . . . to be whipped or punished . . . to be raped on a hard floor," as she had been by George. When she felt too much tension in her body or too much sadness, she wanted to be numb, she wanted me to "screw her for the hour."

In the second 3 months of therapy, which now occurred twice weekly, the content of the sessions was largely concerned with the ongoing, seemingly endless crises created by Jennifer's family. It became apparent that George was in financial and legal trouble. Jennifer was disillusioned because she had always thought of George as a source of security. When these problems led George to threaten to discontinue financial support of Jennifer's psychotherapy, she decided to pay for herself. Subsequently, George said he could pay for the psychotherapy, but would do so only if Jennifer approved of his planned marriage to a girlfriend who was younger even than Jennifer.

A second development during this period was that Jennifer's mother decided to come to Boston. Despite Jennifer's ongoing complaints about her mother's emotional unavailability, she uncomplainingly worked hard to find local accommodations for her mother.

A third development occurred when Jennifer got in touch with her biologic father. While it was clear that he was nervous about this contact, due to his now stable attachment to his second wife and their children, he eventually consented to meet with Jennifer. Jennifer's mother accompanied her on this visit and eventually, to Jennifer's amusement, had intercourse with her ex-husband.

Emerging from these ongoing events was a growing appreciation of Jennifer's lifelong disappointment in her mother's unavailability and her covert resentment toward those who had taken her mother's attention from her. It became clear that she had used her sexual relationship with George as a replacement for her mother. It also became increasingly clear that Jennifer's self-esteem was closely connected with her perceived sexual attractiveness and that she turned to this source of gratification defensively whenever she felt angry or helpless in her basic wish to be mothered.

By 8 months in treatment, Jennifer's ongoing complaints about Mark's failure to assume a maternal role and her resultant temper tantrums or manipulations took a turn for the worse. Mark began to call me, saying that Jennifer was suicidal. This occurred at about the same time that George phoned Jennifer to say that he had married his young girlfriend.

Jennifer would come to the hour, tell me that she was suicidal, and insist that she would tell me about it only if I promised not to stop her. I told her that we needed to explore her distrust of me and that, while she had a right to take her own life, I thought her suicidal feelings were complex and that we needed to understand them. She insisted that she had to know if I cared: If I ended a session by saying that I would see her the next time, it meant I cared and then she could go on living. Our sessions were filled with endless, fruitless arguments about her insistence that I permit her to commit suicide. With some asperity, I finally told her that I considered our work important and that, if she killed herself, we could not continue it. She assured me that she would call me to discontinue therapy before she killed herself! Innumerable sessions ended with her storming out of the office, leaving me uncertain about whether I would ever see her again. I felt helpless to clarify what the suicidality was about and unable to establish a relationship with her in which we could try to look at it together. Moreover, I was bewildered about how to deal with these affective storms in which I seemed to get swept up despite my best efforts. Ultimately, I simply tried to clarify her angry motives and hoped to ride out the storm.

Frequently, Jennifer or her husband insisted that I see them together. Each time, I would confront them with their mutual provocation and they would leave the office somewhat calmer. However, the patient began to be more violent at home, hitting Mark, throwing furniture, sweeping things off his desk.

The sessions were also filled with rage at Mark. Therapy was used solely to revile him, and I told her so. She turned her anger on George, who had deserted her by marrying another woman, so that he no longer bolstered her feeling of being attractive by his interest in her. But she realized that her relationship with him had also been a source of trouble: "It was too limiting to have your boyfriend be your father." She wanted Mark to make up for what she had lost with George. She insisted that her marriage had to end, but she was too frightened to be with other men; she felt small and powerless with Mark.

A new fantasy emerged: If Jennifer had a child, there would be someone to depend on her and then she would not have to kill herself. She no longer wished to see me with Mark because she was unwilling to share me. She noticed that she became depressed when she wasn't angry at Mark; as she began to feel safer with her anger, her depression diminished. She began to worry about my responses when she was angry at me and started to wonder what I was like as a person. She thought she was beginning to trust me even though all of her previous relationships with men had been sexual. When she was depressed, she wanted me to take care of her and tell her what to do. She wondered about having a sexual relationship with me but decided that sex would destroy the therapy. She believed that good therapists were harder to find than good lovers.

This development elicited new memories of George. Jennifer had felt used by him, like a prostitute, since he told her what to do but never allowed her into his life. After sex with him, she felt guilty. I commented that she may have been experiencing feelings of an intensity that she could not manage at that early age. She agreed but felt sad that in letting go of George, she had also lost him as a father. Following this session, Jennifer quit her job and abruptly became increasingly suicidal. I told Mark that it was their decision whether to hospitalize her. When he called his mother to ask for help, Jennifer felt that he was abandoning her. She was not hospitalized. Only later did Jennifer relate this particular flareup to an article in a national newspaper about George's indictment for fraud.

Soon thereafter, Mark phoned at midnight to tell me that Jennifer had taken an overdose of aspirin and he had rushed her to a nearby hospital. I phoned the patient in the emergency room. Jennifer told me that she had tried to kill herself, that marriage was too difficult, that her mother was depressed, and that she felt that she could not cope. When I asked her if she felt entirely unable to cope, she responded that she thought she might be able to work the next morning and that she would come to her next session that day. I decided not to press for hospitalization.

In the next session, she asked me if I had been irritated by her suicide attempt and its timing. I answered truthfully that I had been both concerned and irritated. She said she had feared that Mark was more interested in another woman than he was in her, so she had taken the pills, assuming that she would just go to sleep and die. When she had not fallen asleep, she had become worried and told Mark what she had done. I told her that I felt we could not work together if she continued to act on her suicidal ideation, that it was like having a loaded gun at my head, and that while I understood that similar stressful times might recur, she would have to call me and we would discuss it before she took any action. She agreed. Mark again wanted Jennifer to be hospitalized, but this time I stated that I thought she could continue on an outpatient basis.

Further work on her sexual experiences with George followed. She recognized that in sex, and only in sex, George had usually bargained with her rather than forcing her. Thus, she had felt responsible for the incest. Now she began to question whether in fact it had all been her responsibility. Her present fear that Mark would leave her for another more attractive woman repeated the fears she had felt with George.

Although the difficulties with Mark continued, Jennifer was less angry. She recognized her wish to have Mark guess her desires without her participation. If he failed, she would express her anger through passivity. She believed that if she were overtly angry, he would leave her. We could see that she tried to forestall his feared abandonment by turning her anger on herself; this action, however, led her to become suicidal. She was also angry at Mark for not shielding her from his intrusive mother. She remembered how George had similarly failed to protect her from her mother's demands, while she had tried so hard to help both of them. She wondered how her mother could have let the incest happen. She believed that she had taken the responsibility for holding their marriage together by keeping George at home.

Jennifer knew it was wrong, but she did not want to feel blamed for the ending of another marriage, as she had with her mother's first marriage. She had turned her own marriage into a recapitulation of her involvement with George: She had to comply at all times, and sex was the preferred mode of communication and love. The patient was amazed to see the repetition but felt unable to alter the pattern. Indeed, she became suicidal and canceled a session by phone, but agreed to come after I told her that she was behaving childishly. When Mark forgot to come home from work and drive her to my office, she phoned again and told me that she had decided that she would not try to commit suicide because she was certain that she would be unsuccessful.

Jennifer felt that if she aroused a man sexually, it was her fault, and consequently she had to help him discharge his excitement. But if she felt aroused or derived pleasure from sex, she knew it was wrong; she felt guilty even with Mark if she enjoyed sex more than he did. She recognized that to enjoy sex was to be with George. She was quite pleased with her new realization that the experience with George had inhibited her ever since. She acted out her new information and the transference by calling a man with whom she had become aroused, having sex with him, and enjoying it. Afterward, she became preoccupied with suicide again. I did not comment on the obvious transference acting out, since she was so fearful of experiencing any feelings that would suggest to her that she needed or wanted me. In fact, she later told me that she believed she had become suicidal to prove to me that she did not need the therapy, that is, that she was not dependent on me.

At the end of the first year of therapy, Jennifer became very involved with a neighbor's daughter, Cindy, whose father had abandoned her and her mother. She told Mark that she wanted to have a child of her own. When he replied that his education had priority, she became so furious that she began to hit and bite him. He left the apartment. Alone, she feared that she would harm herself. Instead, she began to comfort herself as she had in childhood: She cried, touched her face, and smoothed her hair the way she wished someone had done when she was a child. She commented, "I wished that someone was there—not my mother, but my idea of my mother." Thereafter, when desperate, she called people or remembered her love for her grandmother, rather than acting self-destructively. These methods calmed her. She began to notice that she was not helpless. Prior to this time, Jennifer had always used rhythmic activity to comfort herself. In overdosing, she had taken the pills in rhythmic fashion; music and thumb sucking were rhythmic; and even fellatio, the preferred mode of sex in her extramarital affairs, was done in rhythmic fashion. These habits were related to early memories of thumb sucking, rocking, and the use of music to console herself.

Year Two: First Half. As we entered the second year of therapy, despite sporadic sessions in which we seemed to work collaboratively, Jennifer still insisted that she would eventually kill herself. I felt frustrated and irritated, unable to understand what she was trying to tell me. I began to confront her suicidal ideation as a disguise for her anger at me. This seemed helpful. She was angry because she felt that whatever she told me about herself she would lose. She began to see her secret affairs as a way to be angry at Mark. She also began to be more directly angry at Mark's mother for her interference. Anger was easier than intimacy for Jennifer because "being close means losing a part of yourself, being submissive." She was angry at her own mother's inappropriate demand that she help to care for her half-siblings. As she became able to tolerate hostility, she could also be alone more comfortably. She began to feel more confident in her interpersonal relationships, particularly in her work, and in the tranference felt a new wish to have me respect her.

Fourteen months after we began therapy, Mark's graduation from school neared and he found employment in Denver. Jennifer informed me that she would have to terminate.

During the last 4 months of therapy, Jennifer was able to work more continuously. She began to wonder if I had feelings about her and about her leaving. She entertained the idea that I might suggest that we end the therapy by having a sexual relationship. However, it suddenly occurred to her that were I to do so, she could simply walk out of the office. Unlike her experience with George, she was not trapped. She told me more about her experiences early in therapy, particularly about her suicidal ideation: If I had continued to argue with her about suicide, she would have suicided in order to be stubborn. She said that after her attempted suicide, she had been frightened that I would be angry. She believed that I had been angry, but she had also been certain that I had not stopped liking her, and so she had decided to continue.

In the last 2 months of therapy, Jennifer became preoccupied with Cindy. She had fantasies of taking her to Denver so that Cindy would not feel abandoned. As her concern about Cindy escalated, she began to speak about suicide again. I commented that Cindy made her feel worthwhile. She was furious because I did not support her wish to adopt Cindy. She calmed down when I suggested to her that she could either leave Cindy as she had been left—with the feeling that it was because she had been bad—or she could leave Cindy with a careful explanation of her reasons for the departure so that each could remember the other with positive feelings. She continued to be furious and, on one occasion, even counted out some pills she was going to take. Finally, she and Mark resolved the problem by deciding that they would pay for 1 year of Cindy's private school.

Up to the very last session, Jennifer had difficulty articulating her feelings about termination directly. She believed that I might ask her to act on any feelings she articulated. She commented that we had battled and that she had survived. Like Cindy, she did not feel abandoned, at least consciously. We terminated 17 months after we had begun.

Interval History

Two weeks after her departure, Jennifer was again depressed and suicidal. When she and Mark called for help, I told them that I could not be helpful at long distance. She phoned and wrote me a number of times over the course of the following year to tell me that she was depressed. She and Mark saw a couples therapist during some of this time and an individual therapist for an additional few months. Jennifer reported that her therapist had given her "permission to stop an affair." In that letter, she also informed me that she had written her mother to tell her about the incestuous relationship with George. Her mother's response had been that "she was sorry; if she had known earlier, she would have divorced him much sooner."

A year after leaving, Jennifer phoned me and told me that she and Mark were moving back to Boston in another year because he was returning to graduate school for more training. She was getting along well with him. She thought she might want to see me again regarding some sexual problems.

Two years after leaving Boston, she returned. Soon thereafter, she phoned me, weeping, to say that she had tried to manage life on her own and could not. We resumed therapy on a once-weekly basis 26 months after we had "terminated."

Second Phase of Therapy

Year Two: Second Half. When we resumed our meetings, Jennifer told me that she had again become alternatively passive and provocative with Mark in order to get him to respond. She would hit him and he would have to pinion her in order to calm her. She thought she had had difficulty in ending therapy with me when she had moved to Denver, and there were some feelings about me that she still needed to explore. She left feeling depressed and angry. Following that first session, she called an old lover but then decided not to see him in order to show me, she said, that she could be different.

Her major reason for seeing me again was Mark's unresponsiveness. As she spoke about this for several sessions, she became depressed and suicidally preoccupied again. This time, however, she recognized that living or dying was her choice; she would choose to live. She told Mark that she was suicidal and was pleased when he said that he did not want her to die, that he needed and wanted her. It became clear to her that she became suicidal when she felt she had not done enough for Mark and he was punishing her with unresponsiveness; she would then get depressed and become suicidal. Her persistent feelings of failure and the wish to kill herself were connected to a memory: George had been so angry at her when she had failed her biology course that he told her he would kill her if she continued to fail. After this initial turmoil abated, she began to wonder why she was still seeing me in therapy.

Though Jennifer was not certain that she could explore her feelings about me without tangible evidence that I cared for her, she thought that her feelings were important. She wondered if she could experience and express those feelings without entering into a sexual relationship with me. Mark had commented that she seemed sexier after our sessions. If any session ran over by even a minute, , she became frightened that I was trying to seduce her; she imagined that I wanted to end the therapy so that our relationship could change. I wondered if she might be trying to attribute some of her feelings to me. She concurred; if she were able to blame the man in a sexual relationship, she could ignore her feelings and act without hesitation. Since George had first approached her, she had developed the fantasy that she was irresistible to men, and when, at 19, one man had resisted her, she felt "more put down than she had ever felt before."

This sexual material, with its connection to self-esteem and maintenance of object ties, resulted in the emergence of more of the history of the incestuous triangle. She remembered George showing her nude pictures of her mother and asking her to wear high heels like her mother's; she refused. She did not want to compete with her mother; she wanted to help her. Though George and her mother had separated while she was in high school, they reconciled for her graduation. "I really did hold the marriage together," she asserted. This was confirmed when George had an affair right after she announced her marriage. She understood that she had played a more active role with George than she had let herself believe.

As this material emerged, Jennifer became more depressed and angry with me. She was outraged that I refused to relieve her of responsibility for her feelings and actions. She acted out her wishes by seducing a male friend. She struggled with sexual feelings in the sessions. For example, after one particularly erotic session, she ended by saying, "Well, it's cold outside. I hope it will cool me off. I hope you feel better; you have a cold."

Jennifer briefly considered her relationships with women, especially her need to act like a little girl with them. She wondered if she had felt competitive with her mother and began to think about surpassing her mother by having a career of her own. As she came to feel less guilty, she expressed more directly her resentment at having to be sexually pleasing to a man. She began to see that she had associated sexuality with George, trying to recapture their relationship and being tormented by her guilt. All this time, she could not tolerate arousal of any sort in the sessions, having to act it out immediately. She began to notice, however, that her acting out left her feeling disappointed and sad. It seemed to her that the empty feelings she had had throughout her life were being replaced by sadness. Though she felt frustrated if she did not act, she began to experiment with efforts to tolerate the frustration.

I suggested that she had perceived only two possibilities in interpersonal relationships: to be a man like George and take whatever she wanted, or to be a passive woman like her mother. Jennifer said that now she did not know what she wanted; she had always tried to become whatever men wanted. I suggested that she was keeping George with her by continuing to hold on to goals that he had set for her, and I wondered if she could pursue a career of her own choice. She could again speak of her little girl's love for George. He had taken care of her, though she had not been his daughter. Her depressions, rages, and promiscuity came to be seen as identifications with George.

Year Three. Seven months after resuming therapy, Jennifer saw a television program on incest that awakened her fury at George. She wished that George had impregnated her so that she could show everyone what he had done to her, but instead she felt "he had gotten away with it." She began to experience guilt about her own extramarital relationships and to notice a sense of alienation from her mother. She still denied feeling any anger at her mother, but she now noticed her fear of doing something wrong when Mark's mother was with her. It reminded her of feeling like an adult when she took care of her siblings and then becoming "a kid again when mother came home."

One month later, Jennifer's half-brother Ken, on a long "visit" to Boston, was sent to a psychiatric prison facility for assaulting a man in a bar; he begged Jennifer to help him find a lawyer. Her mother immediately left town for a high school reunion, saying that Ken had spoiled her entire life and she would not permit this incident to spoil the weekend. For the first time, Jennifer was consciously angry at her mother. She felt that she had excused her mother too often. She was able to help Ken, but recalled that her mother had often taken credit for the work that she, Jennifer, had done. She now knew that in order to keep her mother's love, she had made herself passive and permitted herself to be deprived of satisfaction with her own accomplishments.

While Jennifer's arguments with Mark continued, they were more episodic and were rarely accompanied by suicidal ideation. Their sexual life improved, and Jennifer felt closer to him. A crisis occurred when Mark required minor surgery and his mother insisted on being present against Jennifer's wishes. She felt that her ability to take care of Mark was being questioned by his mother, just as her adequacy as a caretaker for her siblings had been invalidated by her own mother. She did not know what to do and insisted that I tell her. When I did not, she threatened to go to a motel and commit suicide. I told her that she would have to choose between understanding and action.

The issue of trust reappeared when Jennifer found Mark speaking too "personally" to another woman. Again she called me and insisted that I tell her what to do. I told her that I would not confirm her helplessness. She became furious; she said she could not trust me, that only men who wanted her sexually were trustworthy. It seemed to her that, if Mark trusted her, she would have to reciprocate by trusting him totally. She would have to be responsible for her actions, and she was not ready to do so. Her paranoia about Mark increased, and she broke into his office to look for incriminating letters. She scheduled several extra sessions. Finally, she risked asking Mark directly about the other woman; he assured her that it was merely a business relationship. Her trust in me was now somewhat firmer because I had again not acted with her. She said she believed I could not be seduced. She wondered if she precipitated crises in order to have a valid reason to see me and thus be able to deny that she wanted to see me. She expressed discomfort at feeling as if our meetings were hidden from my wife, as she and George had hidden from her mother.

Later that year, Jennifer learned that George had tried to commit suicide. She was angry because I would not tell her whether she should go to visit him. She spoke to him on the phone and realized that he was psychotic. With great sadness, she spoke of her love for George and her anguish that he did not reciprocate. She became enraged at her mother for not having taken better care of George and recognized her anger as being the same anger she had felt toward her mother as a teenager. Her relationship with Mark became more committed, and she became aware of how sad and helpless she felt when he withdrew from her. She began to make friends with women and recognized that this was the first time since she had begun to date men that she was at all interested in female friends.

Halfway through the third year of treatment, Jennifer could better tolerate both her own anger and that of others. As a child, she had felt humiliated if a grownup were angry at her. If Mark were angry at her, she would feel depressed and suicidal. She said, "If someone is angry at me, I feel alone, cut off from people around me. . . . Mark's mother is like my mother. If you go along with her, she likes you and if you don't she doesn't, so her love is conditional. I didn't feel that with George. . . . I tried to be good as a little girl." I suggested to Jennifer that her sexual relationships, running away, and suicidal preoccupations might all have been ways of coping with her helplessness. She began to wonder if all those feelings were not more connected to her experiences with women than with men. She felt more and more committed to her husband: "I feel I have decided to be just with Mark and that makes me more vulnerable—he can hurt me. I know it is insane to go through his wallet or his datebook."

Though there was a brief period of erotizing her relationships with men at work, Jennifer began to acknowledge that these were attempts to act out her feelings about me. She imagined that if she could have intense feelings without acting on them at work, perhaps she might be able to explore those feelings with me. She told me how she had felt earlier in the therapy:

> . . . there was a time I wanted you, at first, to take me over and solve things. Then there was a time I wanted you to screw me and screw me until I was numb. Then recently I said nothing I could do would make you move out of your chair and you said 'I didn't believe it'. . . . Seeing you here, it is like she [my wife] is excluded, it's like when I was younger and my mother was excluded and I felt guilty. . . . I feel that if I turn a man on, I'm cheating him if I don't fulfill my obligation. . . . I feel I shouldn't be here. . . . I don't think I love you. . . . I'm happier than ever before. But if I don't love you, why should I feel I shouldn't be here . . . it's sexual to get so close . . . it's like with my mother.

Jennifer had to cancel the next three weeks because her grandfather had had a sudden heart attack and she went to see him. When she returned to Boston she began to wonder again about becoming pregnant and about whether pregnancy would interfere with her career. She began to talk about discontinuing treatment. I left the decision to her, and she decided to continue for a few more months. She began to sew clothes for herself and to take a greater interest in her appearance. She considered taking the Graduate Record Examination but this time believed that, if she failed, she would not have to kill herself. Yet when Mark had to leave on business for several weeks, she felt so abandoned and frightened that she had to isolate herself in their apartment. She thought that trying to remember him during that time would only make her more angry. She noted that in photographs of herself when her father left at age 4, her appearance suggested that "it was the end of the world." She decided to see me for another 4 months and then to consider termination.

Mark had an opportunity to return to Denver for an entire summer of work and asked Jennifer to accompany him. She wished to remain in Boston and was furious that Mark would consider leaving her. She threatened suicide, and Mark comforted her. She understood now that in suiciding she would be leaving him rather than being left; she felt like a little girl. Without a man, she felt as if she were nothing. It was "not real" to be with a woman unless the primary relationship were with a man.

Jennifer began to insist that Mark impregnate her. At the time that she would have terminated with me, near the end of the third year of therapy (18 months into the second phase of therapy), she became pregnant. Mark insisted that she have an abortion because if she were pregnant they would lose her income, which was needed to support him through graduate school. Jennifer remembered her first intercourse with George and her fantasy that if they continued, she would have a baby—a baby that was hers, as her half-siblings had never been;

a baby that she could use to punish George; a baby that would make it possible to exclude her mother from her relationship with George. She noted that it was as if "the' past and the present get mixed up."

She called her biologic father for advice; he recommended abortion. She wondered if her father had had the same thoughts when her mother was pregnant with her, and she felt furious at men. Nevertheless, she was quite surprised that, in the midst of her anger, she did not "jump into bed with another man" and also, that although she threatened Mark with suicide, she also told him that she did not mean it.

Just as Mark began to accept her pregnancy, Jennifer began to hemorrhage. She consulted her gynecologist, who told her that he did not believe she had ever been pregnant. She then reported one of the few dreams she had had during the therapy: A woman was masturbating her, and she felt aroused. Her association was of turning to women because men were so disappointing. In the next session, she told me of lying in bed waiting for the hemorrhaging to stop; she felt helpless and imagined that this would be her experience in pregnancy. She was frightened of being in an operating room to deliver a child, of being helpless and exposed. She had always been terrified of helplessness and had used affairs, suicide, and even the thought of pregnancy in order to defend herself against it. She was devastated that she had not been pregnant and decided that she wanted to continue therapy in order to sort out her feelings about being a mother.

Year Four. As Mark prepared to leave for Denver, Jennifer increased the frequency of her sessions to twice a week. On one occasion, Mark accompanied her to the session but remained in the waiting room. Jennifer was aroused. Again she was with a man, as she had been with George, and someone else was excluded. When Mark left for Denver, Jennifer imagined that he would never return and remembered her fantasies that her parents would be killed whenever they went out. She then denied Mark's absence. Eventually, she became more able to experience and tolerate her own anger, and the expected depression did not occur.

Jennifer's confidence and competence at work increased significantly. Thoughts of having a baby now recurred, this time as part of a childhood fantasy: If a man truly loved a woman, he would give her a child. George had given them to her mother and not to her. Also, to have a baby was to gain her mother's love through identification rather than competition, by being a mother. Gradually, the baby entered the transference and Jennifer began to articulate what clearly had been a long-held but fearful fantasy: She wanted a baby from me as proof that I cared about her; it was to be my gift to her. I was the father she would have liked to have, but in order to maintain me in that role, she had to inhibit her erotic feelings. How could she have me cuddle her and give her a baby? I was depriving her of both experiences.

Lately, the baby began to appear as her due compensation for supporting Mark through school. When Mark visited her from Denver, she pretended that she was pregnant. She felt he was withholding a baby from her, that he was depriving her, as both her mother and George had done.

Now, midway through the fourth year of therapy, Jennifer could feel more anger at George for not protecting her against her mother. She no longer wanted a baby boy, as she had with George. She now wanted a baby girl. She longed for a mother who would have protected her against George; she had longed for this mother since the age of 11, when she had begun her incestuous relationship with George. She thought that perhaps if she had told her mother about it earlier, her mother would have divorced George at once and then she could have had her mother all for herself. Jennifer's memories and feelings were becoming more vivid, and she could remember turning to George for the love she had so needed. She oscillated between fury at George and fury at her mother. Jennifer felt certain that her mother knew about the incest but was unworried because she knew that Jennifer could not get pregnant; George had had a vasectomy.

Mark suffered an attack of severe abdominal pain on his return from Denver. Jennifer's reaction was complex and confusing to her; she feared he might die, she was furious that he might abandon her, and she felt she loved him. It seemed to her that she could both love Mark and be angry with him. Her childhood fantasy that anger caused loss of love no longer seemed accurate. She began to wish for boundaries in her life, boundaries between Mark and his parents, between her sexual feelings and actions, between fathers and lovers. When Mark's illness continued to be undiagnosed, she became depressed and suicidal, and again began to think about having affairs.

When I suggested that Jennifer's relapse was related to Mark's unavailability, she became calmer. Mark held her in a way that made her feel safe; this had been one of her main reasons for marrying him. After Mark's condition was finally diagnosed and treated, she remained more aware of her longing for nonsexual contact and for her mother. She related fantasies of being touched and held by me that were accompanied by intense anger at her mother. Jennifer turned toward me, wishing both to have a baby by me and to be my baby.

As Jennifer's obsession about having a baby reappeared in full force, she experienced intense despair. Any interventions I made regarding possible meanings she interpreted as being for my gratification, not for her, just as George had told her what she felt in order to persuade her to have intercourse with him. A baby would console her when Mark was less available. Therapy became permeated by her insistent demands that I satisfy her wish to have a baby. She would kill herself if she were not given what she wished. At times, her thinking was nearly psychotic as she imagined she did have a baby but was keeping it a secret in order to prevent its being taken from her.

I felt helpless to understand her insistence. I suggested that her relentless demands were connected to her childhood feeling that wishing would make it so, because in fact her fantasies about George had come true. She explained, in a brief moment of lucidity, that she had been grieving for the baby that would now have been born if she had really been pregnant earlier. She felt that if she could get through this period successfully, she would not need me anymore.

Jennifer decided to decrease the frequency of therapy to one session a week, and I did not demur. She feared that if she held on to her obsession about the baby, she would lose both me and her sense of reality. She said that she wanted to drive her car into a bridge to show her anger at Mark and at me for refusing to give her a baby, but she did not wish to die. She spoke sadly of feeling that nothing had ever belonged to her in the way a baby would. I was forcing her to abandon all her fantasies. She feared she would end up with nothing, just as she had during her childhood and early adolescence.

With each painful session, there were minute gains in reality testing—for example, the realization that Mark had not tricked her into an abortion; she had never been pregnant. But her fierce insistence was unabated; she challenged Mark to either leave her or give her a baby. Again they began couples therapy. Struggles over control predominated. Jennifer refused to have intercourse if either of them was using a contraceptive device. Her earlier anger with George for leaving her without a baby now found expression with Mark.

Jennifer herself realized that her insistence on having a baby felt exactly like her intense urges to have an affair; both were supposed to fill her internal emptiness. She decided that she no longer wished to be "good" with me, as she felt she had been with her parents all her life in order to prevent them from abandoning her. Jennifer became increasingly angry at me, refusing to leave the sessions and insisting that I make her feel better. One theme remained: She either wanted to be taken care of as a child (to be mothered) or else to have a child to care for (to be a mother). In the first phase of therapy, her anger with me for not gratifying her had been expressed through affairs, which she was certain I did not think were in her best interest. I had not given her what she wanted. Therefore, she had found other men who would. Mark and George had both first staked their claims to her vagina and then proceeded to ignore it; she experienced it as an empty hole that someone else had to fill. Despite this, she imagined herself, as she had in her previous false pregnancy, depressed after giving birth. Though still furious with me, she decided that she was having more difficulty in functioning and again wished to see me twice a week. I agreed.

Year Five. Jennifer began to wonder about the quality of her relationships. She now wanted more comfort in heterosexual relationships without the need to erotize them or make them exclusive. Her
fantasy had been that any marriage would be like her relationship with
her mother and any affair like her involvement with George. Jennifer
began to experience her relationship with Mark more fully, missing
him when he was away rather than feeling depressed or hopeless.

She began to feel more competent at work and applied for promo-
tions. In the past, competence had frightened her: It had meant that
our relationship would become sexual. As though to confirm this suspicion, Jennifer considered seducing another psychiatrist. I confronted
her with her wish to have me respond to her either as a helpless little
girl or as a *femme fatale;* perhaps there was more to her than either
of those roles. She said that at times she felt that the latter was true.
She developed a pattern of canceling each session that had been pre-
ceded by one discussing her erotic transference.

Jennifer's interest in her appearance and her pleasure in her beauty
returned, though I perceived it to be in some conflict with her wish
to be pregnant. As she began to spend more money on herself, she
sent less to her mother. On one occasion when her period was late,
she was certain that she was pregnant; when she discovered that she
was not, she decided to terminate therapy. I confronted her with the
connection between the hoped-for pregnancy and her feelings about
me. She said that she was uncertain if she would have the baby with
me or for me; what mattered most was that, if she were pregnant, she
would have a family of her own and so have a reason to refuse her
mother's demands on her. I continued to emphasize her anger at me
for not giving her a baby. She replied that if she was pregnant, she
would feel safe with me; now when I identified her wish to have a
baby by me, it sounded like George's bragging that he could "do it
better than anyone." I began to emphasize her distrust and its very
early development in her biologic father's abandonment of her and
George's betrayal. She felt George had betrayed her twice, once as a
stepfather who became a lover and more recently as an idealized protector who proved unable to take care of himself.

Halfway into Jennifer's fifth year with me (almost 3 years into the
second phase of therapy), George phoned Jennifer to say that everything had been his fault, that he now wanted to be the parent she had
wanted as a child. She called to tell me about it, distraught, wanting
to believe that he meant it and fearing that he did not. George had
betrayed her trust; what he had done with her in the past had been
"crazy." She said that she had phoned me in order to tell me about
it, not to beg me to take away her pain. She wanted me to know that
she was hurt; sharing it with me made her feel better. She said she
felt she could touch me and allow herself to be touched by me in a

way that her mother had never permitted; her mother had only allowed George to touch her incestuously.

George was now perceived as a lonely, deprived man whom she had taken care of and who, in return, had taken care of her. She longed to have a real father. She painfully remembered how important it had been that after George masturbated her, he would kiss her goodnight. She could tolerate the pain now and even have some hope for the future. I suggested that she had wished to tell her mother about George in order to show her mother that George knew how to love her. I said that the first betrayal had come from the mother who she felt did not love her. She remembered her mother saying, "Don't let yourself get emotionally dependent on anyone." I suggested that her mother was like a cold, smooth stone that could not be warmed. Jennifer sobbed and said that she had competed with her mother for George's love. As she became more aware of these feelings about her mother, she also recognized that in each of her jobs she had experienced her employer as the disapproving mother. The jobs were all attempts to gain love, and all men functioned as stand-ins for her mother.

Mark's employment opportunities dictated that they would have to leave the Boston area. As termination of therapy loomed, Jennifer wondered, "How do people replace their parents? Do they feel loved enough that they don't need them anymore, or do they always need them? I guess Mark has his parents and I have you." She said that if I left her, she would have "nothing." She began to cry and feared that she would weep without end. What else would she have to do for me? She had discontinued her affairs for me, and she had stopped the crises. Would ending therapy be good enough for me? How could she remember me after we stopped? If she could have a baby while in therapy, it would always remind her of me. She wanted to be pregnant before she left; her fantasies had been of being pregnant by me, and she felt physical sensations in her vagina as she spoke about them. She still felt that only by being sexual could she show me her love. She was not sure if she was safe with me.

Year Six. Five months before termination (3.5 years after beginning the second phase of therapy), Jennifer became pregnant. Coincidentally, George phoned her again in the hope of reestablishing a relationship. She realized that there had been several Georges in her life. She wanted the presexual one who had loved her as his daughter, but she always remembered the sexual one who had betrayed her. Now she wanted George to "find me attractively married." He visited her and she recognized that she did not understand him, that part of her difficulty was in confusing her own fears and wishes with his: She wanted his love and she feared a sexual relationship. It felt the same with me.

Once Jennifer's pregnancy was medically confirmed, she felt closer to Mark. But she feared that if she truly loved him, she might lose him. She had used sexuality not only to prevent separation anxiety but also to maintain her self-esteem in the face of her fear of abandonment. Jennifer now recognized that she had used affairs as a "pacifier": She laughed, realizing the meaning of fellatio in her affairs. She could now link some of her wishes for exhaustive sexual orgies to the way a baby nurses to exhaustion. What she wanted from a man was what she had not received from her mother.

Jennifer realized that she had lived as though all of her troubles—her father's leaving, the incest, George's divorce—had been her fault. Her suicidal thoughts were in part a confirmation to herself of her mother's statement that she should never have been born. She recalled feeling that it was her fault that her mother had become pregnant with her and that she needed to make reparations for that calamity. Her unconscious fantasy had been that she had been born before her mother had intercourse with her father, and consequently her mother had to marry her father; now she knew that she had been born *because* of her mother's active participation in intercourse with her father. I challenged her conviction that she was serving an indeterminate sentence for being bad. George and her mother had blamed her for so many things that Jennifer had assumed that Mark would do the same; now she believed that she "didn't have to live in her imagination anymore."

Jennifer's relationship with me now became more trusting and less focused on gratification, perhaps because the intensity of the transference was diminishing as we neared termination. She wished to see me three times per week for the last 2 months of therapy. As she wondered about her purposes and motivations, she realized that she was attempting to ward off separation feelings. She decided that the work we still had to do could still be accomplished in twice-weekly meetings.

Two months before termination, the manager of the firm at which Jennifer worked left; Jennifer applied for and was selected as the interim replacement. Shortly after that, Mark was hospitalized again for abdominal pain; a fistula was discovered and treated. Mark's mother came again, and this time Jennifer felt secure about sharing his care. At that time, Jennifer reported the second dream that she had had during the therapy:

> She was a little girl trying on clothes. George, in the guise of helping her with her clothes, had sex with her. She was frightened that her mother would appear at any moment. Her mother did appear and Jennifer ran away, feeling guilty that her mother had found her. She was terrified of what her mother would do and cringed as her mother approached. But her mother merely told her that the TV program that Jennifer had been waiting for was on. Her mother was totally unsuspecting.

She was relieved that she had dreamed about George rather than about me. The dream was so vivid that it reminded her of the first time George had caressed her sexually. She had been fascinated that he had the temerity to do that, it was so private. George was all hers and it did not feel bad; she imagined that all fathers did it. They had intercourse in the parents' bedroom. Jennifer remembered feeling "bad" but not guilty. She felt as though she were his mistress; he treated her as if she were; he confided in her and asked her to exhibit herself in her mother's shoes and nightgown. She laughed at herself for sleeping only in flannel pajamas now. Her past fears of men looking at her as she walked were related to these episodes with George. She had imagined that if people looked at her, they could see that she had had intercourse with George. If she had orgasms with any man, he would know that she had had intercourse with George. So she had allowed herself to have orgasms only with "faceless men that she would never see again." She became generally calmer; her feelings about George had lost much of their intensity.

Jennifer found it difficult to discuss termination because she was so concerned about her pregnancy. She still spoke openly of her wish to have a baby with me. George had given babies to her mother, but all he had given her were career aspirations she could not fulfill. I, on the other hand, had helped her to become a woman, had helped her to find a career for herself, and had made it possible for her to become pregnant. She had wanted me to be her good father. All negative feelings about me were displaced onto Mark.

Approximately a month before termination, Jennifer canceled the entire week because she and Mark were given a free week at a vacation house. On her return, she wondered if I was angry at her for leaving. If I had asked her to stay, she would have remained for me. I suggested that projecting her feeling of abandonment onto me had permitted her to leave without taking responsibility for her own action. Jennifer said that now it felt "okay to have her own feelings. She didn't know why she didn't think so before; it was as if she had gotten lost."

As termination neared, she did not want to leave. She feared having a sexual relationship with me but acknowledged that those wishes were not those of the real Jennifer. She now felt like a grown-up daughter; still, if she did not have intercourse with me, perhaps it was because she was not sexy enough. In the final session, she wondered if I could know how much she appreciated the therapy if she did nothing except thank me verbally. At the door, she realized that perhaps thanking me was sufficient. It was 7 years after our first meeting.

Follow-Up

About 3 months after termination of therapy, Jennifer called to tell me that she had given birth to a daughter and was very happy. The baby's name was the same as her sister's. About a year later, she called me because she was furious with Mark about a disagreement regarding whose mother would get the child if they were both to die. I suggested that there might be more to the issue than that. She calmed down and said she would talk about it with Mark. Three months after that, Jennifer visited Boston and came to see me for 10 minutes to show me the baby. She spoke about some of the difficulties she was having separating herself from the baby, and we both remembered that we had discussed this issue earlier in the therapy.

About 2 years after termination I wrote to Jennifer, requesting permission to write up our work. In her letter of conditional permission, she told me about her current life. Things were going well with Mark. Even when they had arguments and she became jealous, she continued to believe that he was faithful to her. She remained faithful to him. Though there were still difficulties in separating herself from the baby, she was taking small steps to leave her with babysitters. She had a job, was enjoying it, and believed that it made her more interesting to Mark. She was making friends, particularly with another woman. She had written to her biologic father, asking him to lend her money for a house. He had invited her to visit him, and she planned to bring the baby to show him. She observed that she was "obsessed" about buying the house, but her wish no longer had a life-and-death quality; she did not feel that her father owed it to her. She wrote, "How could anyone's father owe them anything when one is 33 years old?"

Case Discussion

Jennifer meets the DSM III criteria for the diagnosis of Borderline Personality Disorder. She presented for treatment with seven of the eight characteristics of the disorder outlined in DSM III: impulsivity, unstable intense interpersonal relationships; inappropriate and poorly controlled anger, identity disturbance, affective instability, intolerance of being alone, and physically self-damaging acts. These were long-standing problems, and they significantly impaired Jennifer's social and occupational functioning. However, Jennifer had been able to work steadily in the past, and so was less functionally impaired by her psychological state than are many patients who warrant the borderline diagnosis. She had no history of psychosis. However, her belief that she was pregnant and her later transference demand that the therapist impregnate her were at times so intense and so refractory to reality testing as to have been considered quasi-delusional.

Jennifer had no significant paranoid, schizoid, or obsessional features. She exhibited narcissistic features—namely, entitlement, egocentricity, and lack of empathy—but these were not the primary features of her disorder. She was quite histrionic, and it might be argued that she meets the criteria for the diagnosis of Histrionic Personality Disorder. Certainly, her self-esteem hinged on her sexual evocativeness. However, her anger, self-destructiveness, and impulsivity are more suggestive of a borderline disorder than a histrionic one.

Jennifer brought considerable *strengths* to her psychotherapy. She was more functional at the start of treatment than the other patients in our group in that she was capable of steady work and had managed to sustain a marital relationship. She was bright and curious about her inner life. She entered treatment already assuming that there was some relationship between the past and the present, and her interest in psychodynamic issues prompted her to work on them outside of treatment hours.

Her marriage proved to be an asset to the treatment, since her husband could sometimes act as the therapist's ally. In many respects, Jennifer's husband provided a container for her between sessions in that he gave her a place to "decompress" at home and was relatively unmoved by her histrionics. The therapist likened this arrangement to the role of an inpatient unit; the husband performed functions for Jennifer that an inpatient staff might have done in a hospital setting.

Jennifer relied heavily on primitive defenses at the start of treatment, most notably projection, denial, splitting, grandiosity, eroticization, and acting out. She possessed little capacity for self-soothing when she entered treatment and could manage seemingly intolerable affects only by enlisting the aid of a sexual partner. Her holding and soothing introjects (to use Buie and Adler's concept) were poorly formed and left her vulnerable to massive anxiety when she perceived important people to be unavailable to her. Her impulsivity threatened her life and her marriage; her judgment was often poor. Her ego functioning varied markedly with her affective state, but she saw no connection between the two. Her amenability to analytically oriented therapy, as assessed retrospectively by the authors, was somewhat mixed (Figure 6–1). While she was rated highly on intelligence, motivation, and psychologic mindedness, she was scored much lower on self-discipline, impulse control, and empathy.

Jennifer's therapist was an interesting match for her in that he was comfortable working within the context of an eroticized transference. He was able to respond to and value her sexual evocativeness as one aspect of her personality without resorting to reaction formation, hostility, or an enactment of the transference. He was verbally quite active, yet slow to take action in the treatment (e.g., limit setting), and this style may have been particularly well suited to a woman who had suffered sexual abuse at the hands of a parent.

The therapist was also tolerant of Jennifer's self-destructive threats and he was capable of bearing with a fair amount of uncertainty about her safety. This prompted him to resist another form of action—hos-

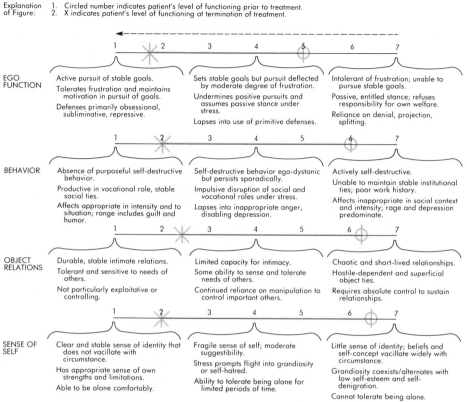

Explanation of Figure:
1. Circled number indicates patient's level of functioning prior to treatment.
2. X indicates patient's level of functioning at termination of treatment.

EGO FUNCTION

1 — 2 — 3 — 4 — 5 — 6 — 7

Active pursuit of stable goals.
Tolerates frustration and maintains motivation in pursuit of goals.
Defenses primarily obsessional, subliminative, repressive.

Sets stable goals but pursuit deflected by moderate degree of frustration.
Undermines positive pursuits and assumes passive stance under stress.
Lapses into use of primitive defenses.

Intolerant of frustration; unable to pursue stable goals.
Passive, entitled stance; refuses responsibility for own welfare.
Reliance on denial, projection, splitting.

BEHAVIOR

1 — 2 — 3 — 4 — 5 — 6 — 7

Absence of purposeful self-destructive behavior.
Productive in vocational role, stable social ties.
Affects appropriate in intensity and to situation; range includes guilt and humor.

Self-destructive behavior ego-dystonic but persists sporadically.
Impulsive disruption of social and vocational roles under stress.
Lapses into inappropriate anger, disabling depression.

Actively self-destructive.
Unable to maintain stable institutional ties; poor work history.
Affects inappropriate in social context and intensity; rage and depression predominate.

OBJECT RELATIONS

1 — 2 — 3 — 4 — 5 — 6 — 7

Durable, stable intimate relations.
Tolerant and sensitive to needs of others.
Not particularly exploitative or controlling.

Limited capacity for intimacy.
Some ability to sense and tolerate needs of others.
Continued reliance on manipulation to control important others.

Chaotic and short-lived relationships.
Hostile-dependent and superficial object ties.
Requires absolute control to sustain relationships.

SENSE OF SELF

1 — 2 — 3 — 4 — 5 — 6 — 7

Clear and stable sense of identity that does not vacillate with circumstance.
Has appropriate sense of own strengths and limitations.
Able to be alone comfortably.

Fragile sense of self; moderate suggestibility.
Stress prompts flight into grandiosity or self-hatred.
Ability to tolerate being alone for limited periods of time.

Little sense of identity; beliefs and self-concept vacillate widely with circumstance.
Grandiosity coexists/alternates with low self-esteem and self-denigration.
Cannot tolerate being alone.

F i g u r e 6–1. Standards for assessing levels of functioning—baseline and outcome: Jennifer.

pitalization—and to insist on her autonomy in the face of life-threatening behavior.

Jennifer's *transference* to her therapist was predominantly eroticized and idealizing. During much of the treatment, she felt that she and he were involved in an exciting and illicit affair. She saw him as able to give her a baby, and as a source of power and pleasure. She also saw him as withholding what he could give her, similar to her view of her stepfather's role in her life. This image of the therapist as withholding shifted from a predominantly paternal to a more maternal transference as the treatment progressed. Her hostility and her wish to control the therapist became more evident in her self-destructive threats and behavior, but were less fully explored. Interestingly, Jennifer did not develop a coherent and *sustained* negative maternal transference to her therapist. Rather, she used splitting to maintain a predominantly idealized paternal transference to the therapist and projected most of her negative transference onto her husband.

Like the transference, the therapist's *countertransference* was predominantly eroticized. The patient's incessant sexualization in the early phase of therapy created an atmosphere that the therapist found highly charged and unsettling. He also felt genuinely fond of her, he respected her intelligence, and he was gratified by her growing capacity for self-analysis. He commented that Jennifer's constant pleas for help generally made him feel valued and capable rather than helpless. He reported feeling overwhelmed and helpless only when his interventions had no discernible effect on Jennifer's suicidal threats or on her wish to have a baby by him.

Jennifer's therapist employed a variety of *techniques* in the treatment. His model of her psychopathology was somewhat mixed. Both conceptually and technically, he saw her as having ego deficits due to poor mothering and inconsistent fathering. Accordingly, his interventions emphasized the reality of her traumatic childhood experiences and the real deficits in the quality of caretaking in her primary relationships. He paid very little attention to Jennifer's contribution to her disturbed primary relationships, that is, to her defensive distortions of those relationships. He did, however, clarify her misperceptions of important early events.

Jennifer's therapist also employed a model of conflict in understanding her psychopathology, and his interpretations were often aimed at elucidating conflicts. His style was the most purely interpretive of any of our five cases. His use of interpretation was active but gentle, nonconfrontive, and nonintrusive. In this respect, as in his relative reluctance to take action, his work might be described as the most classical of the therapists in our group. Similarly, he placed more constant emphasis than any of the others in our group on the relation between the patient's past and her present. However, a classical psychoanalytic approach would probably have involved more consistent attention to transference (particularly negative transference) than was present in this case.

The therapist did not directly address the nature of Jennifer's object relations in her current life. And most surprisingly, he paid little attention to Jennifer's reactions to separations from the therapist during the course of treatment. This was due, in part, to Jennifer's blanket denial of any feelings about the therapist's comings and goings. The therapist allowed Jennifer to control the therapy with respect to both the material discussed and the frequency of sessions. He did not succumb to the patient's manipulations; however, he did not interpret her manipulativeness and her often cruel efforts to control him or her husband. His focus was primarily on her desperation rather than her sadism.

The therapist's technique in dealing with her erotic transference was consistent with what has been discussed so far in that he did not enact the transference with her. Nor did he interpret it vigorously, since he felt that the patient would experience that response as a re-jection. He expected that this issue would be more fully explored in the final stages of treatment, which never occurred. When Jennifer moved to ease the crisis centering on her demand for a baby by cutting down her sessions to once a week, he neither protested nor interpreted.

The therapist's work with Jennifer's husband was probably an important factor in protecting the treatment. From the beginning, he encouraged the husband to meet with him and enlisted the husband as an ally in times of crisis. Less deliberately, the therapist also allowed the husband to bear the brunt of much of Jennifer's negative trans-ference during the course of therapy. He viewed the three-way meetings as a means of helping Jennifer feel that she did not have to choose between her therapist and her spouse. This case raises the general question of whether it is particularly important for a male therapist working with a young married woman to have contact with her family.

Jennifer's self-destructive threats were frequent and caused her therapist considerable anxiety throughout the early phases of the treatment. Nevertheless, he refused to assume responsibility for her life and did not vigorously set limits on her self-destructive behavior (e.g., by insisting on hospitalization). His strategy was to provide her with sessions as frequently as needed during times of intense suicidal ideation. He believed that their strong therapeutic alliance and her eroticized attachment to to him enabled him to maintain a connection with her and to take the risk of keeping her out of the hospital during times of crisis. When Jennifer was suicidal, he clarified her angry mo-tives (the primary occasions on which negative transference was ex-amined) and reminded her, "If you kill yourself, you won't be able to see me anymore." In this respect, he emphasized Jennifer's separate-ness and their inability to control one another. We wondered whether Jennifer may have interpreted his reluctance to hospitalize her as a statement that he valued their relationship more than he valued her safety, but the therapist did not agree. He believed that regression might ensue with hospitalization, and that the patient needed to be confronted with the fact that her safety was in her own hands.

The therapist's relative lack of limit setting was evident in his han-dling of contact outside of scheduled sessions. Jennifer called him frequently during some phases of treatment, and he reports that he was "responsive" on the telephone, talking to her for up to 25 minutes. Later in treatment, he began to ask her about the reasons for her calls. Without interpretation or limit setting in regard to this practice, the phone calls virtually ceased after 3 years of therapy, to recur only in the termination phase.

Jennifer made substantial gains during the course of her psycho-therapy. She developed a less punitive and more tolerant superego, which functioned more consistently than it had when she first came

	Unfavorable	Favorable

1. Friendliness −5 −4 −3 −2 −1 | 1 2 3 4 5
   hostile · amiable *(marker at 1)*

2. Likeability −5 −4 −3 −2 −1 1 2 3 4 5
   below average · above average *(marker at 3)*

3. Intelligence −5 −4 −3 −2 −1 1 2 3 4 5
   below average · above average *(marker at 2/3)*

4. Motivation −5 −4 −3 −2 −1 1 2 3 4 5
   indifferent · motivated *(marker at 3/4)*

5. Psychological-mindedness −5 −4 −3 −2 −1 1 2 3 4 5
   low · high *(marker at 4/5)*

6. Conscience factors −5 −4 −3 −2 −1 1 2 3 4 5
   antisocial; deceitful; vengeful · values; good moral sense *(marker at 1)*

7. Self-discipline −5 −4 −3 −2 −1 1 2 3 4 5
   low; chaotic · high *(marker at −2)*

8. Impulse control −5 −4 −3 −2 −1 1 2 3 4 5
   craving; impulsivity · high *(marker at −2)*

9. Defensive style −5 −4 −3 −2 −1 1 2 3 4 5
   drugs; action · intropunitive *(marker at −3/−2)*

10. Externalization/Internalization −5 −4 −3 −2 −1 1 2 3 4 5
    paranoid · capacity to admit fault *(marker at 1)*

11. Empathy/Narcissism −5 −4 −3 −2 −1 1 2 3 4 5
    contempt; entitlement · ability to care about and resonate with others *(marker at −2)*

12. Parental factors −5 −4 −3 −2 −1 1 2 3 4 5
    brutalization, exploitation, indifference · warmth, support *(marker at −4)*

13. Social supports −5 −4 −3 −2 −1 1 2 3 4 5
    absent-disruptive · stable *(marker at 3)*

FIGURE 6–2. Amenability to psychotherapy: Jennifer. (Adapted from Stone's Amenability for Analytically Oriented Therapy Scale (Stone, 1985).

to treatment. She learned to anticipate the consequences of her acts and to see a relationship between her behavior and its consequences. A lessening of her reliance on denial, projection, splitting, and primitive idealization opened the way for more stable interpersonal relationships characterized by a greater capacity for empathy and mutuality. Her capacity to attend to and tolerate feelings of anger, loneliness, and sexual excitement without acting on them increased markedly.

By the end of the treatment, Jennifer was still seductive, but she was much more appropriate in her displays of sexuality and appeared much better "put together" in dress and demeanor. She had come to see more clearly her unconscious fantasy of being given a baby by a powerful father figure and of wishing to *be* the child of that father figure. Her longing for the fulfillment of these fantasies was never fully sublimated into her marital relationship. Even at termination, she half believed that she might be expected to have sex with her therapist.

Prior to beginning this treatment, Jennifer had no concept of a trusting, nurturant relationship in which exploitation did not play a major role. Her failure to coerce her therapist out of a professional stance frustrated her wish to control him but also enhanced her self-esteem and her sense of being loved. In this way, the therapy provided a corrective experience for her.

Certainly, there was much work left undone when this treatment ended prematurely. Jennifer's infantile wish to have a child by the therapist was incompletely worked through, both because of her premature termination and because of her pregnancy during the final phase of therapy. She did not completely resolve her reliance on sexual evocativeness as a major prop for her self-esteem. Because her negative maternal transference was never fully examined, her aggression toward her mother was left incompletely explored. Given the relative lack of emphasis on experiences surrounding separations, it is not surprising that Jennifer did not do appropriate work on the grief surrounding the termination itself.

Figure 6–2 shows our retrospective ratings of Jennifer's level of functioning on four separate scales before and after treatment. She made substantial gains in ego functioning, behavior, and object relatedness. Interestingly, we rated her as having made the greatest change in her sense of herself, moving from a severe identity disturbance to a more stable and realistic sense of her own strengths and limitations by the end of the treatment.

The therapist's follow-up with Jennifer at the time of this writing indicates that she has made a good life adjustment: She has two children with whom she experiences only minor separation difficulties; she has remained faithful to her husband; and she reports being able to put minor affective storms into perspective without acting on them.

CHAPTER 7

Susan
Case Report

Susan was a 23-year-old single undergraduate student from western Pennsylvania who was hospitalized at McLean for the first time after an episode of depersonalization. She was referred to the hospital by the mental health service of the local university at which she was enrolled in summer school after an 8-day stay in the university infirmary. I was assigned to do the standard extended psychiatric evaluation given to new inpatients.

At our first meeting, I encountered a tall, attractive, neatly dressed woman who seemed eager to engage in the work of the evaluation. She reported that she was in the hospital "because I haven't been able to do anything with my life."

She said that her troubles began at the age of 17, when she moved away from home to a dormitory at a local university in Pennsylvania. Within a month of this move, she had swallowed 56 pills one at a time (including Darvon and several antibiotics), while her roommate handed her the contents of their medicine chest. Susan told me that she had recently read Sylvia Plath's book, *The Bell Jar,* and stated that she had no idea what prompted this drug overdose. She was hospitalized briefly but reported that no one took her distress seriously and that she had no follow-up care.

Out of the hospital, she became increasingly depressed, abused marijuana and amphetamines, and became pregnant by her boyfriend of 3 months. She obtained an abortion, dropped out of school to work, and returned the next fall to complete her freshman year. Susan describes these 2 years, during which she lived with her boyfriend, as the most stable years of her life. During the following summer, she worked as a fashion model in Acapulco and recalled feeling "high, like I was capable of anything, full of energy." Returning to school for her sophomore year, she again became pregnant, ended her 2-year relationship with her boyfriend, and obtained an abortion. That fall she made many extracurricular commitments at school, spent moderate amounts of borrowed money on clothes and weekend trips, and lost 10 lb. She had no history of a thought disorder at that time and no other vegetative signs. She became depressed when she went to her family home for Christmas that year and spent the spring semester "feeling like I was in the middle of a black hole, doing nothing but crying and drinking."

In the fall of her junior year she transferred to a university in Texas, noting, "I needed to start over." Sitting alone in her apartment in a city where she knew no one, she became severely depressed and for the first time experienced episodes of "spacing out," during which she felt that she ceased to exist and became invisible to others. These episodes lasted for several minutes, occurring most often when she was alone or under stress, and particularly when she was alone in crowds "because the lack of feedback from people makes me wonder if I exist at all." On one occasion, she found herself riding her bicycle the wrong way in the middle of rush hour traffic "because I did not exist and there was no reason to avoid cars."

At age 21 she returned to the same university in Pennsylvania where she had started, changed her major for the fourth time, and referred herself to a local female psychiatrist, whom she saw in weekly psychotherapy for 6 months. She took imipramine at this time and reported that it was of no help. The focus of her psychotherapy was on immediate issues of academic survival and peer relationships. Therapy ended when her insurance benefits were exhausted, and Susan reported that her father would not pay for further treatment. Susan felt nothing about having to terminate the therapy at the time, but in retrospect felt angry at her therapist for not continuing to see her without charge.

The summer before her last year of college, she traveled alone to Haiti "to learn French." There she suffered a ruptured appendix and subsequently a ruptured uterus, which required surgical interventions. These conditions resulted in chronic pelvic inflammatory disease (PID), from which she continued to suffer at the time of her first admission to McLean. During her final semester of college, she completed only two of her five academic courses due to depression and remained one semester short of credits for her B.A. degree. In April of that year, a male graduate student who had been her coach and whom she admired was killed in an auto accident, and she noted that "the shock made me vomit for days." Shortly thereafter, she had dinner with a cousin who used self-induced vomiting as a means of weight control, and Susan decided from then on to do the same. By the time of admission she claimed to be unable to stop vomiting after meals, despite a stated desire to do so.

Two months prior to admission, having failed to complete her degree requirements, she moved to Boston and enrolled in summer school to take premedical courses and thereby complete her B.A. degree. Upon arrival there she became increasingly depressed, eating in binges and vomiting. After an episode of fainting while jogging, she went to the university infirmary, where she was hospitalized prior to referral to McLean.

Background Information

Susan was born in western Pennsylvania. Her father, of Scandinavian descent, was a public relations executive. Her mother was of Egyptian ancestry, and was a music teacher who died of ovarian cancer at the age of 35 when Susan was 4 years old. She described her mother as strong, outgoing, vivacious, and someone who had many friends. She described her father as a "wishy-washy Mr. Rogers type who smiles constantly, denies the existence of problems, and avoids all painful subjects." Susan has one sibling, a brother 2 years younger than she, with whom she described having a vacillating but close relationship during adolescence. This relationship became more distant when her brother "decided to become superstraight and rigid when he went to college."

By her father's report, Susan's infancy was unremarkable, and she was a "happy, healthy baby." Her mother became ill when she was 3 years old, and at that time she and her brother were sent to live with their maternal grandparents in a nearby town. When her mother died, Susan was told that she had gone to live with God, and she recalled wondering why her mother liked God better than her own family. Much of her preschool period was spent in the home of her maternal grandparents, where she recalls crying constantly. Her father began to abuse alcohol heavily after her mother's death, and she recalled him as alternately abusive and smotheringly affectionate. She described her father as unpredictable in his availability, often leaving the children with a housekeeper and not appearing for dinner in the evening when he was expected home. She reported that her constant fear as a small child was that her father, too, would decide to go and live with God.

She started school without problems and did well academically. She described herself as a shy schoolgirl who felt like "a big dark-haired lunk—bigger than all the other kids," and felt fit to associate only with other "outcasts" in school. She and her brother spent their summers with their maternal grandparents but otherwise lived with their father and a series of housekeepers. When she was 12, her father (then 45 years old) married a woman who was 17 years his junior. According to Susan, both partners drank heavily and fought violently. The marriage ended in a separation after 4 years, when Susan was 16.

Susan reached menarche at age 13. At age 15 she became involved with a boy with whom she began having unprotected intercourse. She became pregnant by him at 16, and her condition remained undetected until she was 4 months pregnant. This delay necessitated a saline abortion, which she recalled as quite traumatic. She said that her father took her to a hospital in a nearby town for the abortion and registered her there under an assumed name. She recalled spending the rest of her high school days "getting stoned in my room because no one noticed," doing well in school without trying, and continuing her relationship with her boyfriend until age 17, when she graduated from high school one year early and began college.

First Year of Therapy

Once the initial evaluation was completed, Susan's treatment team at McLean recommended that she remain in Boston for at least 1 year in order to continue in psychotherapy with me. Upon hearing this recommendation, Susan requested that I be replaced by a female therapist. She began to talk of my failure to provide her with any answers, and related this fact to her sense that people always failed her. When a consultation was arranged with a female psychiatrist, she was both pleased and dismayed that her request had been taken seriously, and was relieved when the consultant told her to stay in treatment with me.

Plans for an orderly transition out of the hospital did not materialize, since Susan decided to leave against medical advice before finding either a place to live or employment. She planned, in the first week after leaving the hospital, to find an apartment, find a job, return to her alma mater to clear up some administrative details related to her degree, and fly to Illinois to see her most recent boyfriend. I commented that she was attempting to deal with her anxiety about leaving by engaging in a whirlwind of activity.

She returned after a frenzied week out of the hospital—depressed, with no job, and having moved in with Jonathan, the brother of her boyfriend. As she began to explore job possibilities, she again thought that she might want to become a physician, and decided to get some experience working in a hospital. She found a job as an operating room assistant at a local hospital, "because I'm most afraid of blood and I need to prove to myself that I can overcome the fear." When she began to feel overwhelmed by this work, she received a transfer to a secretarial job.

We then began several months of struggle over meeting times. There appeared to be innumerable conflicts between her other commitments and her twice-weekly psychotherapy hours. Work, friends, and a pottery class all posed insurmountable obstacles to continuing with me in treatment, and my repeated refusals to change her hours were met with rage, tears, and insistence that she was never coming back. She saw me as being completely arbitrary and, like her father, having no understanding of her difficult situation. At such times, I simply stated that I would be waiting for her at our next appointment. On several occasions, I was convinced that she had slammed my office door for the last time, only to discover her in my waiting room at our next appointed meeting. She seemed surprised and pleased that I had not taken her threats (which were quite convincing) at face value. I commented that she continually placed obstacles in the way of therapy as a means of avoiding the problems that she was there to work on. She stated that she always wanted to say "fuck you" to people before they could get to know her, because if she stayed, they would find out how terrible she was. She acknowledged her pattern of running, saying that "I'm afraid that if I stay in one place, I will be totally consumed by the sheer terror growing inside me and be just a shell filled with terror, no mind." She reflected that she had been testing me to see if I would put up with her. I commented that she might keep us busy with tests for many months as a means of avoiding the work of therapy.

Susan told me that I had passed her tests for the time being, and began to talk of her fears as a child of losing her father. She felt that she had to be "great" for him in some unspecified way to keep him around, "because he was all I had." She revealed fantasies that her mother's cancer was psychologically induced—that is, that her mother chose to get cancer and that if Susan had been a better little girl, her mother would not have elected to die. I related these fears to her anger when I arrived late for an appointment, and to her persistent belief that I would one day stop appearing for our appointed therapy hours.

Her relationship with Jonathan deepened. The two of them began sleeping together without having intercourse. She described this as the perfect relationship, "close but with some distance." At the same time, she complained that Jonathan was not there for her whenever she wanted him and that she was not the most important person in his life. She had several episodes of unprotected intercourse with Jonathan, and in reporting this to me, she reminded me that her gynecologist had warned against pregnancy at a time when her PID was still active. I wondered with her why she might want to create a crisis situation for herself at this time, and contrasted my concern for her health with her own seeming indifference. I related this situation to her wish to engage her father's attention when she became pregnant at age 16, an interpretation that met with considerable disdain. Soon thereafter, Jonathan told Susan that he was gay—a revelation that hurt her and made her feel increasingly inadequate.

Three months into the therapy, Susan began to talk with great urgency about the need to leave Boston, and arrived at our meetings announcing that she had plane reservations for Cairo, Madrid, Rio di Janiero, and California. When I discussed with her what such trips would accomplish, she became increasingly frustrated and angry, sensing that she was in a no-win situation: Neither staying put nor leaving the city would alleviate her distress. Finally, she began to talk of wanting to put her hand through a pane of glass, "because there's pressure building up and I need to feel something to relieve the pressure." She acted on this impulse, suffering superficial scratches, and her friend Jonathan came to her aid.

At this point, we began a cycle that continued for nearly 2 years: her veiled or direct threats of self-destructive behavior and my attempts to get her to determine how she might keep herself safe. Threats commonly occurred at the end of sessions and before the weekend, usually several times each month. At these times, she felt quite frightened of being alone during the days between therapy sessions. I often questioned her about what she might do to keep from acting on impulses to overdose, run in front of a truck, or cut herself. She was angry because I would not tell her what to do, and at the same time vehemently denied that I could be of any help. These dialogues often carried us beyond our appointed therapy times by 5, 10, or even 15 minutes. She was angry that I was not available to see her on weekends. We agreed that if she felt unable to keep from acting on her self-destructive impulses, she could contact me via the hospital outside of working hours. She did this roughly once or twice each month, and our telephone conversations mirrored our dialogues in therapy: She insisted that she could not contain her self-destructive impulses due to the hopelessness of her life, and I asked her to determine with me how she could keep herself safe in order to remain out of the hospital. I occasionally succumbed to the temptation to suggest ways in which she might alleviate her anxiety (e.g., by getting exercise), and any suggestion I offered was met with disdain and the insistence that my foolish suggestion was of absolutely no help to her. (I was forced to admit to myself that she was right.) My own reaction to these suicidal crises was one of profound helplessness.

During the Christmas holidays we did not meet for 1 week, and she reacted to this separation with anger. She insisted that she could no longer trust me and that it felt as if we were "starting from scratch" because she no longer knew me. One week later, she left a message at my office canceling her appointments for the foreseeable future, since she had gone with her boyfriend to California and did not know how long she would stay. The next day, she called from California to say that she was feeling hopeless and suicidal, that the trip had not helped, that she was stranded with no money, and that she did not know what to do. I insisted that she needed to be in therapy and that she must return to Boston immediately, borrowing money for plane fare if necessary. She did return, by train. At our next meeting she noted that twice-a-week sessions were not enough, and without much discussion I agreed to meet with her three times per week. We continued on this schedule until treatment was interrupted 3.5 years later.

I was seeing Susan through the Hospital Outpatient Clinic. Six months into the therapy, I realized that she was not paying any of her clinic fees. She had run up a considerable bill, and when I confronted her with this situation, she insisted that she had to stop therapy. Again she made airline reservations to a variety of destinations and talked of her rage at having to pay for therapy that had clearly made her worse rather than better. Despite several weeks of discussion, we came to no resolution about how the bill could be settled, and I interpreted this situation as one more obstacle she had put in the way of the work she needed to do. To complicate matters, she decided that she could no longer tolerate her job and quit, taking a new position on a factory assembly line.

I decided that it would be best to enlist her father's support directly at this point in order to protect the treatment. When I proposed that we meet with her father, Susan made no protest. We arranged a three-way meeting at which Susan asked him for financial assistance to take care of her bill, and he readily agreed. Our arrangement was that she must pay her fee before each session; failure to do so would result in an interruption of treatment. From that time on, she paid her fees promptly. However, immediately after the meeting with her father, she became depressed and announced plans to leave for a 2-month stay in California. I interpreted her fears about committing herself to stay in treatment with me, and she again challenged our set appointment times.

By this point in the treatment, it had become clear that she was not simply subject to dramatic mood changes, but that she experienced herself and me differently depending on how she felt during a given session. At best, she was a cooperative and engaging woman who could work collaboratively with me; and at such times she viewed me as well-meaning and friendly, if unthinking and ineffectual, tool of the mental health system. However, during other periods (sometimes in isolated sessions and sometimes for weeks on end), she presented herself as a rageful, tearful, helpless person; and in her eyes I became inattentive, exploitive, and sadistic. My sense of myself during the hours vacillated in corresponding fashion between that of a caring and competent therapist and that of a weak and depriving voyeur. Most striking was the fact that during stressful times, her memory of our more collaborative sessions appeared to have no emotional reality whatsoever. This was also the way in which she experienced others. My persistent attempts to knit these states together in the treatment were repeatedly dismissed by Susan as irrelevant.

After many months of battling over time, money, and Susan's self-destructive threats, her impulsive acts diminished and she began to talk in greater depth about her sense of defectiveness. She believed that had she been more interesting, more engaging, and "less awful," her mother would not have died and her father would not have become an alcoholic. She also spoke with considerable pain about craving attention as a child from the many housekeepers and girlfriends whom her father introduced into her life. She was ashamed of how much she craved love and of her despair when these women did not provide it. Slowly she delved into memories of having been sexually abused by an uncle at age 10, recalling how much she enjoyed his attention to her and how frightened she was by his sexual advances. She told no one of this, fearing that she would not be believed, and that she would be scorned or simply ignored. I related this episode to her constant concerns about what it would take to keep me interested in her and her longings for both closeness and distance.

Second Year of Therapy

Susan's maternal grandmother died at the beginning of our second year of work. She had been one of the few positive and relatively constant presences in Susan's early life. The news of this loss came on the eve of my departure for several days' vacation and at a time when Susan's friend Jonathan was not in town. She began to experience profound depersonalization, along with urges to cut herself, and willingly agreed to hospitalization when I recommended it. She left the hospital within 5 days and changed jobs again—this time working as a gardener's assistant, spending her days outdoors doing vigorous physical labor.

When I took a month-long vacation the following fall, Susan began to speak about leaving Boston to finish her B.A. degree at a university in Florida. She insisted that since she would be leaving therapy shortly after I returned from my vacation, it would be best to quit immediately. I remarked that she was again dealing with her anger and fear about an impending separation by running away. She continued to be rageful and depressed. On one occasion, she began to scratch her forearm to the point of drawing blood while sitting in my office. I told her firmly that I would not allow her to hurt herself in my presence, and if she wished to continue our session, she would have to stop. She did. She spoke of her yearning for someone who would always be there for her: "I want someone who'll always be there to come back to when I leave, so it's okay if I come and go."

When I returned from my vacation, she was making plans for her move to Florida. We began to explore her fears about completing her undergraduate degree, as well as her fears about leaving therapy. For the first time she acknowledged feeling dependent on me, as well as her wish and fear that she might be in therapy with me forever. She became extremely suicidal at this time, lacerating her wrists and abdomen superficially, and at one point went alone to the seashore on a chilly Saturday night and walked into the ocean in an attempt to drown herself. Waist high in water, cold and frightened, she turned around and returned home to telephone me. I actively interpreted her concern about being under my control, along with her fear that she needed me too much and was bound to be disappointed by me. I was concerned about her self-destructiveness, but the telephone contact and interpretive work appeared to ease her distress, and hospitalization was narrowly averted.

With the issue of Susan's move still unresolved, she underwent a laparoscopy to assess the state of her PID. At around the time of this procedure, she had frequent telephone contacts with me and scheduled extra sessions. She used the time to explore her difficulty in attending to bodily sensations, her humiliation at what she felt was the defectiveness of being female, and memories of her inability as a child to get her father to notice her medical problems (e.g., fevers, toothaches) until they had reached crisis proportions and she was in agony. She also reported dreams in which I was one of a series of doctors who stood over her as she lay splayed out on an operating table.

Shortly after the laparoscopy, she decided that she would not move. She still feared that I was an incompetent therapist, but she reluctantly admitted to herself and to me that I was the reason she was staying in Boston. Once this decision was made, we entered a period in which she felt safer and became more playful: She arrived at one session with her mouth filled with bubble gum, and she took delight in showing me her talent at blowing bubbles. She talked increasingly about sex. She spoke of orgasm as losing control. She said she resented men who only wanted her for sex, but put up with sex because she needed men. She related this situation to her having tolerated the advances of her uncle during her childhood because she craved love and attention.

She spoke with increasing rage and depression about not getting what she wanted from anyone in her life, and complained about Jonathan's and my unavailability to her. She became acutely suicidal, made numerous phone calls to me outside of working hours, and requested several extra sessions, which I granted. One day she came in announcing that a friend could obtain a cyanide capsule for her from a local scientific laboratory, and that she had an airplane ticket to Morocco but could not decide which of these options to take.

Her episodic inability to sleep became prolonged and severe, and I prescribed several capsules of flurazepam (Dalmane), which temporarily alleviated the insomnia. In the midst of this crisis, she had a dream in which I hugged her and she felt better. My clarifications regarding her longing for care and protection and her rage at not receiving what she wanted from me did not lessen her frustration. She finally had me paged one Saturday night, and while we discussed her sense of hopelessness about the future over the phone, she informed me that she was cutting her wrist even as we spoke. I insisted on hospitalization, which I arranged by phone.

This hospitalization—her third—lasted for nearly 3 months. During that time, several antidepressants as well as methylphenidate (Ritalin) were prescribed, but none was given an adequate trial due to Susan's sensitivity to their side effects and to noncompliance. We continued our regular therapy hours while she was in the hospital, and she accused me of "dumping her" on the inpatient unit so that I would no longer have to worry about her. She informed me that she was cutting herself on her abdomen even while she was in the hospital, and became angry when I informed her that either she or I would need to tell the ward staff about this behavior. With some humiliation, she told them herself. She continued to insist that she would either kill herself or flee to Florida as soon as she was released from the hospital, and insisted that I tell her which of these options to take. She did, however, begin to look for more appropriate employment, and was able to take pride in being considered suitable for a responsible position utilizing her intellectual abilities. Pleased with herself, she asked me, "If I feel different tomorrow, will you remind me of how I'm feeling today?"

I began to address more vigorously Susan's use of suicide threats to manipulate me. I became careful to end our therapy appointments on time rather than extending them by 5 or 10 minutes to talk about her suicide threats. Echoing her ward administrator, I insisted, each time she talked of suicide at the end of a session, that she wished "to leave me dangling on a hook until next time," and I wondered with her why she needed to do that. She was less angry at these comments than she was embarrassed by them, and began to talk of feeling "slimy" because she needed so much from people that she felt she had to get things from them by manipulation. I interpreted her use of suicide threats at the end of the hour as a way of getting something extra from me and as a way of avoiding separation.

When Susan was discharged from the hospital, she continued a job search that included only white-collar jobs that paid reasonably and involved some measure of responsibility. She arranged for her father to come to Boston to meet with her and an alcohol counselor from the hospital, in an effort to confront him with his alcoholism. She was pleased that she was able to tell him directly, for the first time, how much his drinking upset her.

In the next 2 months, she talked about taking a 2-week vacation in Costa Rica with a woman friend from college. When I did not insist that she was running away from therapy and needed to stay put, she became confused and frightened. She made plans for the trip but began to have trouble falling asleep, fearing that a black hand would come up through a crack in her bedroom floor and grab her in the middle of the night. I addressed her wish for me to intervene to stop her from leaving on vacation and her wish for me to protect her. She expressed considerable anger at me for controlling her life and said that she felt humiliated because she needed me and therefore had to do everything on my terms.

As the date of Susan's trip approached, she became more openly frightened about going away: "I'm afraid I'll die." The week before her departure, she reported the following dream:

> We were in an airplane. I was the pilot, and a girl from work was the copilot. We were testing a dive bomber, bouncing it off the surface of the ocean. Then I pushed a button and destroyed the world without meaning to. It turned to ash. So we flew through the ash, but we had nowhere to land, because there was nothing but ash. We had to fly on forever, and I had to keep my hand on the throttle or we'd go into a free fall.

Prior to her departure, I was persuaded to prescribe several capsules of Dalmane once again to help her sleep. She returned from her trip having enjoyed herself and having used considerable good judgment to keep herself out of possibly dangerous situations.

Third Year of Therapy

Susan took a responsible job at a local newspaper, and for the first time earned a salary that allowed her to stop receiving monthly financial support from home. She functioned well at this job despite her fear that people would discover she was "worthless."

Prior to my month-long August vacation, she again requested and received a prescription for a small number of minor tranquilizers to relieve her persistent insomnia. Five days before I was scheduled to return, she impulsively took all of these capsules, along with other pills that she had saved up from previous prescriptions. She called the physician who was covering for me, and he hospitalized her. Upon my return, my efforts to explore the circumstances of the overdose met with blanket resistance. She could not recall any of her feelings or thoughts prior to or during the overdose and was sure that my absence had little to do with it. I interpreted the overdose as a power play and insisted that the response of her various treaters did not tell her what she wanted to know—whether they cared about her. I also noted her anger at my departure, her inability to express this to me directly, and her need to vent her anger at me on the colleague who was covering for me in my absence. I suggested that my giving her the medication may have given her the impression that I was trying to get rid of her by pacifying her with pills. She reluctantly reported the following dream: "I was in a room full of pills, and you forced me to swallow them, even though we both knew that if I did, I would die."

Susan was discharged from the hospital after 2 weeks. She soon renewed her request for sleeping pills, and when I again agreed, she became increasingly suicidal. I acknowledged to her that when I felt anxious about her welfare, I sometimes did things (like prescribing Dalmane) that were not in her best interest. She was visibly upset by this idea and by my comment that in prescribing antianxiety medication, I had colluded with her in keeping her dependent on me.

Her rage at me for refusing subsequent requests for medication resulted in a flurry of phone calls. Instead of talking with her as usual on the telephone about the distress that had prompted her call, I began to ask what she hoped to gain and what she thought I could do over the phone. She became embarrassed by her inability to answer these questions, and insisted that I had never been of any help to her and never would be. She said she had begun to feel that it was "slimy" to call me, and the phone calls largely ceased for the remaining years of treatment. She began, however, to talk of men as "fucking assholes—they're all alike, they'll only meet you on their own turf." I noted that it was she who insisted on meeting people on her own turf.

At this point, she became involved with a man at work and acceded to his requests to have intercourse, only to refuse all contact with him after they had sex. She began to fear that someone would come into her bedroom at night to murder her. I remarked that she had wanted "to fuck this man over" by letting him have sex with her and then cutting him off, and that she feared retaliation. She did not deny these assertions but elaborated on her rage at this man.

I commented that by taking actions such as overdosing, she wanted to fuck me over as well for my failure to be a perfect caregiver. I noted that with me and others in her life, she was more often a tyrant than a helpless victim, and she acknowledged that she recognized this aspect of herself. Susan recalled that she had hoped that her overdose the previous August would make me look bad, and her fantasy was that if she killed herself, I would forever have a black mark on my curriculum vitae. I told her that I would be sorry if she killed herself, but that my life would go on.

I became more active in highlighting the indirect ways in which Susan made demands of me. On one occasion, she began a session by asking if I thought it was hot in the room. She then complained that the ashtray near her chair was full, and wondered if I ever took the trouble to empty it. I responded by saying, "Jump, Doctor! Speak, Doctor! Roll over, Doctor!" Despite her anger, she laughed at this and similar interventions. I wondered with her why she needed to see if she could make me do her bidding at such times and what might be reassuring about my response when I acquiesced to her demands. She talked more openly about her fantasies of beating me over the head with the heavy glass ashtray in my office, imagining that I would take the beating passively without reacting.

At the same time, she spoke about fantasies of wanting to take her mother's corpse and tear it to shreds "because she left—willingly and without warning." She immediately said that she expected to get sick and die, and I commented on the cycle of getting angry at important people and turning the anger back on herself. She then began to wonder what her mother's experience had been prior to her death, noting with some surprise, "My God, she didn't choose to die—she must have been terrified!" She spent several weeks exploring her lifelong fantasy that her mother and God were watching over her from heaven, and she recalled many instances when, as a child, she had placed objects in certain places and waited for them to be moved "as a sign that God was there and paying attention." She experienced considerable pain in realizing that this fantasy had little basis in reality and that if omnipotent figures were watching, they were passive and not helpful.

During this period, she continued to function responsibly in her full-time job and began course work toward the completion of her bachelor's degree. Despite considerable *sturm und drang* about her inability to do the work and numerous crises centering on examination dates and paper deadlines, she invariably performed at the top of her class. As she discussed academic matters and thoughts about a future career, she expressed an interest in how I had managed various career choices and even how I had learned to type. While I did not answer most of her questions directly, I was obviously more eager to help her explore these matters than I had been to discuss the pros and cons of her jumping into a gorge in Peru.

In January, Susan again began to talk of leaving, allegedly to finish her degree requirements elsewhere. I suggested that this was a way of dealing with her fears about what would happen when I left the Hospital Outpatient Clinic in July. Immediately she demanded to know what her fee would be when I left the clinic. She insisted that she needed to leave treatment at once, since she would never be able to afford a fee increase. She noted with pain and scorn that I obviously did not care about her, because if I did, I would not even consider raising her fee. Through the winter and spring, discussion of her rage at me and her fear of losing therapy occupied most of our work. I eventually set a fee for her that was reduced but still significantly more than what she paid through the clinic. She reacted with fury and made suicidal threats for the first time in several months, but she did not act on them. She immediately arranged two consultations with other psychiatrists at McLean. When the consultants informed her that my procedure was not unusual, she returned to me, complaining that "all you psychiatrists back each other up."

Susan began to insist that my unwillingness to see her for what she could afford to pay and my willingness to let her go meant that she could no longer trust me. I interpreted this to mean that she was terrified to realize that she could not control me, and she was enraged because I insisted on attending to my own needs in this matter, even though they conflicted with hers. When I noted her reluctance to ask her father to help her financially, she dismissed this as impossible, saying that he was too unreliable, she did not want to become dependent on him again, and he could not afford it. The crisis culminated on a weekend when she called me at home, feeling desperate and suicidal. When she requested hospitalization, we both discovered that her insurance coverage had lapsed and she was eligible only for admission to a state facility. She refused this, and was enraged when I would not prescribe medication to sustain her through the weekend. She came to our appointment the next Monday angry and frightened. She left my office and went to a telephone booth in the building, where she attempted to hang herself with the telephone cord. There was a dinner for hospital psychiatrists going on across the hall, but no one noticed her dramatic attempt. She then decided to use the telephone to call her father and ask him for money to continue in therapy. With considerable drama and tears on both their parts, he agreed to help out.

This appeared to be another turning point in the treatment. Susan's self-destructive threats ceased, as did most of her telephone calls and other attempts to seek increased contact with me beyond the limits of our therapy hours. Susan also began to talk about therapy positively for the first time, and the anger and devaluation that had been her constant stance toward me were no longer prominent. She recalled early memories of her mother drawing her close when pictures were being taken "simply to show how close the family was." She noted that her mother always took care of herself before anyone else. She was impressed by her father's willingness to help with the cost of therapy, and worked to gain some perspective on him. She acknowledged that her father really was there at times when she needed him, but that what she could expect from him was limited. He would probably always drink and at times disappoint her.

She planned and took a 2-week vacation just prior to my transition to private practice. Again, I did not interpret this action as running away from therapy, but discussed her fears about fending for herself while she was away. She suffered a severe lower back problem while on vacation, and upon her return she acknowledged that her feelings about being away from therapy may have had something to do with this condition.

The transition to private practice was surprisingly uneventful. Susan paid my subsequent bills promptly and without comment.

Fourth Year of Therapy

Susan spoke haltingly and for the first time of feeling sexually attracted to me; this material came up primarily in dreams. She also stated that she feared the power of her anger toward me: "If I showed you my real anger, it would flatten you against the wall, and then I'd be left alone." She said she was frightened by her new efforts to be a more autonomous adult. She knew that she could no longer call me at home when she was feeling bad, because it was not what she needed and was more frustrating than helpful. When she discussed her need for extensive inpatient insurance coverage, I questioned her assumption that she would require hospitalization in the future. She was both frightened and pleased that I did not assume the inevitability of future hospital admissions and opted for less extensive coverage.

Prior to my August vacation, Susan began to talk of binge eating, a problem that had been chronic and intermittent but seldom explored during our work together. She reported binging "because I have to grab onto people and food since I never trust that they'll be there when I want them." She said she enjoyed ripping food with her teeth, noting that this allowed her to vent some of her anger. She managed my absence better than she had in the past, missing several days of work but functioning adequately overall. At our first meeting after my return, she remarked, "I couldn't believe you were coming back, but I told myself that you wouldn't die, and that was helpful."

During this period, she developed a friendship with a woman who was about her age and quite successful in her career. This was the first enduring friendship with a woman that she had been able to establish since treatment began, and she struggled with the fact that this friend was both important to her and at times unpredictable and disappointing in her behavior. Nevertheless, she realized that this woman had something to offer her. She saw that her friend had personal problems too, but did not feel the need to discuss her difficulties with others at work or to assume a helpless posture in order to get support.

At this time, Susan also developed a sexual relationship with a married man in his late forties. The affair was tumultuous, and she constantly feared his efforts either to establish more closeness or to put more distance between them. It was, however, mutually beneficial to a limited extent, since they shared certain traits of temperament and intellectual interests. Prior to this time, she had formed only unstable, unpleasant, and short-lived relationships with emotionally distant men.

She spent the fall finishing her course work for completion of her bachelor's degree, taking graduate school entrance examinations, and applying to graduate schools. She managed to do all of this while working full time. While her complaints about her ability to cope with this work load were extensive, and while recurrent episodes of depression threatened to undermine her activities almost weekly, she managed to complete her degree and tolerate the frustration involved in ironing out considerable administrative problems with her alma mater. She began to wonder if all of this achievement was nothing but an effort to please me and her father with activities we approved of, and was concerned that she was giving in and becoming "mainstream." In this context, she reported the following dream:

> I was lost in Africa. I was in the jungle without my bicycle. A young man with a crew neck sweater and a tweed jacket came along, and said he could help me—he could get me a bicycle. He took me to a place where there were other people who could help, but they weren't home. So I was left on my own again.

We talked at length of her fear of having taken the wrong path by staying in therapy, of her fear of abandonment as she functioned more autonomously, and of her belief that she could neither function alone nor trust others to help her. As receiving the degree became a certainty and admission to graduate school became increasingly likely, she observed, "Now would be the time for me to throw everything over and run."

We entered another period in which Susan tested the framework of our treatment, insisting that it would be easier to talk to a female therapist. I interpreted her wish to avoid facing the prospect of terminating therapy in order to go off to graduate school. She then insisted that I give her medication that would "help" if she went to graduate school in another city. I again interpreted this request as an avoidance of the choice she must soon make. When she sought and received a prescription for an antidepressant elsewhere, I confronted her with the fact that she could not be in treatment with two psychiatrists at once—particularly while she insisted on keeping the other physician unaware of my existence and ignorant of her previous psychiatric history. She stopped using the medication, but to this date has kept it "for safety" in her medicine cabinet.

When graduate school acceptances came in the spring, Susan struggled with the problem of whether to enter a program in Boston that she did not like or to accept a place in a more desirable program in San Diego. She asked me to tell her what to do but acknowledged that I could not make the decision for her. She wondered if she was ready to leave therapy, and I did too. She noted that she still had great difficulty sustaining relationships with people, particularly with men, and wondered if she would ever be less isolated. I agreed with her assessment that she could benefit from doing more work in treatment and told her that I did not know whether leaving treatment made sense at this time. I noted that whenever she decided to leave treatment, there would be unfinished business. I remarked that she must weigh her need to try out a separation from me against her need for more therapy. I was uncertain about how she would fare without the support of our therapeutic relationship, but believed that at this point I had no reason for insisting that she remain.

Susan put off her decision about graduate school until the early summer. When she chose to go on vacation with Jonathan during this period, I interpreted this as a flight from the dilemma she faced. While on vacation, she was forced to have sex with a man who had offered her a ride back to her hotel, and when she returned, she was able to wonder about her own role in provoking this incident and her wish to be a victim.

She finally decided to accept a place in the graduate program in San Diego and with great trepidation set a termination date 2 months in the future. She noted, "I'm afraid to leave therapy, because I'm afraid to be without the security." She again experienced the fear of someone coming to murder her in the night, which I interpreted as a fear of the consequences of leaving me. I recalled her dream of being a test pilot and inadvertently destroying the world.

During the final months prior to Susan's departure, she spoke with some warmth and understanding about her father's increased helpfulness, as well as about his limitations. When I pointed out the difference in her present view of him from the picture she brought with her to treatment, she noted, "I felt he was so evil, and anything good that he did made me want him to be wonderful. I loved him so intensely. I think I had to give up the intense love before I could give up the intense hatred." She began, too, to acknowledge openly that therapy had helped her and that, within limits, I had been of some use.

One month prior to Susan's departure, she became angry with me and did not know why (a quote from one of her therapy sessions):

> I don't know why, but it feels like it did when you changed your rates. I was in bad shape for a long time. The resolution came that weekend when I had no insurance and would have had to go to the state hospital. I realized the situation was what it was, and I couldn't change it. You wouldn't change. If I accepted that, then I had to accept other things, like living normally without having to show everyone how angry I was at the world. It did no good to show everyone. But at that moment I felt really alone. It was hard, because I was angry at you then, but you had also helped me. I didn't know *how* to feel, because it was confusing to hate you and to need to see you.

I suggested that she was angry about the forthcoming separation and at the realization that she and I were not tied to each other—that she could go and I would let her go. She insisted that treatment was not really ending, since she would come back to visit me once over her winter break. I countered with, "But this really is goodbye." She agreed that it was. She spent several hours demanding that I allow her to end our sessions early, "because there is nothing left to say except goodbye," and insisting that I prescribe medication for her. She acknowledged that it was easier to pick a fight with me than to be sad.

The week before we ended our meetings, she said, "I'm afraid I'll do something awful, that I'll murder someone or be indirectly responsible for someone's death. Maybe I've already killed somebody and don't know it." I related this fear to her persistent belief that she had killed her mother. I again brought up the dream of the test pilot and her fear that when she separated from important people, she and/ or they would be destroyed.

During the last month before Susan's departure, I became aware of how much I would miss working with her. Our last two sessions were warm and quite sad. In our final meeting, she recalled my comments about the two of us not being inextricably intertwined: "For the past few months, I've been seeing you as more separate." She noted that it was not so hard to leave therapy but that it was hard to leave *me*, and that it was unfair that she became so attached to me and then it had to end. I replied that she was surviving the separation and that the experience might make her more free to become attached again. She said she was not sure about that. She asked if she could call me and I replied that she could, but that it would certainly not be in her interest to rely on a long-distance relationship. At the close of the hour, she said, "So, I guess I just get up and leave now, huh?" At the door, I gave her a hug, and she walked away in silence.

Interim Year

Susan moved to San Diego with her father's help and took an apartment by herself. This was the first time she had lived alone, and she found this an enjoyable change from her previous group living situations. She quickly made several friends, whom she came to rely on for emotional support throughout the year. Her first 3 months of school were exciting, and she was enthusiastic about her work. Professors were impressed with her comments in seminars, and two teachers indicated to her that they considered her to be one of the brighter and more capable members of her large class.

Three months into the semester, I received a phone call from Susan, informing me that she was again depressed and feeling suicidal. She said that she did not intend to do anything self-destructive, but she was obviously disappointed that these feelings had returned and frightened about her ability to handle them. She was happy to hear my voice, and while she said I could do nothing to help her, she nevertheless seemed heartened by our telephone contact. She informed me that her current depression had prompted her to seek psychotherapy in the San Diego area.

I did not hear from Susan again until she returned to Boston during her winter break. She made an appointment to see me, and we spent an hour catching up. Her semester had been tumultuous. Subsequent to her phone call, she found herself increasingly unable to study efficiently. She failed to complete several of her final examinations, most notably in subjects where she had previously impressed her professors. Paradoxically, she did outstanding work in a course that required little class participation or interaction with peers or professors. She ended her first semester with a "C" average, which put her on academic probation.

In addition to making female friends, she developed relationships with three men. She seemed genuinely to enjoy their company, and some intimacy was possible without the anger and terror that had accompanied many of her previous relationships. She saw people socially virtually every day, and used these friendships both for support and to avoid facing the work situation, which was becoming more and more of a problem for her.

Susan informed me that she had begun psychotherapy three times per week with Dr. Thomas, a male psychiatric resident at an outpatient clinic in San Diego. In addition to psychotherapy, he prescribed lithium carbonate in an effort to stabilize her moods. She said that she felt like a traitor because she believed I would disapprove of her taking medication, given my refusal to prescribe it prior to her leaving Boston. I let her know that I approved of her receiving treatment, including the trial of lithium.

When Susan raised the possibility of coming back to Boston to study the next year, she asked if she could be in treatment with me again, and I agreed.

I next heard from Susan in May, when she informed me that she would be returning to Boston. She reported that during her second semester, she had been unable to study, had stopped going to classes altogether, and spent every day with classmates, drinking heavily and avoiding work. She reported enjoying herself during this time but feeling guilty and disappointed about her inactivity and what it meant in terms of her academic career.

She claimed that psychotherapy with Dr. Thomas had been of little help, except insofar as it lent some stability to her life. She described him as well-meaning but "unable to see how bad things really were." She wondered if she had been unable or unwilling to give him a clear picture of her distress. Both she and Dr. Thomas agreed that the lithium had not brought about any change in her moods. She terminated therapy, as well as the 6-month trial of lithium, when she returned to Boston.

Fifth Year of Therapy

Susan arrived in Boston and immediately wished to resume intensive treatment with me. I informed her that while I could still offer her a reduced fee, it would have to be higher than that of the previous year.

Initially, she insisted that she would have to seek treatment at an out-patient clinic. However, she eventually secured a part-time job and enlisted her father's financial support to cover my fee on a twice-weekly basis.

Course work and the part-time job occupied virtually all of Susan's time in the fall, and she managed both quite efficiently. She was puzzled by her failure to function well in San Diego, and my interpretation that this had to do with her being away from Boston and from me met with little enthusiasm, serving only to make her feel more hopeless about ever functioning more autonomously. She made some contacts with her new classmates in Boston, but did little to extend herself socially and kept her relationships superficial. She spoke of feeling that there was something about her that made other people shun her.

Once she settled into her work with me, our sessions were punctuated by her repeated insistence that twice-weekly therapy was not enough, that she no longer felt connected to me, and that we ought to stop treatment. I interpreted this as reflecting her persistent fear that she could not get what she needed from me and as a maneuver designed to elicit a holding response from me. She cited this interpretation as "proof" that she was no better and that psychotherapy had made no difference in her life. I pointed out her anger at me for not seeing her more frequently at a lower fee.

A major theme during these months was Susan's belief that I was no longer available to her when she needed me. She perceived me as moving ahead with other interests, and therefore as having less interest in her situation. I clarified her belief that autonomy and assertiveness on my part or hers were tantamount to abandonment. She was so concerned about my perceived lack of availability and involvement that she did not feel safe to do much beyond rail at me for what I was not giving her. She reported a dream in which she came to tell me that she was suicidal, but found me upset about another patient who had committed suicide, and felt she had to keep silent so as not to upset me any further. These issues were intermittently tied to her sense of responsibility for her mother's death and her father's subsequent alcoholism.

Susan feared that she would "clutch" on her examinations, as she had in San Diego. Much to her surprise, she did very well in her first-semester work and finished near the top of her class. A professor took an interest in her work and urged her to pursue specialized studies in his field. She was pleased but also afraid, feeling that her accomplishment was a burden: "Now they all expect me to perform like a normal person, and I can't sustain it." She spoke with increasing fear and anger about having to live up to her professors' expectations.

This was the prelude to 3 months of markedly impaired functioning. Susan further isolated herself from her classmates, not answering her telephone and refusing most social engagements. She found it increasingly difficult to concentrate on work and finally stopped altogether. She reached a crisis point in which she was unable to get out of bed for an entire day. She began to have thoughts of suicide, but made no particular plans and did not behave self-destructively. At the same time, she began to insist that she was going too deeply into debt, that she could no longer afford treatment with me, and that twice-weekly therapy was not helping her enough to warrant increasing her debt still further. She insisted that she would need to terminate treatment.

Because of my unacknowledged wish that she be healthy enough to function without me, I sensed a reluctance in myself to address the degree to which this regression reflected her perception of me as rejecting. Eventually, however, I began to interpret her behavior as a clear message that she was not ready to leave treatment and that she was afraid of losing me if she functioned more autonomously. I noted that she saw me as using her progress as a cause for self-congratulation and as no longer having any genuine interest in helping her. I also pointed out that she was afraid I would let her go, as I had when she went to San Diego. Immediately following these interpretations, her distress diminished; she began to study again, and her mood improved markedly. She acknowledged that she was afraid I would let her go, that she felt unable to take steps toward more independent living, and that she did not know if she would ever be able to make it on her own.

I commented on her repeated attempts to wrest herself away from me in an effort to prove to herself that she could survive on her own. I contrasted this behavior to the model with which I was operating, whereby she would gradually grow out of our therapeutic relationship at a pace with which *she* felt comfortable. This image impressed her, and she became curious about how my own life had gone until now. She wondered how I had managed to remain in the same city for many years and, at the same time, to grow out of old roles and attachments and form new ones. She wondered if she would ever be capable of such gradual transitions.

Susan now more seriously entertains the possibility of remaining in therapy for the foreseeable future. Nevertheless, she continues to struggle with her fear of being dependent on me. Our shared perception is that we have more work to do.

CASE DISCUSSION

Susan fulfills the DSM III criteria for Borderline Personality Disorder. Indeed, at the time she presented for treatment, she exhibited all of the traits cited in DSM III as diagnostic of the disorder: impulsivity, unstable intense interpersonal relationships, inappropriate and poorly controlled anger, identity disturbance, affective instability, intolerance of being alone, physically self-damaging acts, and chronic feelings of emptiness and boredom. These were enduring traits that severely impaired her ability to function in social, academic, and work settings. Moreover, she had a history of transient ego-alien psychosis that took the form of dissociative episodes.

The *differential diagnosis* in this case must include Axis I as well as Axis II disorders. Susan has a family history of alcoholism and major psychotic illness (a paternal uncle was diagnosed as schizophrenic and has been chronically dysfunctional for several decades). These conditions raise the question of a possible genetic vulnerability to an Axis I disorder. There is no doubt that she meets the criteria for Dysthymic Disorder and may fulfill the criteria for Cyclothymic Disorder as well, given her swings from depression to mild elation and increased activity.

Whether Susan meets the criteria for a major unipolar or bipolar disorder is less clear. While her history is suggestive of possible manic episodes in the past (e.g., when she went to Acapulco to work as a model, and lost weight and spent money), careful exploration revealed no striking excesses in her activity level, nor did she report pressured speech, racing thoughts, or other symptoms characteristic of full-blown mania. Her history of recurring depressions with somewhat atypical vegetative signs (early insomnia, bulimia) suggested major depressive episodes. However, these periods of depression seemed to be both context dependent and rapidly shifting. For example, she emerged from a severe depressive state over the course of 12 hours when her therapist returned from a vacation. Trials of antidepressant medication and carbamazepine were never adequate, due to Susan's sensitivity to their side effects. Her trial of lithium, though lengthy, was of no appreciable benefit in stabilizing her moods.

The differential diagnosis among Axis II disorders is less problematic. While Susan presented with pronounced histrionic features, her functioning was more impaired and she was more overtly self-destructive than would be typical of someone with a Histrionic Personality Disorder. Similarly, her entitlement, her covert grandiosity, and her difficulties in maintaining self-esteem in the absence of important others suggest profound narcissistic issues. However, her poor impulse control, her social and occupational dysfunction, and her hunger for nurturance are less typical of Narcissistic Personality Disorder than they are of Borderline Personality Disorder. Susan also exhibits some schizoid features, particularly in times of distress, but her relationships are too intense and stormy to warrant a diagnosis of either Schizoid or Schizotypal Personality Disorder.

Susan was a bright and engaging woman who brought many *strengths* to her psychotherapy. Her intelligence and curiosity about herself prompted her to search for the causes of her difficulties long before she entered treatment. She demonstrated the capacity for insight, although her use of denial impaired her ability to exercise this capacity early in treatment. She was also increasingly capable of allying with the therapist in the task of looking at her behavior. She possessed a good sense of humor and, despite very fragile self-esteem, was capable of laughing at some of her own foibles. Susan also brought adaptive obsessional defenses to her treatment, so that she was capable of a certain degree of self-discipline and organization when not overwhelmed by affect. Despite her protests to the contrary, she also brought a modicum of social support to her therapy. Her father turned out to be less unpredictable and more financially supportive of treatment than either Susan or her therapist expected him to be.

Susan's psychological difficulties at the start of treatment were considerable. She had little capacity for self-soothing and relied on binge eating, alcohol and drug abuse, and other impulsive behaviors to manage her feelings of aloneness and panic. Her sense of object constancy was tenuous, and she clearly articulated the feeling that people ceased to exist for her during times of separation from important others. She demonstrated profound lapses in judgment with respect to her own well-being. She was impaired in her ability to attend to her bodily sensations and needs. Her impulsiveness and dissociative episodes put her at significant risk of harming herself inadvertently.

Susan relied heavily on primitive defenses when she entered psychotherapy. Denial was paramount, particularly in regard to her self-destructiveness and the relationship of affect to action. Acting out was a major defense against unpleasant affect. She also used primitive idealization and devaluation. She projected unacceptable hostile and aggressive impulses onto those close to her, and she relied on manipulation to try to control others and thereby manage her fears of closeness and abandonment.

Susan's amenability to analytically oriented therapy was rated by the authors on the scales shown in Figure 7–1. She was rated highly on personable qualities, intelligence, motivation, and psychological mindedness. She was rated as having very poor impulse control and a defensive style that was quite action oriented. With respect to social and familial supports, her situation was difficult, but a modicum of support was available to her.

Susan's therapist was a warm, outgoing person who felt comfortable in a caretaking role and enjoyed feeling that he was all-important to his patient. He had a high tolerance for frustration, as well as for Susan's self-destructive threats and actions. He was less comfortable with sexual feelings (his own and Susan's) that arose in the treatment, and was

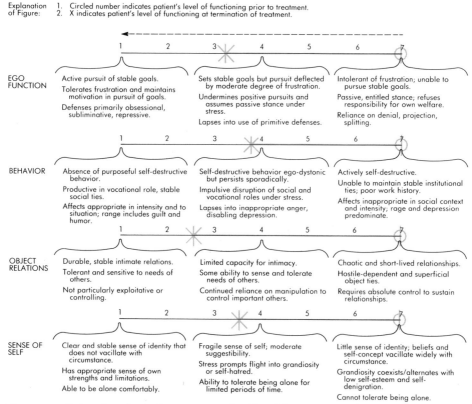

Explanation of Figure:
1. Circled number indicates patient's level of functioning prior to treatment.
2. X indicates patient's level of functioning at termination of treatment.

EGO FUNCTION

Active pursuit of stable goals.
Tolerates frustration and maintains motivation in pursuit of goals.
Defenses primarily obsessional, subliminative, repressive.

Sets stable goals but pursuit deflected by moderate degree of frustration.
Undermines positive pursuits and assumes passive stance under stress.
Lapses into use of primitive defenses.

Intolerant of frustration; unable to pursue stable goals.
Passive, entitled stance; refuses responsibility for own welfare.
Reliance on denial, projection, splitting.

BEHAVIOR

Absence of purposeful self-destructive behavior.
Productive in vocational role, stable social ties.
Affects appropriate in intensity and to situation; range includes guilt and humor.

Self-destructive behavior ego-dystonic but persists sporadically.
Impulsive disruption of social and vocational roles under stress.
Lapses into inappropriate anger, disabling depression.

Actively self-destructive.
Unable to maintain stable institutional ties; poor work history.
Affects inappropriate in social context and intensity; rage and depression predominate.

OBJECT RELATIONS

Durable, stable intimate relations.
Tolerant and sensitive to needs of others.
Not particularly exploitative or controlling.

Limited capacity for intimacy.
Some ability to sense and tolerate needs of others.
Continued reliance on manipulation to control important others.

Chaotic and short-lived relationships.
Hostile-dependent and superficial object ties.
Requires absolute control to sustain relationships.

SENSE OF SELF

Clear and stable sense of identity that does not vacillate with circumstance.
Has appropriate sense of own strengths and limitations.
Able to be alone comfortably.

Fragile sense of self; moderate suggestibility.
Stress prompts flight into grandiosity or self-hatred.
Ability to tolerate being alone for limited periods of time.

Little sense of identity; beliefs and self-concept vacillate widely with circumstance.
Grandiosity coexists/alternates with low self-esteem and self-denigration.
Cannot tolerate being alone.

FIGURE 7–1. Standards for assessing levels of functioning—baseline and outcome: Susan.

particularly uncomfortable with the aggression mobilized in this therapy. Thus, he was initially reluctant to see the hostile aspects of Susan's manipulativeness and to acknowledge his own anger at her provocative behavior. It was not until later in the treatment that he became active in interpreting her aggression and in setting limits on it. Susan's therapist shared her sense of humor, as well as a variety of interests (including a fascination with foreign cultures and travel). His academic orientation and personal values were in many respects similar to Susan's. While these similar interests were not shared overtly between patient and therapist, they undoubtedly contributed to the sense of fit between them.

Susan's *transference* must be understood in terms of both her hunger for a protective, nurturing relationship and her sense of her own badness. She felt she could not survive emotionally apart from important others, and so believed that the therapist was responsible for her very existence (a belief she attempted to test repeatedly with self-destructive threats and behaviors). She also harbored the fantasy that she was responsible for her mother's death and her father's alcoholism. Her sense of herself as being "toxic" to others exerted a profound effect on her relationship to the therapist. She felt as though she were living on borrowed time, and that her badness would inevitably be discovered by the therapist and result in his abandoning her. Moreover, she was beset by the fear that this toxic quality would hurt those whom she cared about, and so it was dangerous for her to get close to the therapist. She projected her sadism and hostility onto the therapist, so that closeness threatened her safety as well.

Hence, Susan's need–fear dilemma. Distance from the therapist threatened her with aloneness and psychological annihilation, while closeness threatened to destroy the therapist if he did not destroy her first. This dilemma was largely responsible for her chronic dysphoria in the therapy relationship for the first several years of treatment. She attempted to solve this problem by vigorously manipulating the relationship in an effort to balance closeness and distance. She projected her sense of helplessness onto the therapist, whom she devalued and saw as having nothing to offer. At the same time, however, she made the therapist feel all-important in her life. While negative transference predominated in the early years of treatment, positive transference was clearly present and no doubt sustained both Susan and her therapist.

The therapist's *countertransference* meshed with Susan's transference in many respects. The therapist had a sense that Susan was special among his patients, and that she somehow had the ability to "get inside" him and know him as none of his other patients had. Susan's attempts to shift the responsibility for her life to the therapist were unconsciously accepted by the therapist early in treatment, as he wished to take care of her and felt it his obligation to keep her safe. Moreover, the therapist was genuinely concerned about how much he could help Susan, and so felt increasingly guilty in the face of her devaluation and her belittling of his efforts to be helpful. This guilt undoubtedly interfered with his recognition of the aggressive aspects of Susan's behavior toward him (e.g., her failure to pay her bill) and inhibited him from setting limits on it.

The therapist's *technique* was based on a model of Susan's psychopathology that shifted over the course of treatment. Initially, he thought of her as primarily suffering from deficits of holding/soothing introjects (à la Buie and Adler), and saw himself as providing a holding environment in which she could gradually develop more stable, positive images of caring others. He also saw the etiology of her difficulties as rooted primarily in poor and inconsistent parenting. His model shifted gradually to include psychological conflict (such as the need–fear dilemma described above), and looked more closely at Susan's role in creating her difficulties through distortion of her relationships with primary caretakers (e.g., her distorted picture of her father as completely unreliable and unavailable). With this shift, the therapist relied more on interpretation of conflict than he had previously, and pointed out Susan's contribution to her pathologic relationships with important others.

The initial work of treatment was almost entirely focused on the management of the here-and-now. The therapist made vigorous efforts to link behavior to affects, and worked to focus Susan's attention on the self-destructive and impulsive aspects of her acting-out behaviors, which she so adamantly denied. Much of the work of the first 3 years of treatment focused on the management of boundaries—those of the therapeutic relationship and, by extension, those of Susan's other relationships. The struggles over appointment times, fees, and contacts beyond the prescribed treatment hours were all played out in the service of establishing the reality of Susan's separateness from the therapist. When Susan's challenges to these boundaries seriously threatened the therapy, the therapist enlisted a variety of supports, including her father (primarily for financial help) and the hospital.

Hospitalization played a central role in this case and was used for different purposes at different times. The initial hospitalization was probably essential in establishing enough of a relationship between Susan and her therapist to allow her to continue in treatment on an outpatient basis despite her intense fear of closeness. Hospitalization was subsequently used to help protect the boundaries of the therapeutic relationship, usually at times when Susan's efforts to control the therapist through self-destructive behavior threatened to overwhelm both of them. Her last hospitalization was used by the therapist as a safe place in which to change his therapeutic stance and begin interpreting the aggressive and hostile aspects of her manipulative behavior toward him.

Throughout much of the treatment, the therapist attempted to resist Susan's efforts to make him responsible for her life. Thus, he asked her to determine how she could keep herself safe during times of crisis and reminded her that suicide was always her option. Such interventions did little to ameliorate her self-destructiveness. The therapist did not address the *process* of her trying to hold him responsible for her safety until late in the treatment (after her last hospitalization), and it was at the time of this shift in therapeutic technique that her self-destructiveness diminished significantly.

Early in treatment, the therapist emphasized and worked with Susan's positive transference. He interpreted her acting out as based on her longings for holding and soothing, and focused primarily on her sadness and aloneness at times when she behaved impulsively and self-destructively. For example, he interpreted her efforts to drown herself as based on her fear of abandonment by the therapist, and did not emphasize her anger at him or her wish to control him. In this respect, his technique was similar to that of Martha's and Jennifer's therapists.

The therapist paid some attention to the relationship between Susan's present behavior and her past, but this was not the major focus of the therapeutic work (as it was, for example, in Jennifer's therapy). The therapist attended primarily to Susan's current life situation and her behavior in the treatment. In particular, he tried to help Susan knit together her fragmented sense of self, emphasizing the reality of both Susan's higher-functioning self and her depressed and dysfunctional self. This attempt to enlist her observing ego met with little success, and she continued to experience alternate ego states well into the treatment. However, her self-observing capacities were enlisted more effectively in looking at manipulative behavior, as when the therapist began to call her attention to such maneuvers as bringing up suicidal thoughts at the end of the therapy hour.

Certainly, the most salient feature of the therapist's technique was the shift in the way he handled his own and Susan's aggression. This shift occurred midway through her treatment. He moved from paying little attention to the aggression involved in her "helplessness" to actively interpreting her loss of function as a move to control him and exact a "saving" response from him. He shifted from essentially ignoring her hostility and sadism to making it clear that he saw, understood, and accepted these aspects of her character. Suicide threats were interpreted as power plays. These interventions met with two reactions: shame and relief. Susan was obviously embarrassed by the open discussion of these forbidden impulses, but she was also reassured by the therapist's recognition of and ability to confront her badness.

This shift was manifested in increased limit setting and more precise adherence to the boundaries of the therapeutic relationship. For example, Susan's attempts to squeeze extra minutes out of the therapy sessions with threats of self-destruction were interpreted rather than gratified. Telephone calls were met by the therapist with questions about what she hoped to gain from such contacts. These interventions quickly produced a diminution in her requests for extra contact. They also brought her negative transference more directly into the treatment.

Concurrent with this shift was the therapist's new willingness to acknowledge and talk about Susan's effect on him. He shared with her the fact that when she made him anxious about her welfare, he might do things that were not in her interest. She was visibly shaken by this realization, which seemed to alter the course of the therapy. In particular, this type of intervention seemed to help her move out of the position of victim and rely less on projection of her hostility and helplessness onto the therapist. The therapist's admission of fallibility and susceptibility to manipulation startled Susan and made it increasingly impossible for her to abrogate responsibility for her welfare to him.

Susan made considerable gains during the course of treatment. In the holding environment created by the therapist, she developed a keener sense of her own separateness and of the boundaries between herself and those to whom she became attached. Her primitive defenses—most notably projection, denial, and externalization—gave way, to some extent, to higher-level coping mechanisms. In particular, she learned to mobilize obsessional defenses, to anticipate, and to delay gratification in order to pursue career goals appropriate to her intellectual abilities. She developed a greater capacity to observe and evaluate her own intrapsychic processes.

The shift in Susan's object relationships that occurred in the third year of treatment was particularly striking. Her capacity to tolerate ambivalence increased markedly, as was evident in her development of less stereotyped views of her father and her therapist. This shift in her view of others was reflected in a growing ability to tolerate frustration in interpersonal relationships and thus to sustain close friendships longer than had been possible at the start of treatment. Moreover, her sense of herself shifted, so that she now more openly identified and acknowledged her aggression, and saw herself as more active and autonomous in interpersonal relationships. The therapist's attempts to interpret splitting and to knit together her alternate ego states seemed to be of less value than experiential factors in helping Susan to consolidate her sense of self.

The authors rated Susan's level of functioning before treatment and at the end of year 5 on four separate scales; the results are shown in Figure 7–2. She received the lowest possible pretreatment scores on each of the four scales of ego functioning, behavior, object relations, and sense of self. We assessed her as having made considerable gains in all areas by the end of the fifth year of treatment, particularly in the area of object relations.

One important question is highlighted by this case material: To what extent is it therapeutic to gratify the transference wishes of the borderline patient early in treatment? Susan's therapist actualized many of her transference wishes in the beginning phase of therapy (e.g., complying with her covert demands for extra time and attention, allowing her to neglect payment of her bill). It may be argued that this gratification was necessary to foster an attachment, and that vigorous limit setting and interpretation of Susan's aggression early in therapy would have prompted her to flee treatment. However, it might also be argued that the therapist's gratifying behavior and his failure to

	Unfavorable									Favorable
1. Friendliness	−5	−4	−3	−2	−1	1	2	3	4	5
			hostile					amiable		
2. Likeability	−5	−4	−3	−2	−1	1	2	3	4	5
			below average				above average			
3. Intelligence	−5	−4	−3	−2	−1	1	2	3	4	5
			below average				above average			
4. Motivation	−5	−4	−3	−2	−1	1	2	3	4	5
			indifferent				motivated			
5. Psychological-mindedness	−5	−4	−3	−2	−1	1	2	3	4	5
			low				high			
6. Conscience factors	−5	−4	−3	−2	−1	1	2	3	4	5
		antisocial; deceitful; vengeful				values; good moral sense				
7. Self-discipline	−5	−4	−3	−2	−1	1	2	3	4	5
		low; chaotic				high				
8. Impulse control	−5	−4	−3	−2	−1	1	2	3	4	5
		craving; impulsivity				high				
9. Defensive style	−5	−4	−3	−2	−1	1	2	3	4	5
		drugs; action				intropunitive				
10. Externalization/Internalization	−5	−4	−3	−2	−1	1	2	3	4	5
		paranoid				capacity to admit fault				
11. Empathy/Narcissism	−5	−4	−3	−2	−1	1	2	3	4	5
		contempt; entitlement				ability to care about and resonate with others				
12. Parental factors	−5	−4	−3	−2	−1	1	2	3	4	5
		brutalization, exploitation, indifference				warmth, support				
13. Social supports	−5	−4	−3	−2	−1	1	2	3	4	5
		absent-disruptive				stable				

FIGURE 7–2. Amenability to psychotherapy: Susan. [Adapted from Stone's Amenability for Analytically Oriented Therapy Scale (Stone, 1985)].

address her transference demands openly in the early days of treatment increased Susan's anxiety and prompted more prolonged self-destructive behavior than might otherwise have occurred.

Much work was left undone at the time this case report was written. Susan's profound sense of shame and defectiveness at being female remained largely unexplored, as did her sense of having caused her mother's death. Sexual issues were, for the most part, untouched. Finally, there is the fact that this treatment has not yet terminated. How lasting her gains will be when psychotherapy has ended remains an open question.

Nevertheless, during the course of therapy, Susan moved from a position of chronic social and occupational dysfunction to improved role performance that comes much closer to utilizing her full capabilities. She learned to experience herself as more complex and more autonomous than she did when she entered treatment, and she began to develop a greater mutuality in relationships with others.

8

Diagnostic and Prognostic Considerations

The large and growing literature on psychotherapy with borderline patients is derived almost exclusively from the observations of individual practitioners on patients in their own practices. Therefore, the existing principles of practice, expectations of change, and understanding of the process of change are inextricably tied to the limited clinical samples of these authors. The fact that generalizing from such limited and necessarily idiosyncratic samples can be misleading is clearly attested to by the literature on the psychotherapy of borderline patients.

A major difficulty in evaluating the literature on the psychotherapy of borderline patients stems from the fact that authors use the "borderline" label to describe a wide variety of patients. Masterson's work provides an example of this problem. His early work on adolescents is derived from samples of patients who would be largely identifiable as borderline by modern criteria. Yet in his later work (Masterson, 1976), his case reports describe patients who are much less functionally impaired than those in his previous samples. Moreover, he advocates a more central role for interpretation in the psychotherapeutic treatment of his later patients. Masterson now uses the borderline category to indicate the presence of severe separation problems. As a result, his "borderline" patients cover a broad range of health to sickness. While patients with healthier ego functioning may still have severe separation problems, the interpretive techniques he recommends for their treatment are radically different from those he uses with patients whose abandonment conflicts are combined with major deficits in such ego functions as the capacity to delay, the ability to use repression, and the achievement of object constancy. With this latter group, Masterson himself would argue against the use of interpretation and would emphasize the need for considerable structuring, support, and confrontation both inside and outside the therapy.

An even more radical example of a confusing use of the term "borderline" can be found in the book by Abend et al. (1983). These authors report four patients treated with classical psychoanalysis, all of whom were functioning adults who had successfully completed prior psychotherapy. The authors not only argue for the applicability of psychoanalysis to borderline cases but also, not surprisingly, argue that others have overlooked major oedipal components in borderline psychopathology. The circularity of their argument is obvious. Even cursory inspection of their cases shows that, at most, only one approaches an identifiable borderline syndrome by any modern diagnostic standard.

Elsewhere in the literature, patients described in case reports by both Chessick (1982) and Adler (1981), although closer to being borderline by the usual standards, were both well-functioning adult women with intact career aspirations and some stability in their relationships. Thus, here too, questions can be raised about the applicability of the psychotherapeutic techniques advocated by these authors to the impulse-ridden, dysfunctional borderline patient for whom the DSM-III diagnosis is usually intended.

The cases reported in this book come closer to representing a homogeneous and easily identifiable borderline sample. Finding patients who fit the common usage of the borderline diagnosis and who had successful outcomes that could be related to the processes of a relatively intensive psychoanalytic therapy proved to be difficult. Despite the enormous amount of clinical experience among our colleagues in working with such borderline patients, it was only the exceptional patient who went on to achieve a satisfactory outcome that could be related to ongoing, long-term psychotherapy. In addition to these two prerequisites, a variety of other factors ruled out viable candidates, such as (1) a therapist's wish to discuss this project with a patient who was unwilling or currently unavailable, (2) the presence of a major concurrent treatment (such as couples therapy), which would make it difficult to isolate the effects of individual psychotherapy, (3) the fact that a patient continued in or resumed intensive therapy elsewhere shortly after the "termination," (4) special problems of maintaining a patient's anonymity, or (5) a therapist's reluctance to undertake extensive writing of the report. Still, the conclusion is inescapable that such good-outcome cases are unusual, and few clinicians can point to more than one or two in their practices despite many years of experience.

Diagnostic Ratings

Diagnostic ratings on the case reports were made retrospectively by the authors, using two different methods. The first method is a retrospective form of the Diagnostic Interview for Borderlines (DIB) (Gunderson et al., 1981), which has been adapted and developed for

TABLE 8–1

Diagnostic Interview for Borderlines: Retrospective (DIB-R) Criteria

	Susan	Jennifer	Stewart	Ann	Martha
I. Social adaptation (2-year framework)					
1. School/work achievement: lack of stability in work/school during past 2 years	2	1	1	2	2
2. Special abilities/talent: areas or periods of special achievement effectiveness	2	1	2	1	0
3. Sociable: active social life involving groups of people	1	0	0	2	1
4. Appearance/manner: generally appears appropriate and conventional in a group of socioeconomic peers	2	2	1	2	2
Section Total	7	4	4	7	5
Scaled Total	2	2	2	2	2
(If Section Total Score ≥4, score 2; 2–3, score 1; ≤1, score 0)					
II. Impulse/action patterns (2-year framework)					
5. Self-mutilation: slashed his/her wrist or otherwise mutilated self	1	0	2	2	0
6. Manipulative suicide: any suicide attempt, threat, or gesture made when someone probably would know of the effort (i.e., designed to effect a saving response; can include wrist slashing)	0	2	0	0	2
7. Drug abuse: pattern of serious drug or alcohol abuse	0	0	0	0	2
8. Sexual deviance: pattern of promiscuity, homosexuality, or repetitive sexually deviant practices	2	2	0	0	2
9. Other impulsive pattern (e.g., running away, assaults, trouble with the law)	2	1	1	0	0
Section Total	5	5	3	2	6
Scaled Total	1	1	1	0	2
(If Section Total Score ≥6, score 2; 3–5, score 1; 0–2, score 0)					

III. Affects (3-month framework)

10. Depression: appears depressed or reports recent or chronic depression	2	2	0	2	2
11. Hostility: angry, hot-tempered, or sarcastic	0	2	2	2	0
12. Demanding/entitled	0	2	2	2	1
13. Dysphoria/anhedonia: complains of emptiness, loneliness, boredom, or anhedonia	2	2	2	2	2
14. Flat or elated affect[a]	0	0	0	0	0
Section Total	4	8	4	8	5
Scaled Total	1	2	2	2	2

(If Section Total Score ≥5, score 2; 4, score 2 (only if patient is angry and depressed); if 3–4 (other than above), score 1; 0–2, score 0)

IV. Psychosis* (3-month framework, except as noted)

15. Derealization: things are unreal, changing shape, separated by windows	0	0	2	0	1
16. Depersonalization: feels unreal, outside self	0	2	2	0	2
17. Depressive: drug-free, brief psychotic depressed experiences	1	0	0	0	1
18. Paranoid: drug-free, brief paranoid experiences	0	0	0	0	0
19. Drug-induced: any psychotic experiences while taking marijuana or alcohol or persisting psychosis after using	0	0	2	2	0
20. Hallucinations/delusions[a]: drug-free hallucinations, nihilistic delusions, grandiose delusions, or bizarre delusions	0	0	0	0	0
21. Mania/widespread delusions[a,b]: any manic episodes or periods of persistent, widespread delusions or hallucinations[b]	0	0	0	0	0
22. Past regressions[b]: any transient psychotic experiences that developed in psychotherapy or a clear behavioral regression during prior hospitalizations[b]	0	0	0	0	0
Section Total	1	4	6	2	4
Scaled Total	0	2	2	1	2

(If Section Total Score ≥4, score 2; if 2–3, score 1; if 0–1*, score 0*)

*If there are psychotic experiences that are well organized, stable, enduring, or widespread, the scaled score in this section is automatically 0.

(Continued)

169

TABLE 8–1 (Continued)

	Martha	Ann	Stewart	Jennifer	Susan
V. Interpersonal relations (2-year framework, except as noted)					
23. Aloneness: almost always with people or actively avoids being alone	1	2	0	1	1
24. Isolation[a]: socially isolated: a loner	0	0	−2	−1	−1
25. Anaclitic: actively seeks a relationship that involves taking care of others (e.g., nurse, veterinarian, housekeeper) or is in active conflict about giving and receiving care	2	2	1	2	2
26. Instability: forms intense, unstable one-to-one relationships (i.e., stormy relationships with hostile/dependent features)	2	1	1	2	2
27. Devaluation/manipulation: devaluation, manipulation, and hostility recur in close relationships	2	2	1	2	2
28. Dependency/masochism: dependency and masochism recur in close relationships	2	2	1	2	1
29. Past therapy[b]: ever involved staff splitting, formed special relationships, or evoked noteworthy countertransference problems by a therapist	0	2	0	0	0
Section Total	9	11	2	8	7
(If Section Total Score ≥6, score 2; if 3–5, score 1; if 0–2, score 0) Scaled Total	2	2	0	2	2
TOTAL SCORE	8	8	7	9	10

[a] Characteristic discriminates against the diagnosis of borderline.

[b] Score based on whether the patient has *ever* had these symptoms in the past.

Sources: Gunderson, J.G.; Kolb, J.E.; and Austin, V.: The diagnostic interview for borderline patients. *Am. J. Psychiatry,* **138**:896–903, 1981. Armelius, B.; Kullgren, G.; and Renberg, E.: Borderline diagnosis from hospital records, reliability and validity of Gunderson's Diagnostic Interview for Borderlines (DIB). *J. Nerv. Ment. Dis.,* **173**:32–34, 1985.

making borderline diagnoses from charts. The DIB-R has been used in prior research (Gunderson et al., 1980; McGlashan, 1983, 1984) and has been found to be reliable (Armelius et al., 1985). Using the established cutoff of 7 (out of a possible total score of 10), all five patients scored in the borderline range, as shown in Table 8–1. Those sections of the DIB that are diagnostically most important are the interpersonal relations and impulse/action patterns. With the exception of Stewart, all of the patients scored highly on interpersonal relations, whereas in the impulse/action patterns, there was a somewhat reduced profile. All five patients generally scored quite highly in the other remaining sections.

The second method for establishing a borderline diagnosis consisted in applying the eight DSM-III criteria for Borderline Personality Disorder to the case reports. The patients in our group exhibited between five and eight criteria from this list; at least four out of the five scored positively on every criterion except impulsivity (see Table 8–2). This again suggests that our sample had a somewhat lower level of impulsivity than could be found in other samples of borderline patients. By DSM-III criteria, Ann had the lowest score (5 out of 8). Susan scored highest, fulfilling all criteria for the DSM-III, as she also did on the DIB-R.

Although the patterns and types varied, all five patients had serious difficulties with impulsive action. Susan, Jennifer, and Martha were more severely impulse ridden than Stewart or Ann. All patients except Jennifer had been involved in self-damaging acts including suicide attempts, gestures, threats, and/or self-mutilation. Even Jennifer was involved in suicidal rumination and threats.

All five patients expressed a broad range of subjectively and interpersonally unpleasant affects. Four of them complained of depression, and two were considered clinically depressed to the extent that antidepressant medications were employed. At the time of presentation, the two who were clinically depressed (Martha and Susan) did not manifest the problem of controlling their temper that was apparent in the other three. In retrospect, though, all five patients had a history of extreme anger and poorly controlled hostility. All five had longstanding, chronic feelings of tension, boredom, emptiness, loneliness, or anhedonia. None of them had periods of elation or hyperactivity that would have raised diagnostic questions of cyclothymia.

Three of the five patients had dissociative experiences prior to the beginning of treatment. Curiously, the other two (Jennifer and Martha) developed transferences in the course treatment that were thought to have a psychotic or near-psychotic quality. This observation suggests that the borderline diagnostic category, when properly applied, may be useful in predicting vulnerability to such reality distortions in treatment.

TABLE 8–2
DSM-III Criteria

	Susan	Jennifer	Stewart	Ann	Martha
1. Impulsivity or unpredictability in at least two areas that are potentially self-damaging (e.g., spending money, sex, gambling, substance abuse, shoplifting, overeating, physically self-damaging acts)	X				X
2. A pattern of unstable and intense interpersonal relationships (e.g., marked shifts of attitude, idealization, devaluation, manipulation)	X	X	X		X
3. Inappropriate, intense anger or lack of control of anger (e.g., frequent displays of temper, constant anger)	X	X	X	X	
4. Identity disturbance manifested by uncertainty about several issues relating to identity, such as self-image, gender, identity, long-term goals or career choice, friendship patterns, values and loyalties (e.g., "Who am I?", "I feel like I am my sister when I am good.")			X	X	
5. Affective instability: marked shifts from normal mood to depression, irritability, or anxiety, usually lasting for a few hours and only rarely for more than a few days, with a return to one's normal mood	X		X	X	X
6. Intolerance of being alone (e.g. frantic efforts to avoid being alone, depressed when alone)	X	X		X	X
7. Physically self-damaging acts (e.g., suicidal gestures, self-mutilation, recurrent accidents or physical fights)	X	X	X	X	X
8. Chronic feelings of emptiness or boredom	X	X	X	X	X

172

The interpersonal relationships of these five patients were all marked by intolerance of aloneness, dependency, devaluation, and manipulation. These characteristics resulted in relationships that were unstable and turbulent. Certainly, the severe separation/abandonment concerns that are central to Masterson's use of the borderline category were present and became core issues in the subsequent therapies.

Finally, all five patients had dropped out of school and/or were unemployed when their treatment began. Moreover, these role dysfunctions were clearly secondary to their personality problems rather than vice versa.

Prognostic Considerations

Although all five patients met the standard criteria for Borderline Personality Disorder, there were also many differences. Some of these variations may have significantly affected their prognosis in general and their responsivity to psychotherapy in particular. Existing evidence suggests that the subgroup of borderline patients who remain in treatment will be less symptomatically disturbed at baseline than those who do not remain in treatment (Masterson and Costello, 1980; Skodal et al., 1983; Lynch and Gunderson, unpublished). Other evidence suggests that the borderline patients with better outcomes are those who were healthier at baseline (Masterson and Costello, 1980; Waldinger and Gunderson, 1984; Wallerstein, 1983; McGlashan, 1985). As noted, the diagnostic information presented in Tables 8–1 and 8–2 suggests only that our group of five patients may have been somewhat less impulsive, especially with regard to drug abuse or antisocial activities, than other DSM III/DIB-defined borderline samples might be. These features, however, might be expected to bear upon the aptitude for remaining in and learning from psychoanalytic psychotherapy.

McGlashan's Predictors of Outcome

McGlashan (1985) has recently identified baseline characteristics of a borderline sample (similarly identified by the DIB-R) that were predictive of a good long-term outcome. Although his study does not allow the effects of extensive hospital and psychotherapeutic treatments to be separated from the natural course of the borderline patient's illness, it does provide the first thoughtful investigation in this area.

McGlashan found that the three most important predictors of a good outcome were high intelligence, chronic dysphoria (absence of affective instability), and relatively few prior hospitalizations. Clearly, the five patients in this sample were well above average in intelligence. Despite being unemployed, they had all at least entered college and were perceived to be bright by their therapists. With respect to affect, all of them had chronic emptiness and loneliness, as well as hostility and depression. Only Susan had a history of elation, which McGlashan also found to be predictive of a better outcome. With respect to McGlashan's third predictor, none of these patients had prior psychiatric hospitalizations. On the other hand, three of the five (Jennifer, Stewart, and Susan) had had previous psychotherapy. Hence, of McGlashan's three general predictors, our sample conforms to two (intelligence and few prior hospitalizations) but not particularly to the third.

Four other less important predictors of a good outcome in McGlashan's study were (1) being male, (2) prior heterosexual functioning, (3) absence of alcohol abuse in the family, and (4) absence of devaluative and manipulative features in the patient's relationships. Although the meaning of the association between male gender and better outcome is unclear, our sample was nearly representative of the usual gender distribution patterns of borderline patients (c.f. Gunderson and Kolb, 1978; Sheehy et al., 1980; Kroll et al., 1981). With respect to alcohol abuse in the family, this was clearly present in three of our five (Susan, Jennifer, and Martha). These same three patients may, on the other hand, have been positively influenced by having a history of significant heterosexual involvement, which was not apparent for the other two. On the fourth variable in this list, all five patients were judged to use devaluation and manipulation in their interpersonal relations. In summary, then, by these four variables, our five patients might be considered cross-sectional in terms of expected outcomes.

Stone's Amenability to Psychotherapy Ratings

Stone (1985) has recently outlined 11 characteristics that he believes identify borderline patients as good or poor candidates for psychoanalytically oriented therapy (see Figure 8–1). Modifications were made in four of Stone's original 11 variables (numbers 1, 6, 10, and 13) so that the labels more precisely reflect the content of the scales. One scale (number 5, Genuine Concern) was dropped because it tapped several different dimensions. Finally, as illustrated in our earlier case report discussions, we added three new scales on social supports, intelligence, and likeability (see Figure 8–2). We found that of the 65 independent ratings done on our 13 amenability scales, there was agreement within 2 points on the 10-point scales in 53 instances. On the 12 ratings with a greater than 2-point gap, the differences were discussed and a consensus reached.

The comparative profiles on our five patients with respect to amenability factors are shown in Figure 8–2. In general, these patients scored highly on the initial variables that reflect both amiability (1

	Unfavorable	Favorable
1. Characteristic defensive style	alloplastic	autoplastic
2. Likeableness	−5 −4 −3 −2 −1 hostile	1 2 3 4 5 amiable
3. Motivation	−5 −4 −3 −2 −1 indifferent	1 2 3 4 5 motivated
4. Psychological-mindedness	−5 −4 −3 −2 −1 low	1 2 3 4 5 high
5. Genuine concern	−5 −4 −3 −2 −1 denial; disdain	1 2 3 4 5 genuine concern
6. Conscience factors	−5 −4 −3 −2 −1 antisocial; deceitful vengeful	1 2 3 4 5 values; good moral sense
7. Self-discipline	−5 −4 −3 −2 −1 low; chaotic	1 2 3 4 5 high
8. Impulse control	−5 −4 −3 −2 −1 craving; impulsivity	1 2 3 4 5 self-control
9. Externalization/ Internalization	−5 −4 −3 −2 −1 paranoid	1 2 3 4 5 capacity to admit fault
10. Empathy/Narcissism	−5 −4 −3 −2 −1 contempt; entitlement	1 2 3 4 5 ability to care about and resonate with others
11. Family factors	−5 −4 −3 −2 −1 parental brutalization, exploitation, indifference	1 2 3 4 5 warm, supportive
	−5 −4 −3 −2 −1	1 2 3 4 5

FIGURE 8–1.   Rating scale for amenability to analytically oriented psychotherapy (Stone, 1985).

and 2) and aptitude for psychotherapy (3–6). A notable exception was Ann's lack of introspectiveness. Our patients scored unfavorably on variables reflecting their psychopathology, that is, those that rated their tendency to internalize rather than act out painful affects and situations (variables 6–11). Here, an exception was Stewart, who was less impulse ridden even though he was the most likely to externalize. There was considerable variation on the variables related to supports (12 and 13).

In this latter respect, all five patients had a history of chronically unsatisfactory relationships with both parents, despite persisting strains of emotional and/or financial dependency. Four patients were estranged from their parents; one, Ann, lived at home. Another, Jennifer, was married throughout her treatment. These supports for Ann and Jennifer seemed important in diminishing their need for institutional care. Only Stewart and Ann had consistent, albeit disturbed, relationships with their biologic parents throughout development. Martha, Jennifer, and Susan had lost parents, with no replacement for the mother in Susan's case or for the father in Martha's case. Jennifer's relationship to her stepfather was stably present but disturbed by incest.

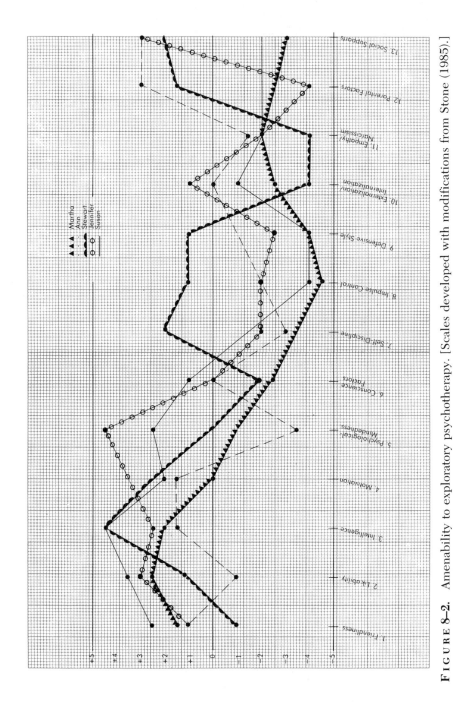

FIGURE 8-2. Amenability to exploratory psychotherapy. [Scales developed with modifications from Stone (1985).]

One characteristic not included in the work of McGlashan or Stone concerns the personality styles of the five patients. It was our impression that the diagnoses of these patients would overlap with other Axis II diagnoses in varying ways. None of the patients could be considered significantly antisocial or schizotypal—both personality types that might have a detrimental effect on therapeutic responsivity (Kernberg, 1967; Stone, 1985). Both Stewart and Martha evidenced strong narcissistic features, with a conviction of their specialness and entitlement. Martha, Susan, and Jennifer were quite histrionic in their use of helplessness to evoke protective care from males and in their use of their sexual attractiveness. More unique were the impressive masochism of Martha, the dependent infantilism of Ann, and the strong paranoid trend seen in Stewart. According to Kernberg (1967, 1975), the masochistic, dependent, and histrionic features indicate a positive prognosis, whereas paranoia is a negative sign. In Kernberg's view, narcissistic qualities are quite variable in their prognostic significance.

Summary

This chapter has examined the diagnostic and prognostic characteristics of this sample of patients. With respect to their diagnostic characteristics, it was clear that all five patients meet the standard DSM-III criteria for the borderline diagnosis. Hence, this sample improves on previous reports of psychotherapies by introducing relatively clear definitions and some boundaries that ensure minimal homogeneity. It is also apparent, however, that the patients differed in a number of ways. Descriptive differences were outlined, and it seemed generally true that this sample of five patients was less impulse ridden than other samples of borderline patients.

A further investigation of these five patients was made to identify features that might have general prognostic significance and, more particularly, features that might affect their ability to utilize the type of psychotherapy provided. These issues address the question of how generalizable the conclusions about psychotherapeutic prospects from our five case reports are with respect to other borderline patients. We used two recent efforts to provide a framework by which to investigate these issues. Among the predictors of outcome identified by McGlashan, these patients clearly had the advantages of high intelligence and little previous hospitalization. In other respects, however, such as their affective profiles, heavy use of devaluation and manipulation, family histories including alcoholism, and even being predominantly female, this sample appeared to be quite representative of a broad prognostic constituency of borderline patients.

With respect to Stone's amenability to exploratory psychotherapy variables, these patients scored generally high in likeability and motivation but generally low in terms of their defensive styles (tendency to externalize, lack of empathy for others, etc.). As a group, they appeared to show a complex mixture of high and low scores on features that might affect their amenability to psychotherapy. This finding, like the prognostic considerations, suggests that results from these five patients might be generalizable to a broader sample of borderline patients.

Finally, we noted that although all five patients would be considered borderline, they had some significant crossovers in terms of character style that included histrionic, infantile, narcissistic, and paranoid traits but no strong schizotypal or antisocial traits.

These considerations of descriptive and prognostic factors are noted without any strong convictions about which of them indicate a successful outcome for exploratory psychotherapy. They provide a method of approach and help to establish a precedent for future studies. In the long run, we hope that these methods will yield information that clinicians can use in assessing candidates for psychotherapy.

9

Patterns of Change

This chapter attempts to review systematically the patterns of change that were observed in all five patients on both a year-by-year basis and in terms of the overall sequence of change. We attempt to do this without looking concurrently at the patterns of intervention employed by the therapists in order to isolate issues of change that may be tied to developmental aspects of borderline psychopathology and to isolate the data on change from our clinical prejudices by which we inevitably tend to explain these changes.

There is a prior literature in which therapists have attempted to delineate phases or patterns of change with borderline patients based on their clinical experience (Masterson, 1976; Volkan, in press; Gunderson, 1984). Our investigation differs from these reports because it examines cases drawn from five different therapists, utilizes systematic ratings, and relies only upon a well-defined borderline sample that achieved good outcomes. It is our expectation, however, that the description of these patterns of change can also be applied to the many borderline patients who do not achieve good outcomes. Moreover, delineation of such sequence and time frameworks for change can provide a guide for researchers in selecting assessment instruments and for clinicians in assessing whether progress is being made.

Change Indices

Table 9–1 lists 51 variables that we have gleaned from the literature and from clinical experience, and that we consider to be potentially useful markers of change over the course of long-term, exploratory therapy with borderline patients.*

The first group of change indices listed in Table 9–1 (Section I) consists of action patterns characteristic of borderline patients. These are arranged hierarchically in terms of severity and in terms of their potentially damaging effects upon both the patient's life and the continuation of psychotherapy. Although the variety of action behaviors

---

*The numbers in the columns refer to years in psychotherapeutic treatment.

TABLE 9-1
Change Indices

	Martha	Ann	Stewart	Jennifer	Susan
I. ACTING OUT					
A. Life-Endangering Actions					
1. Suicidal acts	1–3*		(1)	1	1–3
2. Self-mutilation	1–3				1–3
3. Substance abuse	1–4		3		
4. Reckless driving			4		
5. Promiscuity	1–3		3	1,2	
6. Fights				1–3	
7. Eating disorders (anorexia, bulimia)	1–4				1–5
B. "Testing" Behaviors					
8. Self-destructive threats	1–4	1,3	1	1–4	1–3,5
9. Threats to leave therapy		1	1,2,4	5	1–5
10. Unscheduled contacts (phone calls, visits)	1–3	1–3		1–3,5	1–3
11. Absences (missed sessions, excessive travel)	1			1,3,5,6	1,2
12. Payment conflicts			2–4	1	1
13. Schedule conflicts			2–4	1	
C. Acting "In"					
14. Lying	?1	1	1		
15. Withholding	?1	1			
16. Silences		1	2,4	1,2,5	
17. Lateness/refusal to leave		2	1,4	4	1,2
18. Seductiveness		1		1,2	2
19. Other (posturing, positioning, eating, etc.)	3	1	1,2		

II. SEPARATION RESPONSES

20. Flight/action	1-3	1-3	1	1-4	1-2
21. Replaces therapist (interim therapist, moves into holding unit, new relationship)	5→	4→	2,3	1	1-4
22. Anxiety	3→	4	3→	1-3	1→
23. Intensely emotional (anger/depression)	5→		5	1-5	
24. Tolerates being along				5→	

SOCIAL ROLES

A. Work

25. Steady work	3→	2	2→	1→	2→
26. Career (future) oriented	4→	5→	4→	5→	3→

B. Relationships

27. Nonsexual, nonpatient friends	6→	2	5→	3→	4→
28. Sexual relations, mutual, caring	5→	5→		6	

III. AFFECTS

29. Depressed	1-3		1→	1,2	1-5
30. Anxious	1-4	1	5	1-4	
31. Guilty/concerned			3,5	3,5	4→
32. Humor	5→	4→	4	5→	3→
33. Envious					
34. Angry	1-3	2-3	1-4	1-4	

IV. RELATIONSHIP TO THERAPIST

35. Suspicious/distrustful			1-3	1,2	1-4
36. Devaluative/blaming		1	1-4	1	
37. Idealized therapy/therapist	1→	1→		1	

(Continued)

181

TABLE 9–1 (Continued)

	Martha	Ann	Stewart	Jennifer	Susan
38. Directly expressed hostility	4→		2–4	2–4	2–3
39. "Owns" sadism	4→		4→	3,5→	3→
40. Defiant/demanding	1–2	1–4	1,2,4	1,4	1→
41. Manipulative	1–3	1–3	1,3,4		1–4
42. Trust	1→	5		3,5→	
43. Explicit dependency	1→	1–4	3–4	1,4	2→
44. Explicit belief in specialness	1→	1–5	5	2,4	
45. Craving love/nurturance	1–6	1–3	1	1,4–5	2,5
46. Perceives therapist as positive, lovable person	1→		3,5	3,5→	3→
47. Feels lovable/worthwhile to therapist	5→		5	6	3→
48. Alliance present	3→		2→	2→	4→
49. Recalls memories/dreams	1→		2→	1→	2→
50. Alternating views of self/therapist	2–4	1–3	1–4	1–4	1–3
51. Loves/hates therapist at same time			4	4→	

*Numbers in columns refer to specific year(s) of psychotherapeutic treatment during which each symptom or quality was evident.

found in any sample of borderline patients is extraordinarily large, these categories capture most of the significant action problems that are observed in these patients. At least one of our patients manifested each of the 19 variables that were rated in this section at some point in the course of treatment.

Suicidal acts represent the most severe type of acting out. They engender the greatest concern among treaters, and they are usually the most immediate targets for change in psychotherapy. The sustained, potentially life-endangering actions of borderline patients (items 2–7 in Table 9–1), such as substance abuse, promiscuity, and eating disorders, are often seen as more self-destructive by therapists than by the patients themselves. Hence, they commonly create tension in psychotherapy because the therapist feels that he is taking responsibility for the patient's life under circumstances in which the patient either denies the danger or seems unconcerned about it. These life-endangering acts all involve what Masterson (1972, 1976) and Stone (1985) have called an "alloplastic defensive style," which allows borderline patients to avoid attending to internal dysphoric feeling states.

Testing behaviors of borderline patients (variables 8–13 in Table 9–1) have been the focus of much of the literature on psychotherapy with such patients. Testing behaviors are almost paradigmatic for the borderline diagnosis, to such a degree that many therapists would doubt the validity of the diagnosis in their absence. Variables 8–13 consist of behaviors that many therapists consider testing of the "boundaries of therapy" (e.g., Masterson, 1972, 1976). Like life-endangering acts, testing behaviors are more apt to be seen as such by the therapist than by the borderline patient. These behaviors are consistent with an alternative conceptualization in which, rather than consciously trying to see what he or she can get away with (as the term "testing" suggests), the patient is attempting to enlist the therapist in enacting the transference and thereby attempting progressively to establish a new relationship (Gunderson, 1984).

The so-called acting-in behaviors (items 14–19 in Table 9–1) are not specifically characteristic of borderline patients. Rather, they represent types of psychotherapeutic resistance encountered in borderline and nonborderline patients alike. Nevertheless, in psychotherapy with borderline patients, they can create major impediments to a successful outcome. Examples in our sample were Jennifer's overt seductiveness, Stewart's insistence on playing a game during the hour, and Martha's taking a photograph of her therapist. Such behaviors do not, however, involve the same danger to physical safety created by the more severe types of action behavior described in variables 1–13.

Section II (items 20–24 in Table 9–1) rates the patient's separation responses. Obviously, separation issues are critical to many dynamic formulations of borderline psychopathology (Masterson and Rinsley,

1975; Buie and Adler, 1979; Gunderson, 1984). Separations are also repeatedly introduced at regular intervals in psychotherapy and constitute predictable stressors. Hence, they provide a naturalistic experiment—a periodic stressful event to which borderline patients can be expected to respond and from which change can be readily observed. The five variables in this section represent a hypothetical hierarchy of the adaptiveness of the response. Hence, one would expect that a borderline patient who habitually handles separations with a low-level response such as flight or action would eventually be able to tolerate being alone as improvement occurs during the course of therapy.

In Section III (items 25–28, Table 9–1), we predicted that steady work would be expected to precede the development of career-oriented work; while nonsexual, nonpatient friendships would be expected to precede sexual relations that are mutual and caring.

Among the variables of the remaining two sections, (items 29–34 and 35–51 of Table 9–1), no hierarchy of severity or sequence is involved. In these sections, each variable stands by itself as a putative change marker that might be expected to show alteration over time in its own right, and its relationship to other variables in the section is unclear or too overlapping to permit the development of a hierarchy or sequence.

Ratings

The ratings in Table 9–1 indicate, on a year-by-year basis, whether each of the 51 variables was considered to be significantly present during a given year of treatment. For example, item 16 (Silences) may have been present in the first 3 years, whereas item 39 ("Owns" Sadism) may have been intermittently present in years 2 and 4 but not in the other years.

One of us (J.G.) initially rated all five patients from the case reports. The advantage of having a single rater was that a uniform perspective was brought to bear on all five cases. The disadvantages were the potential idiosyncrasy of that rater's judgment and the variable amount of attention paid to each of the 31 change indices in the case reports. Because of the latter, each of the therapists was asked to make similar ratings on his patients. In most instances, when therapist ratings did not agree with those by the single rater, the nonconformity was due to material not included in the case reports. In some instances, such as the presence of an alliance (item 48), variations seemed to be more closely related to differing definitions of the variable itself. The ratings in Table 9–1 were achieved after consideration was given to the origin of differences when they occurred (e.g., if differences were due to incomplete information in the reports, the therapists' ratings were used).

Two complementary methods of interpreting the results were employed. The first was to review the patterns of change on a year-by-year basis; the second was to look for recurrent patterns (sequencing) of changes that occurred across cases regardless of differing time frames. The first method, as shown in Table 9–1, is more easily documented and provides a data base that displays the range of progress likely to be observed in borderline patients on their way to achieving successful outcomes. The second method represents an adaptation and extension of the observations made on a year-by-year basis and comes closer to synthesizing issues of therapeutic process.

Year-By-Year Pattern of Changes

Year One The first year of treatment is marked primarily by a broad range of acting-out behaviors (Figure 9–1). Two patients were involved

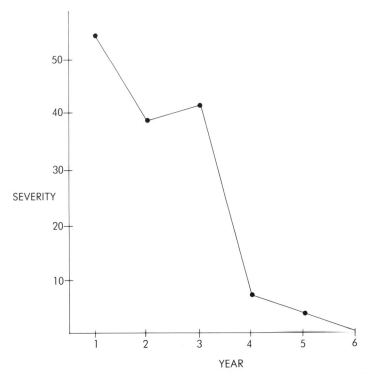

FIGURE 9–1. Self-destructive actions. Suicidal acts = 20; self-mutilation = 10; self-destructive threats = 3.

in suicidal acts and four in self-mutilation, and all five made threats of self-destruction. Beyond suicidality, issues of promiscuity, threats to leave therapy, absences from treatment, failure to talk meaningfully, and a wide variety of other actions characterized the treatment situation (Figure 9–2). In all instances but one, the patients initiated a pattern of contacting the therapist between sessions on an unscheduled basis.

The patients' early relationship to the therapist was intermittently devaluative, defiant, demanding, and manipulative. This was a period in which rapid fluctuations were seen in the patients' view of the therapist and themselves. Therapists were generally idealized as powerful people (rescuers, protectors, directors, nurturers) who were beseeched to provide care and nurturance or, alternatively, seen as cruelly withholding and renounced for this trait. They were not, however, idealized as especially gifted, admirable, brilliant, or intuitive. The great power consistently attributed to all of the therapists was sometimes accompanied by significant distrust about their genuineness, care, and ability to be useful. In every instance, this clearly distrustful but markedly hopeful attitude reflected a paternal transference constellation; retrospectively, it was seen as modeled upon expectations, hopes, and fears related more to the patients' fathers than to their mothers.

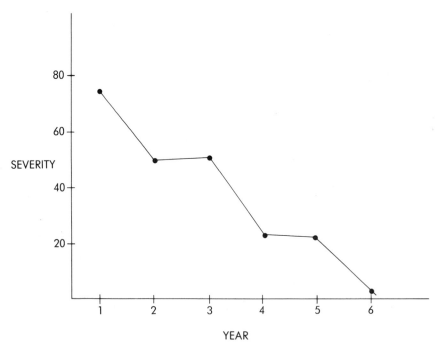

F I G U R E 9–2. Testing behaviors. Self-destructive threats = 6; threats to leave therapy = 5; unscheduled contacts = 4; absences = 3; payment problems = 2; schedule problems = 1.

In general, the social role performance of the patients was extremely dysfunctional; only two (Ann and Jennifer) found employment during the first year. Almost all patients responded to the stress of separation by flight or increased acting out, without being aware of the relationship to the precipitant. Affectively, patients during the first year were characterized by a mixture of anger, depression, and anxiety.

Year Two Year 2 saw a continuation of significant acting-out problems, including serious ongoing self-destructive behavior. The two patients who had previously been protected by extended hospitalizations (Stewart and Martha), showed measurably increased acting-out problems. All five patients continued to explore the boundaries of the treatment by extratherapeutic contacts or within-session behaviors that tested the limits of the therapist's tolerance for continuing the treatment in the face of defiance of the rules (Figure 9–2). Separations from the therapist continued to be managed primarily by action.

The second year witnessed a clear improvement in role performance. All but one patient found steady employment in circumstances that required consistency and a willingness to follow directions. The job usually involved routine tasks rather than those that expanded or tested their intellectual or social abilities. In several instances, the incentive to work was clearly related to the need to pay for the therapy.

The second year saw some diminution of the craving for love or nurturance from the therapist and was associated with a more explicit acknowledgment of dependency on the therapist. It was also a year in which a number of the patients began to express more direct hostility toward their therapist. Despite these changes, however, the prevailing impression was one of highly volatile therapeutic relationships in which defiance, demands, manipulations, and distrust were still clearly evident.

Year Three There was a sharp decline in the severity and frequency of self-destructive activity in the third year (see Figure 9–1). At the same time, there was a continued—perhaps even intensified—high level of testing behaviors around and within the therapy. There was less action in our patients' responses to separation, and more anxiety, anger, and depression were associated with these disruptions than in the earlier years.

By the third year, the patients had established relationships with their therapists in which rudimentary trust was evident. This trust was based on the belief that the therapist was interested in them, and also on the pattern of reliability and consistency that the therapist had established over the preceding 2 years. Hence, a minimal alliance was now consistently present that had been only erratically present earlier.

In the third year, the patients continued the process begun in year 2 in which they increasingly experienced and expressed feelings of dependency and hostility. Hostility was expressed in reaction to the limitations of the therapeutic relationship (i.e., based on the inevitable disillusionments of transference wishes) and in response to the therapist's real failures in providing attention, reliability, or understanding. These expressions of hostility were in some instances associated with "owning" sadistic motives (such as enjoying the therapists' discomfort or controlling them) that had previously been inferred to exist. The patients' views of themselves and of their therapists continued to fluctuate dramatically between devaluation and overvaluation. The idealization of the therapist that had been characteristic of the early period of treatment remained largely untouched.

Year Four By year 4 self-destructive activity was rare and was associated with an equally dramatic decline in testing and acting-in behaviors (Figures 9–1 and 9–2). Absences by the therapist were now managed without action, without hospitalizations, and, with a few exceptions, even without recourse to phone contacts. Intense angry and depressive affects were sometimes still present.

Outside of therapy, the fourth year was the time in which most patients significantly changed their social role performance. A second incremental advance was observed in employment. There was some variation in the exact time (between the third and fifth years), but during this period the patients shifted from stable, low-level work situations to ones that were more oriented to the possibility of advancement and long-term satisfaction. Indeed, their performance at work was now equal or superior to that of any time in their prior history. This was also a time in which patients began to develop and report nonsexual friendships with persons other than their fellow psychiatric patients. Previous friendships had been highly contaminated by the artificiality of enforced living situations or by the patients' use of "friends" largely as buffers to provide allies for or against various therapeutic goals.

The patients now consistently saw their therapists as people who cared about them. It was possible to identify stable, cooperative working alliances, which now took the form of earnest involvement in the process of self-examination. The enormous amount of anger and testing that had previously characterized the relationship with the therapist was no longer predominant. Testing, manipulation, and hostility still occurred, but these episodes were now intermittent and were accompanied by much more insight into their dynamic significance. There was now a clear diminution in the fluctuationing (very good, very bad) views that patients had of themselves and of their therapist.

Year Five By year 5, acting-out behaviors characteristic of the earlier years of treatment had ceased, and the patients had assumed responsible vocational roles. At this point, psychotherapy and the relationship to the therapist became the arena in which patients exhibited the most change. In addition to the emergence of humor, there was also the progressive emergence of guilt and concern for others.

The alternating views of themselves and the therapist were no longer in evidence. In fact, patients now generally felt themselves to be worthwhile and lovable to their therapist. This was also a period when envy, anger, manipulation, and defiance were no longer characteristic. Finally, responses to separation were now limited to more appropriate expressions of less intense affects and, in some instances, to an emerging ability to tolerate the experience of aloneness.

These changes within therapy were evident in the development of more intimate, caring sexual and nonsexual relationships in the fifth year—although this pattern was by no means uniform or complete.

Overall Sequencing of Changes

Although the amount of time required for individual patients to change in the ways specified in Table 9–1 was variable, there were some patterns in the sequences of change that were common to all of the patients in our group. These sequences of change offer an opportunity to identify the more invariant evolutions of borderline psychopathology during treatment, which may, in turn, reflect these patients' developmental templates.

Early Phase The clearest and safest generalization that can be derived from these five cases concerns the progressive diminution of action behaviors over the course of the first 4 years of therapy. Figures 9–1 and 9–2 clearly illustrate the overall decline in both the amount and severity of such behaviors. The reduction of serious acting-out behaviors during the first 3 years was more evident with respect to severity than frequency. Generally, such reductions, while definitely present, were modest in scope. They were accompanied by an equally clear but modest increase in role performance, since all five patients now had steady (if not stable) working situations. There was also a shift during this early phase from a depressed, anxious affective picture to a more clearly angry picture. Within the therapy, the initial distrust was replaced by overt dependency.

These changes are consistent with theories of the therapeutic process that view the action behaviors of borderline patients either as efforts to ward off underlying dependent wishes or as indirect expressions of hostility. Such explanations are consistent with the idea that the acting-out behaviors are primarily defensive (e.g., Kernberg, 1968; Masterson, 1972, 1976; Gunderson, 1984). The changes in acting out are also consistent with theories suggesting that when the relationship with a therapist has proven steadfast and benevolent, a patient willingly gives up his or her efforts to make unreasonable and coercive demands. This second explanation conceptualizes the borderline patient's acting out as an effort to recapitulate and/or create a tolerable relationship (e.g., Adler, 1979; Giovacchini, 1979; Chessick, 1982).

These cases failed to reveal the pattern described by Masterson (1972, 1976), whereby the acting-out behaviors early in treatment are a defense against an underlying depression, which emerges as the action decreases. Depressions were common at the outset of treatment in our five patients and generally diminished together with the level of acting-out behaviors.

Middle Phase This phase was characterized by a continued decrease in action and by a growing awareness of affects—which are given increasingly direct expression.

During the third and fourth years, a dramatic shift occurred characterized by a rapid diminution of acting-out behaviors, of feelings of dependency, and of expression of aggression toward the therapist. In many instances, this transformation appeared to be related to both the patients' growing ability to own their own hostility and sadism and to the increasing recognition that efforts to control (possess) their therapists were both futile and maladaptive.

Middle-Late Phase In the wake of this shift away from action, dependency, and hostility, more positive affects within the therapy became apparent for the first time, and more positive employment goals emerged. The patients' relationships to their therapists were no longer characterized by clinging hostility. Instead, patients came to see the relationship as more optional, that is, as chosen by them, and as based upon the belief that their therapist found them of value and that they had profited from therapy. As an outgrowth of these changes, the patients were eventually able to establish more positive and mutual relationships with their peers, and they began to be able to tolerate the experience of being alone.

Late Phase We have already traced the progression in the patients' views of their therapist from initial devaluation and mistrust (early phase) to dependency and a severe need for the therapist (early-middle phase), and then to the recognition of the therapist as benign and caring (middle-late phase). As an outgrowth of this progression, the patients became more explicit in their belief that the therapist valued, appreciated, and cared for them. Only in an even later phase did the patients openly express feelings of a caring and positive nature toward their therapist. Only then could they express guilt and concern about past or present transgression toward the therapist.

In all but one case (Jennifer), patients began to explore as dystonic their belief that they were special to their therapist. While this belief reflected an inflated view of their value (a narcissistic issue), this change was not accompanied by a shift toward a more narcissistic character style. Rather, it was as if a prior denial or repression had hidden a dystonic grandiosity that, when revealed, was an object of curiosity and shame. There was no concurrent increase or shift toward a more arrogant, entitled, exploitive, distant, cold, interpersonal style, such as characterizes the Narcissistic Personality Disorder (Ronningstam, 1985). In this regard, then, the opening up for exploration of grandiosity did not signify a change in the patient's psychopathology toward greater narcissism, as has been suggested by Adler (1981) and Rinsley (1983).

Applications and Implications

This analysis of patterns of change may be of interest to clinicians, since it offers a possible framework for assessing improvement in psychotherapy. The conclusions drawn here must obviously be tempered by the small size of our sample, the biases of therapists' and patients' retrospective assessments, and the possibility that other borderline patients might recover by patterns not observed in these cases. Despite these limitations, however, we were encouraged (and surprised) by the fact that the broader patterns of change were common to all five cases. Moreover, the patterns that emerged seemed sensible from a theoretical perspective.

Clinicians should expect to see at least a modest diminution in the severity of acting out generally and of self-destructive behavior specifically in the first 2 years of therapy. The ratings done here actually demonstrate this diminution even less convincingly than they would if the ratings had taken into consideration the baseline level of such activities (i.e., during the period shortly before entering therapy) and/or broke down time sequences into smaller intervals (i.e., 3- to 6-month intervals instead of 1-year intervals). Hence, the clinical impression noted elsewhere (Gunderson, 1984) that decrements in self-destructive behaviors are an important index of progress in the early years of psychotherapy is supported by the results of this examination. Failure to show improvement in this area by 2 years probably indicates that a significant revision in the treatment program is needed.

Another clinical implication of this analysis involves the finding that explicit and positive dependency upon the therapist is an important stage that patients should be expected to enter. This reflects a shift away from the distrust, counterdependency, and denial that precede this stage. This overt dependency seems to set the stage for more direct expressions of hostility toward the therapist and the development of a collaborative working alliance. This is useful information for clinicians to draw upon, since both patients and their families are often suspicious that such dependency represents an addiction that cripples rather than enables potential psychological growth. Our observations are in line with those of Wallerstein (1983), who similarly observed, in his small sample of borderline patients who got well, that their relationship to their therapist was characterized by a period of positive dependency.

A third parameter of change that clinicians can attend to involves progress in social role performance. Although all five patients entered treatment while they were unemployed and out of school, all had found steady (albeit low-level) employment by the second year of treatment. It is difficult to judge whether this return to work reflects psychological growth due to therapy or to the nonspecific supportive functions inherent in the therapeutic relationship (i.e., "transference cure") or is reflective of the adaptive ego strengths of this sample. In its own right, the return to work seemed to have therapeutic merits and was a major source of support for the psychotherapeutic enterprise. It is clearly our clinical impression that borderline patients who are employed in any stable and socially valued role (e.g., worker, student, homemaker) find comfort in the structural and self-esteem supporting aspects of being functional, and that this situation acts synergistically with the goals of psychotherapy. Hence, role performance in the form of employment is probably both a cause and an effect of successful psychotherapy.

In any event, our findings suggest that prolonged and intractable unemployment may indicate that therapy has failed to address this important element of change or that the patient's prognosis in treatment is poor. Thus, psychotherapists whose borderline ptaients remain unemployed into the second and certainly the third year of ongoing therapy should have cause to be concerned and should request consultation to address not only this disturbance in functioning but also the role that the psychotherapy plays in either encouraging or discouraging the patient from assuming a functional role.

10

Patterns of Intervention

This chapter attempts to systematize and quantify the types of intervention employed by the five therapists in these case reports. Consistent with their analytic orientation and training, all of them were committed to establishing a therapy based exclusively on the exchange of words; from the beginning of treatment, they used a variety of techniques in order to get these five patients to conform to the usual contract of psychoanalytic therapy. Namely, they expected the patients to pay their bills, to come to appointments on time, to speak freely about problems of significance, and to depart on schedule without intersession contacts. Obviously, none of the patients conformed easily to this model of therapy.

As noted in Chapter 9, the case reports were analyzed on a year-by-year basis. Unlike the ratings presented in that chapter, which relied heavily on a single rater's evaluation of the material, two raters (the authors) evaluated patterns of intervention. Both of us knew the cases in depth—including much information about the therapists' activities and orientation that was not included in the case descriptions themselves. The ratings, done independently, were in very good agreement on the presence or absence of a given type of intervention for each patient in a given year. Even in instances where the two raters had different amounts of firsthand knowledge about the cases, their ratings were still quite similar.

Table 10–1 outlines the 35 types of interventions that were rated.* Each type of intervention was rated on a four-point scale: 0 (not apparent), 1 (probable, based on inference), 2 (present), and 3 (considered common or important). With the exception of Section V, which dealt with the techniques for managing prolonged separations, the other sections are arranged hierarchically in terms of the degree of departure from the classical psychoanalytic technique of transference interpretation. As such, this represents an effort to develop a rational ordering of what Eissler (1953) called "parameters," that is, all noninterpretive interventions.

---

*Numbers in columns represent years in psychotherapy.

T A B L E 10–1
Table of Interventions

	Martha	Ann	Stewart	Jennifer	Susan
I. Institutional					
1. Hospitalization					
a. ≥ 6 mo	1*		1		1
b. 3–6 mo	2		2–3		2–3
c. 0–3 mo					
2. Partial hospitalization					
a. ≥ 6 mo	2				
b. 3–6 mo					
c. 0–3 mo					
3. Halfway house					
a. ≥ 6 mo	2		2		
b. 3–6 mo					
c. 0–3 mo					
4. Emergency room visits				1	
II. Action Parameters					
1. Physical restraints	1				1
2. Escorting (for patient's safety)	1–3	1–2,5	2	1–?	
3. Family (spouse) contacts	1				
4. Drug administration	3				2–4
5. Consultations					1–3

6. Intersession contacts					
a. Initiated by therapist	1–2	5		1	1–3
b. Allowed by therapist	2–3	1–5		1–5	1–5
7. Altering fee	1,2		2		
8. Altering appointment schedule					
a. Initiated by therapist	1,2	5		1,3	1
b. Allowed by therapist					1,2
III. Verbal Parameters					
1. Limits					
a. Threats (If you .., then I'll ....)	2–3	1	3–4	1,?4	2
b. Directives (stop, you must ....)	2	1–2	2–4		1–2
2. Advice	2–3		3–4	1	2–3
3. Expressed anger	1–3				2–3
4. Expressed concern	1,4		1–5		1,3
5. Expressed warmth, affection	1–2				4
6. Expressed commitment to therapy/patient	1–4			1	
7. Expressed hopefulness about therapy					1
8. Self-disclosure					
a. Regarding background, values	5	5	2–5	1	3–4
b. Regarding countertransference problems					3

(Continued)

TABLE 10–1 (*Continued*)

	Martha	Ann	Stewart	Jennifer	Susan
VI. Verbal Techniques					
1. Behavioral focus	1–5	1–3	1,4	1–2	1–5
2. Relationship focus	1–6	1–5	1–5	1–5	1–5
3. Practical problem focus					1
4. Validation of feelings (affirming, accepting)	1–4			1	2,4
5. Validation of past/present trauma	1–6		1–5	1–5	2
6. Relating past to present			2–5	1–5	
7. Dream analysis				3	2–3,5
8. Negative transference clarified	2–3	1–?2	1–5	1–2	2–3,5
9. Transference interpreted	1–6	1,4	1–5	2–5	1,4–5
V. Vacation Management					
1. Hospitalization	1				2–3
2. Interim therapist (scheduled/available)	1,3		1,2		1–3
3. Scheduled contacts	2	3			
4. Availability by phone or mail	2–5			1–2	
5. Providing a token	?3				
6. Other		3 (patient visits)			

*Numbers in columns represent specific year(s) in psychotherapy during which each intervention was made.

Institutional Usage

Figure 10–1 shows how the use of institutions dramatically decreased over the first 3 years of treatment. In two instances (Martha and Stewart), there was an extended initial hospitalization, with gradual decrease in the use of institutional resources over the next several years. In two other instances (Jennifer and Susan), the hospital was used intermittently at times of crises, although this was much more prolonged and extensive in Susan's case than in Jennifer's. Finally, in one instance (Ann), no hospitalization was used. This range of institutional utilization reflects the range of resource utilization for a broad spectrum of borderline patients.

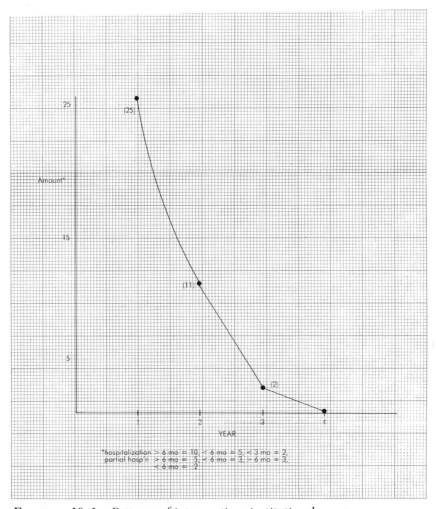

FIGURE **10–1.** Patterns of intervention: institutional usage.

Action Parameters

The term "action parameters" is employed in this context to identify overt behavioral interventions transcending the boundaries of the usual listening position of psychotherapy. Table 10–1 shows that such departures were common.

In no instances were the therapists involved in physically restraining their patients. In one instance (Ann), the therapist had to move in order to avoid being hit, and in another (Stewart) the therapist felt compelled to tell the patient that a physical assault would jeopardize continuation of the therapy. Also, there were no clear instances where the therapist had to be physically present in order to prevent self-injurious acts; the possible exceptions are Martha and Susan, whom the therapists visited on the ward during periods of suicidality. One action parameter that was employed in all five cases was contact between the therapist and members of the patient's family. In one instance (Jennifer), this was exclusively with the spouse, whereas in the other four, it was with parents. These contacts almost always took place in the first 2 years. By year 3 there were only two such events, and the sole instance after that was atypical in that Ann's therapist attended her wedding in year 5.

Contacts with the patient between sessions constituted another common intervention that involved action by/with the therapist. In all five cases, the patients initiated these contacts. In one case (Stewart), this was a single incident; for most of the others, it was an extensive pattern beginning early in treatment and extending throughout most of its duration. In two cases (Jennifer and Martha), the therapists felt compelled at times to initiate contact by calling their patients out of concern for their safety.

The other common form of action intervention involved alterations in the appointment schedule. While such alterations might be common in any long-term therapy, in these cases they were notable because, in two instances (Jennifer and Susan), added sessions or time were frequently used for managing crises, whereas in several other instances, the alterations were initiated by the therapist because of the patients' inability to deal realistically with their financial limitations (Martha and Susan) or as a way of reinforcing the reality of termination (Ann). In contrast, Stewart's therapist threatened to discontinue the treatment if the patient insisted on cutting down the frequency.

Beyond these more common action types of parameters (i.e., family contacts, intersession contacts, and altering appointment schedules), in two cases (Martha and Susan) the therapists were also involved in drug administration, in arranging consultations, and in altering the fee to accommodate the patient's inability to pay. As described earlier (Chapter 2), these two cases, in which the greatest number of action parameters were employed, also involved the most serious patterns of self-destructive acting out and were the longest in duration.

Verbal Parameters

"Verbal parameters" refer to interventions that are made to protect the continuation of the therapy (e.g., limit setting) or to verbal interventions that depart from a traditionally neutral therapeutic stance. The latter category includes the therapist's expression of feelings about the patient, about the course of the therapy, or even about himself. Obviously, as shown in Table 10–1, such verbal parameters were common in these five cases.

The only cases in which limits did not need to be set by the therapist in the first year were those where this function was provided by the hospital (Martha and Stewart). When these therapists took on some of this responsibility, there was an increase in the amount of limit setting required in the second year. Limits were set for a variety of behaviors— most notably for self-destructive actions (e.g., when Susan was told that she couldn't cut herself in therapy) but also with respect to confidentiality (Martha), silences (Stewart), and lying on the floor (Ann). In all five cases, limit setting decreased during the third and fourth years and disappeared thereafter.

Other verbal parameters used in these cases included expressions of concern, of commitment, and of hopefulness. These were mainly used in the early phases of treatment. They were particularly evident in the cases of Jennifer, Martha, and Susan, were present to a lesser degree for Stewart and were absent only for Ann. Advice was given in the middle stages of therapy in three cases. Self-disclosures were not common but were present in most cases—usully in the later stages of treatment. Self-disclosures rarely involved countertransference issues, but were more concerned with the therapist's background or values. This use of advice and self-disclosure during the middle and later phases of treatment is probably equivalent to Masterson's "communicative matching" (1976).

Verbal Techniques

The interventions listed under "Verbal Techniques" (Table 10–1) are those that might be considered to be within the more standard repertoire of psychoanalytic therapists. They include the interventions that have been the focus of most of the attention and debate in the psychoanalytic literature.

While in all five instances the therapist maintained a focus on the nature of the relationship between the patient and himself, perhaps more interesting are the different forms that this focus took. In the case of Stewart, the therapist focused much more directly, emphatically, and unwaveringly upon the negative motives behind the patient's interpersonal behaviors early in the treatment. This approach, more in line with that advocated by Kernberg (1968, 1972, 1979), may, of course, have been due in part to diferences in the patient's psychopathology. Nevertheless, this difference in technique allows us to explore its therapeutic implications. An interesting variation on this technique was observed in Ann's treatment. Here the therapist became increasingly aware of how the patient's actions were manifestations of negative transference. As a result, he later felt emboldened to set strong limits on the behavior. The patient responded quickly to this action, but with little evidence of having worked on, used, and owned the sadistic, controlling, and manipulative motives behind her behavior toward the therapist. By contrast, in the other three cases, transference interpretations, while present from the beginning, were largely directed at identifying the patients' yearning for protection, love, attention, and nurturance, an approach more consonant with that of Buie and Adler (1982), Chessick (1977), and Brandschaft and Stolorow (1984). The three therapies that attended to this aspect of the patient's transference were also characterized by their validation of both the pathogenic significance of early parenting experiences and the importance and value of their expressions of feelings.

Two other traditional components of the usual dynamic therapy were quite variable in these cases. Susan's, Stewart's, and Jennifer's treatments were all characterized by systematic efforts to relate the patient's past to the present, and to some extent they involved the analysis of dreams. These techniques were strikingly absent in the treatments of Ann and Martha. Although the significance of these issues for therapeutic process and outcome will be commented upon elsewhere, it is notable that therapeutic success was not dependent upon their presence in the treatment.

Vacation Management

Because of the central importance of separation and abandonment concerns in borderline patients, a special effort was made to review the interventions that these therapists employed in managing vacations. Based on a hypothesized hierarchy of the range of interventions (see Table 10–1), Figure 10–2 clearly dramatizes the movement from an extreme intervention such as hospitalization early in treatment to the absence of any special technique over a 5-year period. The use of special techniques decreased most dramatically in the third year of treatment. The degree to which such management techniques were employed varied greatly from case to case and depended upon factors such as (1) whether the patient was within an institutional support

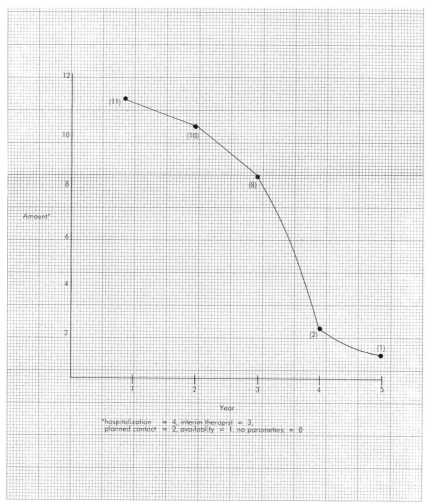

FIGURE 10–2. Patterns of intervention: vacation management.

system, (2) whether the patient lived with significant others, and (3) the perceived likelihood of self-destructiveness.

Clearly, some of the differences in the techniques used were due to differences in therapists' styles. Susan's therapist preferred to arrange interim coverage rather than allow himself to be contacted. Stewart's therapist also offered an interim therapist during the first year, but thereafter did nothing. Under similar circumstances, Martha's therapist first arranged phone contacts and subsequently made himself available. The most dramatic circumstances surrounding vacation management occurred with Ann. Ann phoned her vacationing therapist despite his disapproval; then, perhaps because of his irritation at this intrusion, she made an uninvited visit to him at his vacation site.

Overview: Implications

This review of the patterns of intervention employed by these five therapists offers some fresh perspectives on issues that have been the subject of controversy in the literature. These cases cannot easily be used to resolve debates over the comparative merits of such techniques, since to some degree, the techniques were responsive to each patient's particular psychopathology. Still, these cases do make it clear that there is room for a considerable range of therapeutic techniques. The variations in the techniques employed offer a naturalistic experiment in which some of the theories about the relationship between technique and outcome, and between technique and therapeutic process, can be freshly examined.

The fact that all five of these patients made unusual and significant gains despite major differences in the therapists' approach is in itself notable. It should give pause to any of us who espouse one specific theory of treatment as being the only way. In particular, these case reports give no support to either those who argue for the necessity of early negative transference work (e.g., Kernberg) or to those who argue for reliance on validation (e.g., Brandschaft and Stolorow, 1984).

Another area in which these cases offer some fresh insight concerns the possibility of shifting from more supportive to more interpretive and confrontational techniques over time. Kernberg (1982, 1984), for example, has argued that such shifts are not possible. Our experience suggests that the rationale behind his position stems from the added resistance engendered by such shifts, which derives from having to undo the effects created by previous therapeutic positions. For example, the therapist who has expressed concern for his patient's welfare has set a precedent, so that a subsequent failure to do so under similar circumstances will then be more likely to be experienced as a sign of the therapist's growing distaste or sense of futility. However, these five cases, in particular that of Susan, show that while borderline patients are highly sensitive to shifts in their therapists' approach, they can adapt when the therapist remains consistently committed to the continuation of the treatment. Such shifts in technique are probably far less tenable when derived primarily from feelings of hopelessness or anger.

Technical shifts were in fact evident in most of these cases. The therapists gradually moved toward greater recognition of the hostile, controlling motives behind their patients' behaviors and became progressively more active in interpreting and setting limits upon actions of which they had initially been more tolerant. In a sense, the need for limits emerged from the therapeutic relationship rather than deriving from rigid adherence to an initial contract (to which borderline patients might naively agree but then experience as arbitrary). Moreover, the importance of elucidating negative transference also emerged as the relationship deepened, and was not simply an outgrowth of a theoretical understanding of the patient's disowned motives.

Given the dependence on noninterpretive interventions, these cases cannot be claimed to be psychoanalyses. Indeed, whether the content of the words was accurately understood and useful in the early years of these therapies is hard to know. Clearly, all of the therapists believed that the accuracy, empathy, and focus of their clarification, confrontation, and interpretation were very important in facilitating the development of a trusting, dependable, and positive relationship well before the therapeutic alliance (Zetzel, 1970) was formed.

11

The Quality of Outcome

The extensive literature on psychoanalytic psychotherapy for borderline patients contains very few references to the issue of outcome. This is probably not only because of the relatively small fraction of borderline patients who go on to complete an intensive, long-term course of psychotherapy with a single therapist, but also because of the lack of any standard system by which outcomes are assessed. Moreover, the depth and duration of intimate exposure that are part of long-term analytic psychotherapy may diminish the capacity of therapists to provide the distance and the objectivity needed to make such assessments. Finally, we suspect that both patients and therapists are usually too gratified and grateful when things work out well to do other than sigh.

The present series of five cases provides an opportunity to look relatively closely at the quality of the outcomes obtained in successful long-term therapies. Because of the limitations of any one approach to the assessment of outcomes, we approach this problem through four perspectives. The first (Phenomenologic/descriptive) is the standard type of psychiatric assessment used to evaluate change resulting from a variety of treatments. The second (Structural) and third (Core conflicts/deficits) borrow from psychoanalytic conceptualizations of what issues are central to borderline psychopathology, and these two approaches look more at outcome characteristics that are likely to be the intended focus and target for change in the minds of psychoanalytic therapists. The final approach (Functional) derives from an earlier effort by us to conceptualize the major dimensions of change in successful treatment of borderline patients (Waldinger and Gunderson, 1984).

The divisions between these four approaches are, in fact, quite blurred. A criterion such as intolerance of aloneness in DSM-III taps an issue that comes very close to the abandonment anxiety assessed in the section on core conflict. The lapses in reality testing examined in the structural outcome assessment address the same issue as the psychosis section of the DIB. Likewise, the capacity for sustained goal directedness in the core conflict section overlaps with the ego function area of functional outcome. Many other examples of conceptual overlap between the four systems will be observed.

Despite such areas of overlap, the four approaches are presented sequentially in order to test their applicability to our small sample and to portray their possible usefulness in future prospective studies. Obviously, because of the selection of cases, improvement was assumed prior to our efforts to quantify systematically the types and amount. Thus, the changes that we rated should be viewed with commensurate scientific skepticism. Nevertheless, we comfortably offer them as a small step toward the larger and longer-term goal of doing prospective blind evaluations of operationally definable and clinically relevant outcome criteria.

Although psychotherapy continued beyond the fifth year in two of these cases (Martha and Susan), it was our impression that basic characterologic changes had already taken place by year 5. Thus, we have addressed issues of outcome cross-sectionally by evaluating the patients either at the time of their termination or at the conclusion of the fifth year of treatment—whichever came first.

Phenomenologic/Descriptive Outcome

The diagnosis of any personality disorder in DSM-III requires evidence of significant impairment in social or occupational functioning or subjective distress. Although the level of subjective distress was quite variable in the five patients at the end of the fifth year of therapy, there was no evidence of severe impairment in social or vocational functioning.

Both DSM-III and DIB agree on most of the descriptive characteristics of Borderline Personality Disorder, namely, impulsivity, negative affects, and unstable intense interpersonal relationships. (See Chapter 8 and Tables 11–1 and 11–2.) At the end of 5 years, our patients were involved in relationships that were no longer clearly marked by patterns of devaluation, manipulation, dependency, and masochism. Moreover, all five patients showed a capacity to contain their abandonment anxieties and manifested increased ability to tolerate separations without acting out. More obviously, self-destructive and other impulsive activities had almost disappeared by the end of the fourth year. Another criterion of Borderline Personality Disorder is anger as a predominating affect. This too had undergone rapid and dramatic changes during the third and fourth years of treatment in these cases. Another affective state characteristic of borderline patients in general and this sample in particular involves chronic feelings of emptiness, loneliness, and boredom. While occasionally present in some patients, these feelings were sustained only in Susan. After 4 years of therapy, all five patients experienced periods of self-satisfaction and fulfillment.

TABLE 11–1
DSM-III Criteria at Outcome*

	Martha	Ann	Stewart	Jennifer	Susan
1. Impulsivity or unpredictability in at least two areas that are potentially self-damaging (e.g., spending money, sex, gambling, substance abuse, shoplifting, overeating, physically self-damaging acts)	?	NA	NA		
2. A pattern of unstable and intense interpersonal relationships (e.g., marked shifts of attitude, idealization, devaluation, manipulation)		NA			
3. Inappropriate, intense anger or lack of control of anger (e.g., frequent displays of temper, constant anger)	NA				
4. Identity disturbance manifested by uncertainty about several issues relating to identity, such as self-image, gender, identity, long-term goals or career choice, friendship patterns, values and loyalties (e.g., "Who am I?", "I feel like I am my sister when I am good.")		X	?	NA	
5. Affective instability: marked shifts from normal mood to depression, irritability, or anxiety, usually lasting a few hours and only rarely for more than a few days, with a return to one's normal mood			NA		X
6. Intolerance of being alone (e.g., frantic efforts to avoid being alone, depressed when alone)		?			
7. Physically self-damaging acts (e.g., suicidal gestures, self-mutilation, recurrent accidents or physical fights)				NA	X
8. Chronic feelings of emptiness or boredom	?	NA			?

NA = Not applicable, since the criteria was not present at baseline.
? = Possibly present.
X = Present.
*Outcome: At the end of 5 years of therapy or at termination, whichever came first.

TABLE 11–2
Functional Outcome* (Change Scores†)

	Martha	Ann	Stewart	Jennifer	Susan	Mean
Ego function	5.00	4.50	4.50	3.25	3.75	4.20
Behavior	4.75	3.50	5.00	4.00	3.25	4.10
Object relations	4.50	2.75	4.50	3.75	4.50	4.00
Sense of self	4.25	3.75	3.75	4.50	3.50	3.95
Total Change Score	18.5	14.50	17.75	15.5	15.0	16.25

*Outcome at termination or at the time of the case report.
†Level of functioning scales (Figure 11–1) used: baseline score – outcome score = change score.

In sum, then, by standard descriptive and phenomenologic criteria, none of the five patients could qualify for a borderline diagnosis by the time they entered their fifth year of therapy. These changes are shown in Table 11–1, which displays our ratings of DSM-III criteria at the conclusion of therapy or at the end of the fifth year.

Structural Outcome

Kernberg (1967, 1975) provided three "structural" criteria by which to identify the intrapsychic characteristics of people with a *borderline personality organization*—a category that is broader and more inclusive than that defined by borderline criteria in DSM-III or the DIB. The first of these criteria is *generally intact reality testing*, which can fail transiently under stress. In four of our five cases (all except Martha), such vulnerability in reality testing was apparent either prior to treatment or in response to the stress of the treatment itself. Such vulnerability was not apparent beyond the fourth year of treatment (or subsequently in those cases where follow-up reports were available).

Kernberg's second structural characteristic of borderline personality organization is *reliance upon primitive defenses* such as projection, projective identification, denial, and (most notably) splitting. Projection diminished steadily throughout treatment in all cases. Because of the complexity (notably the subjective contribution and involvement by the object) of projective identification, we felt unable to make judgments about its presence or absence from the available reports. In several instances, however, the therapists did volunteer a description of this interactional process (see, for example, the case of Martha). These instances occurred early in the treatment.

The most evident of Kernberg's primitive defenses was splitting. All five patients shifted between markedly contradictory views of themselves and of the therapists. Susan's perceptions of her therapist shifted dramatically from well-meaning and friendly to inattentive and exploitive. Both Martha and Jennifer evidenced splitting of another type; they divided their object field into good and bad components. Martha preserved her idealization of her therapist by villifying other members of the treatment team, whereas Jennifer maintained her idealized transference by denouncing her husband. As late as the early part of the fourth year, Stewart spent half of his sessions in mute defiance of what he considered an unfair expectation that he speak about what was on his mind, and the other half discussing intimate matters eagerly and willingly, without evidence of distrust or apprehension. Whether these various forms of splitting all reflect the same psychological process is debatable (see Gunderson, 1984), but for our present purposes it is sufficient to note that they were no longer evident after the fourth year of treatment in these five patients. Here again, there is evidence of a basic change that would disqualify these patients from a designation of borderline personality organization by year 5 of treatment.

Kernberg's third criterion, absence of a stable identity, is difficult to judge. This is due in part to the ambiguities in the concept of identity and the problem of reliability in its assessment (Gunderson, 1982). Moreover, while all five patients had identity problems, these did not emerge as explicit issues in therapy in the first 4 years. In several cases, identity disturbance did become a more explicit issue in the later phases of therapy. Ann, however, left treatment without this aspect of her psychology being explicitly worked on, and residual evidence of this problem remained at the time of the follow-up interview. Stewart attended to identity concerns in some respects within his treatment, but his sexual identity was largely unresolved both at the time he left treatment and at the follow-up evaluation. Hence, by this criterion, the achievement of a clear, stable sense of identity was incomplete even at the termination of therapy.

Outcome with Respect to Core Conflicts and/or Deficits

Various authors have identified core issues that they believe are both characteristic of and specific to patients with Borderline Personality Disorder. Among these core issues are extreme separation/abandonment anxiety, a conviction of inner badness/destructiveness, the inability to sustain soothing introjects, conflict over the experience and expression of emotional needs and anger, and failure to sustain goal directedness. Perry and Cooper (1983) have attempted to develop reliable assessment methods for some of these core conflict/deficit areas. Their work, however, depends upon having a videotaped record of a psychodynamically sophisticated interview from which "relevant" material is abstracted and then subjected to a separate rating process. Although these techniques hold promise for use in future prospective outcome studies, they obviously cannot be employed for the current retrospective assessment of these five patients. For the present purposes, we have had to depend upon our clinical judgments.

Separation/Abandonment Fears The centrality of separation/abandonment fears in borderline patients was first suggested by Mahler (1971) and subsequently emphasized in the theories of Masterson (1971, 1972). As noted in Chapter 9, our five patients' reliance on flight and substitution gradually gave way to more awareness of both their separation anxiety and their expressions of anger and depression related to the therapist's absence during the course of the treatment. By the end of the fifth year, none of the patients experienced panic in response to their therapist's departures and, in several instances, found themselves able to manage important losses elsewhere in their lives appropriately (Stewart successfully moved away from home, Martha gave up her clinging need for her mother and stepfather, and Jennifer managed the loss of her stepfather in ways that had previously generated panic.)

Soothing Introjects The ability to manage abandonment fears is closely connected to the core deficit described in Adler and Buie's (1979a, 1979b) theory about borderline psychopathology, namely, the inability of borderline patients to recall soothing memories (to sustain soothing introjects) during periods of separation from important objects. At the end of 5 years, three patients were judged to be able to tolerate being alone comfortably. For the other two patients, Susan and Ann, this issue was unresolved. While Ann did not evidence abandonment fears, it was clear that she had not really dealt with loss and that her marriage provided a substitution that militated against a real termination experience from her therapy. With Susan, separation fears persisted in diminished form, and she remained moderately intolerant of the experience of aloneness, though she no longer acted on these feelings.

Omnipotent Destructiveness In a more recent formulation, Robbins (personal communication, 1984) has stressed the central problem of the borderline patient's conviction of his or her own badness and destructiveness. Gunderson (1984) has likewise written that borderline patients' dependence upon the availability of supportive others is linked to their underlying sense of their own badness, which becomes conscious and prominent whenever important objects are seen as unavailable. Certainly, these five patients all evidenced a profound sense of their own badness. In all five instances, however, this conviction had undergone significant modification by the end of the fifth year. This was evident in their more or less stable sense of their worth (as assessed and reported by their therapists) and in their ability to establish relationships that were not primarily need satisfying. This improved sense of self-worth was also seen in their looking forward to a future that included vocational fulfillment and the possibility of marriage and child rearing. These hopes had not been voiced until the late period of treatment by any of these patients.

Goal-Directedness The improved sense of self-worth (the dramatically diminished sense of badness) is closely connected with the emergence of sustained goal-directed behaviors. All five patients were working toward sustained vocational and personal goals by the fifth year of treatment. These goals clearly stretched their known capacities and reflected their ability to risk failure, as well as a sense of realistic hopefulness about their chances of success. One patient went on to complete college and graduate school; another obtained a professional degree; two sustained gratifying business careers while functioning as wives and mothers; and the fifth also developed a successful office management career and married.

From an ego psychological point of view, this area of outcome is describable in terms of new capacities to plan, organize, and initiate, as well as to endure frustrations, failures, limits, and negative affects. From a public health point of view, it speaks most persuasively to the issue of the potential costs and benefits of psychotherapy for borderline patients. After 5 years of psychotherapy, all five of these patients were self-sufficient and productive members of their communities who were contributing to the welfare of society rather than absorbing its resources.

Functional Outcome

In an earlier report, we surveyed the practices of 11 experienced clinicians who are experts in long-term psychotherapy with borderline patients (Waldinger and Gunderson, 1984). These therapists were asked to rate their successfully treated borderline patients in the following four areas of functioning: Ego functioning, Behavior, Object relations, and Sense of self. Each area is rated on a seven-point scale that is anchored by changes that might be specific to borderline psychopathology (see Figure 11–1). The 11 therapists reported that their successful patients improved significantly in all four areas. The five cases presented here allow us to apply these anchored rating scales under circumstances where the data base is more standardized and where our ratings can be compared.

Both of us (R.W. and J.G.) rated all five patients on these four scales. We disagreed in only 3 of the 20 ratings, and in those cases by only one point or less on the seven-point scales. In the three instances of disagreement, there was a discussion and a consensus was reached (these scores are shown for each patient in their respective case discussions).

Table 11–2 compares the change scores on these four active dimensions. In general, the magnitude of improvement in all four areas was approximately four scale points. This is similar to the magnitude of change reported in our earlier survey of the 11 expert therapists (Waldinger and Gunderson, 1984). While there is no clear cutoff point on these scales by which to determine whether someone is still functionally or is syndromally diagnosable as borderline, these ratings clearly show across-the-board improvement for all patients in all areas. These scores are also consistent with the authors' impression that Martha had improved most, Stewart ran a close second, and the other three patients showed less but still highly significant improvements.

For the most part, the scores at the conclusion of treatment were on

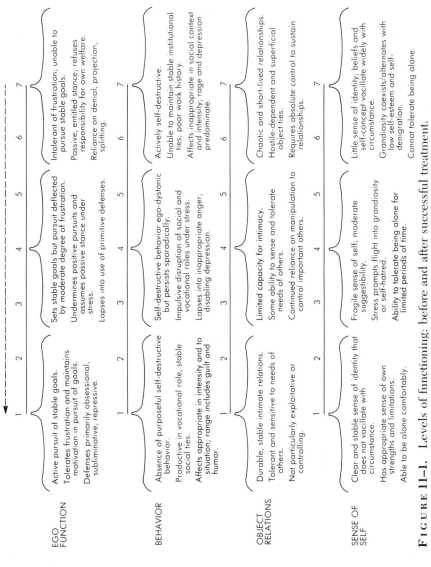

FIGURE 11–1. Levels of functioning: before and after successful treatment. BPD (*n* = 54) (adapted from Waldinger and Gunderson, 1984).

the lower end of the scales—again similar to what our survey had found. There were, however, a few notable exceptions. At the higher (sicker) end, we felt that Ann still had significant problems in her sense of self and that Susan was still significantly impaired in the behavioral area, as evidenced by her recurrent depressions and occasional role disruptions under stress. On the lower end of the scales, we felt that Jennifer had a very stable sense of herself and consistent ego functioning, that Martha had also achieved a very high level of ego functioning, and that Stewart excelled in the behavioral area.

Summary

In this chapter, we have evaluated outcomes using four different clinical and conceptual approaches. As would be expected from the selection of case reports, all of the assessments documented that clinically significant changes were apparent in all five patients.

In the areas of outcome where the four conceptual frameworks overlapped, they seemed to agree in their assessments of improvement. Obviously, this agreement could be due to the fact that the two authors made all of the assessments, hence they were not independent of each other. Nevertheless, the assessments of impulsivity via the DSM-III criteria, the DIB, and the functional scale for behavioral change were very similar.

Congruence was observed among the various methods with respect to borderline patients' perceptions of themselves. Whether this issue was examined using Robbins' core conflict of omnipotent destructiveness or Kernberg's splitting defense, the patients uniformly acquired a more stable and a more benign sense of self; there was a clear loss of the aggressively infused, negatively valued self-image with which they began treatment. The issue of identity was looked at descriptively (DSM-III) and via the sense of self scale of functional outcome. Here there was variability in how close patients came to achieving a coherent, clear sense of self. In most instances, this was judged to have been incompletely attained.

The borderline patient's relationships with others were assessed in the object relations scale of functional outcome, in the interpersonal relations section of the DIB, in the assessment of the separation/abandonment conflict, and indirectly via Kernberg's defenses. Here too, the various assessments coincided in documenting a great deal of change. Every patient's relationships had become more stable and more neutralized—that is, they were not infused with urgent need gratifications. The residual limitations frequently consisted of persistent problems with intimacy, especially the open expression of love. It could be argued that longer periods of therapy might be suitable for bringing about changes in this area as well. The progress observed in Martha's longer-term therapy suggests that this may be the case.

Another impression about outcome involved variations in levels of functioning within each patient and among different patients. For example, it was clear that at the end of treatment, Ann was quite impaired in terms of her self-identity, despite doing well in other outcome areas. Susan, on the other hand, had persistent problems with impulsivity, and Stewart had notable problems with closeness in relationships. These variations in the quality of the outcome raise the question of whether such differences were related to the initial psychopathology of the patients or to the treatment processes in which they participated.

Despite the broadness and significance of the changes observed, it was our impression that at the conclusion of their treatments, these patients could not be considered classically neurotic. Rather, the quality and nature of their changes left them more reflective, certainly more functional, and more open people. Their openness was not just tolerance of the feelings of others; it extended to increased tolerance of tension around basic conflictual issues that remained central to their personality structure. What was different was the degree to which these issues were coped with equably, without impulse discharge, largely because these patients had been able to develop enhanced support systems (both interpersonal and intrapsychic) to help them deal with stresses. This is not to minimize the importance of basic personality structural change that took place, but rather to give more emphasis to the changes in adaptation to core issues. We join Giovacchini (1979) in feeling that the nature of such changes is not understandable in terms of resolution of conflict, but rather in terms of the strengthening of ego functions and adaptive defenses.

12

Overview and Implications

It has been repeatedly noted throughout this book that most discussions of the technique of psychoanalytic therapy with borderline patients are tied to specific writers' theories about the origins and nature of the borderline patient's psychopathology (see Chapter 2). Such theories have been derived from the clinical experience of therapists whose samples are necessarily limited, and have been defined using widely divergent and usually idiosyncratic sets of diagnostic criteria. Hence, theories about psychopathology as well as recommendations about treatment cannot comfortably be assumed to apply to borderline patients meeting the usual current criteria.

In the few instances where authors have provided more detailed series of case reports (Masterson, 1972, 1976; Abend et al., 1983) or where single case reports have appeared (Adler, 1981; Chessick, 1982), it is clear that patients being called borderline are quite variable in their presenting problems, levels of function, and signs and symptoms. Hence, it is not surprising to find variations in the recommendations about appropriate treatment, in the observed processes of change, and in the theories about the sources and nature of the psychopathology.

The five case reports presented here represent a step toward increasing the homogeneity of the sample, the potentially significant variations among these cases notwithstanding. Perhaps more importantly, the interventions and the processes of treatment are described independently by clinicians who each operated within the framework of psychoanalytic therapy, but with otherwise different training, different theoretical orientations, and different personalities. This diminishes the likelihood that theoretical beliefs have organized the data, and it allows more hope that the data can yield new theoretical perspectives. This chapter attempts to summarize the conclusions and to integrate them into broader theoretical frameworks.

Summary of Conclusions

Conclusions drawn from this sample can be expected to be generalizable to most patients meeting modern criteria for Borderline Personality Disorder. Our five patients were, however, more intelligent and possibly less impulsive than might be expected of modal patients meeting borderline criteria. It was also our impresssion that these patients benefited from the particularly strong commitments made by their therapists—more than could be expected for the usual patient in their practices and more than could be expected for most borderline patients.

Some patterns of change were common to all five patients. In all instances, there was a progressive diminution of action, most notably self-destructive acts, along with a progressively explicit acknowledgment of trust and dependency upon the therapist. The emergence of trust and dependency was accompanied by progressively more direct expressions of hostility toward the therapist. These expressions, in turn, gave way to the first acknowledgments that the therapists appreciated and valued them, and to a liberation of energy for improved interpersonal and role functioning. We concluded that these identifiable and consistent patterns provide useful indices that therapists can use to gauge progress or the lack of it in psychotherapy.

These cases made it clear that there is room for a considerable range of therapeutic techniques. All of the patients required the repetitious use of a wide of range of parameters. Observations of the variety of types and the sequence of interventions should give pause to any clinician who espouses a specific theory of treatment as being the only way. Even within a given therapy, many variations in technique were observed over time; therapists often moved from an initial period of acceptance and alliance building toward increasing confrontation and limit setting. The amount of interpretive activity in each treatment was quite variable, as was the extent to which therapists related the patient's past to the present and paid attention to negative transference.

Using multiple approaches to evaluate the outcome, we found that major changes occurred that affected core issues of borderline psychopathology. It was also apparent that the patients had not resolved or covered up the issues that had preoccupied them when they entered therapy. Rather, they seemed to have made useful adaptations that led to improved social supports, markedly decreased self-destructiveness, and enhanced self-esteem. Despite significant variations in the quality of the outcome, none of the patients was manifestly diagnosable as borderline after 4 years of treatment. This is the central observation of this book. Despite the widely cited advocacy of the value of psychoanalytic therapy for borderline personalities, there has been no persuasive evidence that this treatment is actually effective. Previously reported successes have been subject to criticisms that the cases were not really borderline or that the good outcomes were the rare result of a gifted therapist. The cases reported here do not suggest that a successful outcome is common; they do suggest that a variety of well-trained, strongly motivated therapists are able to do such work. This conclusion supports the therapeutic enthusiasm of pioneers such as Kernberg (1968), Masterson (1972), and Giovacchini (1973). It calls into question the beliefs of others such as Knight (1953), Zetzel (1971), Grinker (1968), and Friedman (1975), who have stated that such character change cannot be expected to occur. These practitioners have argued that only a supportive therapy aimed at stabilizing their adaptation is feasible for borderline patients because of their gross ego deficits and their inability to establish or maintain a working alliance.

One question that should be asked in evaluating the effectiveness of these therapies is whether the changes could have been due to factors other than the treatment. The growing evidence about the natural course of Borderline Personality Disorder (Grinker et al., 1968; Gunderson et al., 1975; Pope et al., 1983; Perry, 1985) suggests that a continuation of severe morbidity is expectable over the 3–7 years following the diagnosis (during which these therapies took place). Therefore, it seems safe to assume that the patients discussed in this book would have remained dysfunctional, with continued rehospitalization and chaotic interpersonal relations, in the absence of treatment. Longerterm follow-up studies of borderline patients over 10–20 years report a significant reduction in the level and type of dysfunction (McGlashan, 1984; Stone, unpublished) in many borderline patients. One implication of these longer-term follow-up studies is that favorable changes that are observed after a therapy that lasts for 10 years or more should not be inferred to be due to treatment. A second implication of these studies is that since the borderline patients who were functioning well on follow-up had usually had much prior treatment, the results seen in our cases may endure. An advantage of the intense involvement reported between patients and therapists in these treatments is that there is a coherence and logic to the interaction between them and the changes observed. Hence, these reports provide a face validity for the conclusion the the changes observed were directly related to the process of therapy.

Relating Interventions to Changes and to Outcome

As noted in Chapter 1, Kernberg (1975) has stated that early interpretation of negative transference leads to a more rapid decrease in rage and facilitates a more rapid development of a therapeutic alliance. This belief contrasts sharply to Zetzel's (1971) position that because of the inability to form a therapeutic alliance, borderline patients are unable to use interpretation and should be given nonintensive supportive therapy. The patients in our study certainly proved incapable of establishing a stable therapeutic alliance at the onset of their treatments. The fact that they eventually developed this capacity indicates that it was not a prerequisite for treatment and that it may have been an effect. Whether the development of an alliance was due to the interpretive efforts of the therapists, or whether it grew out of more supportive aspects of the early treatment, is unclear. The patient who had the most early negative transference work (Stewart) did show early evidence of an alliance, as Kernberg predicted. Nevertheless, it was very unstable until late in the therapy. With the advent of new assessments of the presence and quality of an alliance in psychotherapies, future prospective research can address this issue more definitively.

Both Martha and Stewart spent most of the first year of psychotherapy in hospitals. This setting clearly helped contain their acting out and allowed the therapist to establish a working relationship without evoking as much potentially negative transference by having to set limits or frustrate dependency needs. In the case of Stewart, the therapist confronted the patient's manipulations of the staff and his parents early in treatment. By contrast, Martha's therapist remained outside of the ongoing struggles between Martha and her milieu and her family in ways that reflected more acceptance and perhaps more sympathy for her complaints. This difference in approach raises the question of whether it was causally connected to a difference in the patients' subsequent course. In other words, was the sustained pattern of life-endangering behavior for Martha and its lack of recurrence for Stewart (where the therapist sided with the staff) related to whether these patients perceived their therapists as sympathetic or unsympathetic to their motives? Although this question is unanswerable from these cases, it suggests that therapists working on inpatient services should be aware that these stances may affect the extent and duration of such acting-out behavior.

The issue of when to confront or limit manipulative and self-destructive behaviors is highlighted by the cases of Ann and Susan. In both cases, the therapists slowly and with discernible reluctance began to set limits on maladaptive behaviors. The patients clearly responded beneficially to these limits. This observation seems to support the position most strongly advocated by Kernberg, (1968) and to a lesser extent by Masterson (1972, 1976) and Gunderson (1984), that early confrontation and limit setting facilitate therapeutic change in borderline patients. However, it is our opinion that more aggressive confrontation and limit setting early in treatment might have increased the likelihood of premature discontinuance among outpatients who did not have the benefit of the containing function of an inpatient unit. In the cases of Ann and Susan, the absence of these interventions early in treatment did not seem to mean that a therapeutic impasse or a lack of change occurred until the therapist "came around" (as Kernberg, for example, might predict). The responsiveness of Ann and Susan to limits and confrontation seemed to derive in part from their already growing sense that their therapists cared about their welfare and were committed to working with them.

Having thus justified the later introduction of confrontation and limits for some borderline patients, it should be noted that the therapists themselves usually felt, in retrospect, that they could have—and should have—confronted their patients and set limits earlier. However, despite a tendency to use these techniques earlier with subsequent borderline patients in their practices, the therapists did not feel that their results with subsequent patients were enhanced. It may be that the awareness of and comfort with the need to confront and set limits on borderline patients that comes from experience may translate into a readiness to use these methods too early in treatment, causing increasing numbers of dropouts as therapists grow in experience.

It was our impression that the patients' direct expression of anger at the therapists, who proved to be resilient and nonretaliatory, seemed to set the stage for greater trust by the patients, less testing, and the development of a stable collaborative relationship. These changes were evident by the end of the fourth year. This observation is consistent with Winnicott's (1965) concept of the holding environment, as elaborated upon by Modell (1976). Referring to the management and containment of rage, Modell states that limit setting combined with nonretaliatory acceptance of a child's rageful outbursts helps a child learn the limits of his own aggression. Such experience demonstrates to a child that his or her angry impulses can neither destroy nor create the mother (or other parent). This realization permits a developmental process whereby a symbiotic relationship is transformed into one in which autonomy is recognized. In these patients, such an interaction occurred during the middle stages of therapy. It seemed to provide a corrective experience by which the patients came to view themselves and their therapists more benignly and were able to achieve a stable working alliance. These changes appeared to reflect the internalization of a more stable, constant object representation. This shift, however, was not accompanied by a decrease in separation anxiety. Rather, it seemed as if the internalization was completed to the point where the danger of its loss at times of separation could be recognized. Hence, in the aftermath of this corrective expression and survival of aggression, there was less rage and anger but more anxiety associated with separations.

As noted in Chapter 2, the theories of borderline personality development that rest exclusively or primarily on the pathogenic influence of poor parenting view the borderline patient's aggressivity as secondary. One such theory states that preborderline children suffer retaliatory withdrawal in response to their anger or emerging autonomy (Mahler, 1971; Masterson and Rinsley, 1975). The observations drawn from the five cases described in this book offer a fresh opportunity to explore the controversy about whether the borderline patient's aggressivity is primary or secondary. In these patients, there was little reason to support the idea that their hostility was secondary to either the therapist's unempathic techniques (as suggested by Brandshaft and Stolorow, 1984) or to the therapist's efforts to enforce or demand separation or individuation (as might be suggested by Masterson's theory [1972, 1976]). What was observed in these cases was that the therapist's gradually increasing efforts to clarify, confront, and interpret the aggressive motives that were expressed indirectly through action led to more direct expression of this hostility. The corrective experience occurred because of the therapist's tolerant involvement with the aggression. There was little reason to believe that this aggression was generated by and became excessive in reaction to the therapist's inadequate empathy or availability. This suggests that the patients' aggression was in part an inherent component of their personality that needed to find more overt and adaptive forms of expression. These observations are consistent with Kernberg's developmental theory, which emphasizes the pathogenic importance of a misdirected and possibly hypertrophied aggressive drive. These observations are also consistent with a theory in which the affects derived from aggressive drives (i.e., anger, rage) are disowned or split off early in life, as described by Klein (1946) and used in the developmental theory of Kernberg.

The sequence of changes that was observed has parallels in psychoanalytic models of early childhood development. The patients in our group moved from an initial preoccupation with trust and attachment toward relationships characterized by unstable dependency and increasing awareness of and anger about the object's failure and separateness. Although the patients were still operating on a need-satisfying level, immediate gratifications were less essential and dependency became progressively less frightening. Coherent separation anxiety occurred, along with a more positive perception of the therapist's value and a more overt recognition of the therapist's care for them. Facilitating these developmental processes initially was a heavy reliance on acceptance and validation, followed by confrontation and limit setting, then by the provision of corrective experiences in the relationship with the therapist, and finally by experiences involving explanations (linking the past to the present and articulating motives). All four of these processes occurred from the beginning of all of the treatments, but there appeared to be a sequence to their shifting priority in promoting change.

The above statements about developmentally determined sequencing of therapeutic stratagies are similar to those theorized by Gedo and Goldberg (1973). Using Gedo and Goldberg's hierarchy of treatments, the earliest phase of treatment involved primarily unification and the interventions responsive to such patients' fragmented sense of self. The therapist was establishing himself as a central focus around which to organize by virtue of stability, reliability, identification, and being "real." Using a slightly different developmental scheme, the patient's needs were being met by the therapist who served as a transitional object. According to Gedo and Goldberg, disillusionment through confrontation with realities then becomes the active therapeutic process used to assist the patient's movement from transitional object relatedness to whole object relatedness. It was in this period that the patients' grandiose sense of destructiveness was modified by the corrective disillusionment caused by the therapists' survival of their anger. It was only after this stage that the capacity for whole object relatedness was evident in the stable therapeutic alliance and in the ability to rely primarily upon interpretations. At this point, as we have seen, the patient could no longer be considered borderline.

In theory, there should be a correspondence between the use of the accepting, validating techniques advocated by Kohut and a resulting enhancement of self-esteem and productive/creative socioculturally desirable role functioning. With regard to change in interpersonal relationships, Kohut (1971) states that "the increase in the capacity for object love must be considered important but nonspecific and a secondary result of the treatment" (pp. 197–198). In contrast, an approach that pays more attention to the frustrations inherent in relationships and the patient's maladaptive efforts to overcome these frustrations might be expected to have its reward in an outcome marked by improvement in one's relationships with others and in the management of one's aggression (or comfort with authority, competitiveness), rather than enhancement of self-esteem and role performance per se (Gunderson, 1984). This distinction is offered only weak support by the case reports provided here. Stewart, in whose case the most attention was paid to aggression, had serious residual problems in relating intimately to others. By contrast, Ann, in whose case the least attention was paid to aggression and the most consistent validation of her early victimization occurred, showed relatively little improvement in the development of a productive, creative, independent role. In object relations, she showed an improved capacity for stable, intimate relations but retained relatively unclear self-boundaries. She has led a subjectively satisfying life despite her residual dependency and vagueness about boundaries and other aspects of self-definition. Stewart had less subjective satisfaction on follow-up but more clearly defined boundaries. This outcome might seem to have been related to the clear boundaries that were maintained in his therapy. He retains considerable ongoing subjective dissatisfaction. This observation confirms another of Kohut's ideas—that more classical technique may not facilitate the emergence of the "joyful self" (Kohut, 1977).

The very different outcomes of these two patients do not easily fit the theories linking technique to outcome noted above. Instead, we felt that the more confrontative, ego-reliant therapy was correlated with more awareness and greater specificity of conflict and more self-definition. Such observations force one to consider that some more uniform aspects of change like those in self-esteem, role performance, and management of anger may be products of the nonspecific factors (corrective, identificatory, stabilizing, supportive) of long-term psychotherapy. Other areas of outcome, such as self-definition and behavioral control, may be products of the more specific factors (interpretations, limit setting, confrontations, etc.) within such long-term treatment.

Such speculations about the relationship of the types of intervention to the processes of change and the quality of the outcome are obviously very hazardous. They are offered tentatively, with full awareness of the limits of such a sample and the problems of attempting to reconstruct developmental processes through observations of therapeutic change. Such, however, is the data base from which psychoanalytic theories of psychopathology and treatment have arisen and that have provided the stimulus for our interest and study in this area.

We close, then, with apologies for the inevitable limitations that are inherent in this methodology, but also with the hope that this work will take its place alongside previous psychoanalytic studies that have already contributed to an understanding of borderline psychopathology and to an ambiance of greater therapeutic enthusiasm.

Abend, S.; Porder, M.; and Willick, M.: *Borderline Patients: Psychoanalytic Perspectives.* International Universities Press, New York, 1983.

Adler, G.: The myth of the alliance with borderline patients. *Am. J. Psychiatry,* **136:**642–45, 1979.

Adler, G.: The borderline-narcissistic personality disorder continuum. *Am. J. Psychiatry,* **138:**46–50, 1981.

Adler, G., and Buie, D.: Aloneness and borderline psychopathology: The possible relevance of child development issues. *Int. J. Psychoanal.* **60:**83–96, 1979a.

Adler, G., and Buie, D.: The psychotherapeutic approach to aloneness in borderline patients. In *Advances in Psychotherapy of the Borderline Patient.* Edited by LeBoit, J. Jason Aronson, New York, 1979b, pp. 433–448.

Alexander, F., and French, T.: *Psychoanalytic Therapy: Principles and Applications.* Ronald Press, New York, 1946.

Andrulonis, P., et al.: Borderline personality subcategories. *J. Nerv. Ment. Dis.* **170:**670–79., 1982.

Armelius, B.; Kullgren, G.; and Renberg, E.: Borderline diagnosis from hospital records, reliability and validity of Gunderson's Diagnostic Interview for Borderlines (DIB). *J. Nerv. Ment. Dis.,* **173:**32–34, 1985.

Boyer, L.: Working with a borderline patient. *Psychoanal. Q.,* **46:**386–424, 1977.

Brandschaft, B., and Stolorow, R.: The borderline concept: Pathological character or iatrogenic myth? In *Empathy.* Edited by Lichtenberg, J.; Bornstein, M.; and Silver, D. Analytic Press, Hillsdale, N.J., 1984, pp. 333–357.

Buie, D., and Adler, G.: The definitive treatment of the borderline personality. *Int. J. Psychoanal. Psychother.,* **9:**51–87, 1982.

Chessick, R.: *Intensive Psychotherapy of the Borderline Patient.* Jason Aronson, New York, 1977.

Chessick, R.: A practical approach to the psychotherapy of the borderline patient. *Am. J. Psychother.,* **33:**531–46, 1979.

Chessick, R.: Intensive psychotherapy of a borderline patient. *Arch. Gen. Psychiatry,* **39:**413–19, 1982.

Eissler, K.: The effect of the structure of the ego on psychoanalytic technique. *J. Am. Psychoanal. Assoc.,* **1:**104–143, 1953.

Friedman, H.: Psychotherapy of borderline patients: The influence of theory on technique. *Am. J. Psychiatry,* **132:**1048–52, 1975.

Frosch, J.: Psychoanalytic considerations of the psychotic character. *J. Am. Psychoanal. Assoc.,* **18:**24–50, 1970.

223

Frosch, J.: Technique in regard to some specific ego defects in the treatment of borderline patients. *Psychiatr. Q.*, **45**:216–20, 1971.

Gedo, J., and Goldberg, A.: A psychoanalytic nosology and its implications for treatment. In *Models of the Mind: A Psychoanalytic Theory*. University of Chicago Press, Chicago and London, 1973.

Giovacchini, P.: Character disorders with special reference to the borderline state. *Int. J. Psychoanal. Psychother.*, **2**:7–36, 1973.

Giovacchini, P.: *Treatment of Primitive Mental States*. Jason Aronson, New York, 1979.

Grinker, R.; Werble, B.; and Drye, R.: *The Borderline Syndrome: A Behavioral Study of Ego Functions*. Basic Books, New York, 1968.

Grotstein, J.: The analysis of a borderline patient. In *Technical Factors in the Treatment of the Severely Disturbed Patient*. Edited by Giovacchini, P., and Boyer, L. Jason Aronson, New York, 1982, pp. 261–288.

Gunderson, J.: Empirical studies of the borderline diagnosis. In *Psychiatry 1982* (Vol. 1 of *Psychiatry Update*). Edited by Grinspoon, L. American Psychiatric Press, Washington, D.C., 1982, pp. 414–37.

Gunderson, J.: *Borderline Personality Disorder*. American Psychiatric Press, Washington, D.C., 1984.

Gunderson, J.: Review of Abend, S.M.; Porder, M.S.; and Willick, M.S.: *Borderline Patients: Psychoanalytic Perspectives*. *Am. J. Psychiatry*, **142**:509–10, 1985.

Gunderson, J.; Carpenter, W.; and Strauss, J.: Borderline and schizophrenic patients: A comparative study. *Am. J. Psychiatry*, **132**:1257–64, 1975.

Gunderson, J., and Kolb, J.: Discriminating features of borderline patients. *Am. J. Psychiatry*, **135**:792–96, 1978.

Gunderson, J.; Kolb, J.; and Austin, V.: The diagnostic interview for borderline patients. *Am. J. Psychiatry*, **138**:896–903, 1981.

Gunderson, J., and Englund, D.: Characterizing the families of borderlines: A review of the literature. *Psychiatr. Clin. North Am.*, **4**:159–68, 1981.

Gunderson, J., Kerr, J., and Englund, D.: The families of borderlines: a comparative study. *Arch. Gen. Psychiatry*, **37**:27–33, 1980.

Guntrip, H.: My experience of analysis with Fairbairn and Winnicott. *Int. Rev. Psychoanal.* **2**:145–56, 1975.

Hoch, P., and Polatin, P.: Pseudoneurotic forms of schizophrenia. *Psychiatr. Q.*, **38**:248–276, 1949.

Kernberg, O.: Borderline personality organization. *J. Am. Psychoanal. Assoc.*, **15**:641–85, 1967.

Kernberg, O.: The treatment of patients with borderline personality organization. *Int. J. Psychoanal.*, **49**:600–19, 1968.

Kernberg, O.: *Borderline Conditions and Pathological Narcissism*. Jason Aronson, New York, 1975.

Kernberg, O.: *Object Relations Theory and Clinical Psychoanalysis*. Jason Aronson, New York, 1976.

Kernberg, O.: Overall structuring and beginning phase of treatment of borderline and narcissistic patients. In *Parameters in Psychoanalytic Psychotherapy*. Edited by Goldman, G., and Milman, D. Kendall/Hunt, Dubuque, Iowa, 1979, pp. 215–36.

Kernberg, O.: The psychotherapeutic treatment of borderline personalities. In *Psychiatry 1982*. Vol. 1 of *Psychiatry Update*. Edited by Grinspoon, L. American Psychiatric Press, Washington, D.C., 1982.

Kernberg, O.: *Severe Personality Disorders*. Yale Univ. Press, New Haven, 1984.

Kernberg, O.; Burstein, E.; Coyne, L.; et al: Final report of the Menninger Foundation's psychotherapy research project: Psychotherapy and Psychoanalysis. *Bull. Menninger Clin.*, 34:1–2, 1972.

Klein, M.: Notes on some schizoid mechanisms. *International J. Psychoanal.* 27:99–110, 1946.

Knight, R.: Borderline states. *Bull. Menninger Clin.*, 17:1–12, 1953.

Kohut, H.: *The Analysis of the Self*. International Universities Press, New York, 1971.

Kohut, H.: *The Restoration of the Self*. International Universities Press, New York, 1977.

Kroll, J.; Sines, L.; Martin, K.; et al: Borderline personality disorder: Construct validity of the concept. *Arch. Gen. Psychiatry*, 38:1021–26, 1981.

Lynch, V., and Gunderson, J.: Treatment utilization by outpatient borderlines. Unpublished paper.

Mahler, M.: A study of the separation-individuation process and its possible application to borderline phenomena in the psychoanalytic situation. *Psychoanal. Study Child*, 26:403–24, 1971.

Mahler, M.: *On Human Symbiosis and the Vicissitudes of Individuation*. International Universities Press, New York, 1971.

Masterson, J.: Treatment of the adolescent with borderline syndrome (a problem in separation-individuation). *Bull. Menninger Clin.*, 35:5–18, 1971.

Masterson, J.: *Treatment of the Borderline Adolescent: A Developmental Approach*. John Wiley & Sons, New York, 1972, p. 125.

Masterson, J.: *Psychotherapy of the Borderline Adult*. Brunner/Mazel, New York, 1976.

Masterson, J.: The borderline adult: therapeutic alliance and transference. *Am. J. Psychiatry*, 135:437–41, 1978.

Masterson, J., and Costello, J.: *From Borderline Adolescent to Functioning Adult: The Test of Time*. Brunner/Mazel, New York, 1980.

Masterson, J., and Rinsley, D.: The borderline syndrome: The role of the mother in the genesis and psychic structure of the borderline personality. *Int. J. Psychoanal.*, 56:163–77, 1975.

McGlashan, T.: The borderline syndrome, I: Testing three diagnostic systems for borderlines. *Arch. Gen. Psychiatry*, 40:1311–18, 1983.

McGlashan, T.: The Chestnut Lodge follow-up study, II: Long-term outcome of borderline personalities. *Arch. Gen. Psychiatry*, 41:586–601, 1984.

McGlashan, T.: The prediction of outcome in borderline personality disorder: Part V of the Chestnut Lodge Follow-up Study. In *The Borderline: Current Empirical Research*. Edited by McGlashan, T. American Psychiatric Press, Washington, D.C., 1985, pp. 63–98.

Meissner, W.: Notes on the levels of differentiation within borderline conditions. *Psychoanal. Rev.*, 70:179–209, 1983.

Modell, A.: The "holding environment" and the therapeutic action of psychoanalysis. *J. Am. Psychoanal. Assoc.*, 24:285–307, 1976.

Perry, J., and Cooper, S.: A preliminary report on defenses and conflicts associated with borderline personality disorder. Draft manuscript presented before the Panel on Borderline Personality Disorders and the fall meeting of the American Psychoanalytic Association, December 16, 1983, New York.

Perry, J.C.: Depression in borderline personality disorder: lifetime prevalence at interview and longitudinal course of symptoms. *Am. J. Psychiatry*, **142**:15–21, 1985.

Pope, H.; Jonas, J.; and Hudson, J.; et al: The validity of DSM-III borderline personality disorder. *Arch. Gen. Psychiatry*, **40**:23–30, 1983.

Rinsley, D.: *Borderline and Other Self Disorders*. Jason Aronson, New York, 1982.

Robbins, M.: Review of Abend, S.M.; Porder, M.S.; and Willick, M.S.: *Borderline Patients: Psychoanalytic Perspectives*. *Psychosomatics*, **26**:74–75, 1985.

Ronningstam, E.: Narcissistic personality disorder: A comparison of three diagnostic systems. Unpublished paper, 1985.

Searles, H.: Psychoanalytic therapy with borderline patients—the development, in the patient, of an internalized image of the therapist. Paper presented as the Fifth O. Spurgeon English Honor Lecture at Temple University School of Medicine, Philadelphia, April 25, 1980.

Shapiro, E.: The holding environment and family therapy with acting out adolescents. *Int. J. Psychoanal. Psychother.*, **9**:209–26, 1982.

Shapiro, E.; Zinner, J.; Shapiro, R.; et al: The influence of family experience on borderline personality development. *Int. Rev. Psychoanalysis*, **2**:399–411, 1975.

Sheehy, M.; Goldsmith, I.; and Charles, E.: A comparative study of borderline patients in a psychiatric outpatient clinic. *Am. J. Psychiatry*, **137**:1374–79, 1980.

Skodal, A.; Buckley, P.; Charles, E.: Is there a characteristic pattern to the treatment history of clinical outpatients with borderline personality? *J. Nerv. Ment. Dis.*, **171**:405–10, 1983.

Stolorow, R., and Lachmann, F.: *Psychoanalysis of Developmental Arrests*. International Universities Press, New York, 1980.

Stone, M.H., Stone, D.K.: The natural history of borderline patients. *J. of Pers. Dis.* (in press).

Stone, M.H.: Analytically oriented psychotherapy in schizotypal and borderline patients: At the border of treatability. *Yale J. Biol. Med.*, **58**:275–88, 1985.

Tahka, V.: Psychotherapy as phase-specific interaction: Towards a general psychoanalytic theory of psychotherapy. *Scand. Psychoanal. Rev.*, **2**:113–32, 1979.

Thomas, A., and Chess, S.: Genesis and evolution of behavioral disorders: From infancy to early adult life. *Am. J. Psychiatry*, **141**:1–9, 1984.

Vaillant, G.E., and Perry, J.C.: Personality disorders. In *A Comprehensive Textbook of Psychiatry*, Vol. 1, 4th ed. Edited by Kaplan, H.I., and Sadock, B.J. Williams and Wilkins, Baltimore, 1985, pp. 958–86.

Volkan, V.: Six phases of the psychoanalytic psychotherapy with borderline patients. In *The Borderline Patient*. Edited by Grostein, J., Solomon, M., and Lang, J. Analytic Press, New York (in press).

Waldinger, R., and Gunderson, J.: Completed psychotherapies with borderline patients. *Am. J. Psychother.*, **38**:190–202, 1984.

Wallerstein, R.: Psychoanalysis and psychotherapy: Relative roles reconsidered. Paper presented at the Boston Psychoanalytic Society and Institute Symposium, October 29, 1983.

Winnicott, D.: *Collected Papers*. Basic Books, New York, 1958.

Winnicott, D.: *The Family and Individual Development*. Tavistock, London, 1965.

Winnicott, D.: The theory of the parent–infant relationship. In *The Maturational Processes and the Facilitating Environment*. International Universities Press, New York, 1965, pp. 37–55.

Zetzel, E.: A developmental approach to the borderline patient. *Am. J. Psychiatry*, **127**:867–71, 1971.

Zetzel, E.: Therapeutic alliance in the analysis of hysteria (1958). *In The Capacity for Emotional Growth*. International Universities Press, New York, 1970, pp. 182–196.